What reader could fail to be enthralled by the *Iliad* and the *Odyssey*, those greatest heroic epics of antiquity? Yet the author of these immortal texts remains, in the end, an enigma. The central paradox of 'Homer' is that – while recognized as producing poetry of incomparable genius – even in the ancient world nobody knew who he was. As a result, the myth-maker became the subject of myth. For the satirist Lucian (*c.*125–*c.*180 CE) he was a captive Babylonian. Other traditions have Homer born in Smyrna or on the island of Chios, or portray him as a blind and wandering minstrel.

In his new and authoritative introduction, Jonathan S. Burgess addresses fundamental questions of provenance and authorship. Besides conveying why these epics have been cherished down the ages, he discusses their historical sources and the possible impact on the *Iliad* and *Odyssey* of Indo-European, Near Eastern and folktale influences. Tracing their transmission through the ancient, medieval and modern periods, the author further examines qu

CW00607351

JONATHAN S. BURGESS is Professor of Classics at the University of Toronto. He is the author of *The Tradition of the Trojan War in Homer and the Epic Cycle* (2001, paperback 2004) and *The Death and Afterlife of Achilles* (2009).

Jonathan Burgess is a leading figure in the ongoing study of Homeric poetry. He views this dynamic art form within the historical context of its reception in the overall song culture of the ancient Greeks – as also in the literary world of the Classical and the post-Classical eras. Such a perspective, which takes all epic traditions into account, gives the reader an illuminating view of Homer as a grand unifying idea of Hellenic civilization.

—Gregory Nagy, Francis Jones Professor of Classical Greek Literature and Professor of Comparative Literature, Director of the Center for Hellenic Studies, Harvard University

Two and a half millennia of criticism and reception of the indescribably rich Homeric texts make the task of introducing them quite Herculean, but Burgess has managed it superbly. This eminently readable survey covers an enormous amount of ground with tact and insight. Deeply informed both theoretically and philologically, this is an outstanding introduction to possibly the greatest poems in the Western canon.

—Robert Fowler, Henry Overton Wills Professor of Greek, University of Bristol

Jonathan S. Burgess is one of the most important scholars working on Homer today. In this elegant new book he starts with the big picture, introducing readers to the world of ancient epic. He then narrows his purview to focus on the *Iliad* and the *Odyssey*, discussing plot, characters and transmission. Finally, he homes in on one central mystery: the identity of Homer. The learning is vast; the approach nuanced; the writing crystal-clear. Readers will delight in this book, and learn a great deal from it.

—Barbara Graziosi, Professor of Classics, Durham University

Jonathan Burgess has written an admirable introduction, covering with lucid concision all the main issues from the Indo-European origins of Homeric epic to its reception in our own time.

—Richard Seaford, Professor of Ancient Greek, University of Exeter

UNDERSTANDING CLASSICS

EDITOR: RICHARD STONEMAN (UNIVERSITY OF EXETER)

When the great Roman poets of the Augustan Age – Ovid, Virgil and Horace – composed their odes, love poetry and lyrical verse, could they have imagined that their works would one day form a cornerstone of Western civilization, or serve as the basis of study for generations of schoolchildren learning Latin? Could Aeschylus or Euripides have envisaged the remarkable popularity of contemporary stagings of their tragedies? The legacy and continuing resonance of Homer's *Iliad* and *Odyssey* – Greek poetical epics written many millennia ago – again testify to the capacity of the classics to cross the divide of thousands of years and speak powerfully and relevantly to audiences quite different from those to which they were originally addressed.

Understanding Classics is a specially commissioned series which aims to introduce the outstanding authors and thinkers of antiquity to a wide audience of appreciative modern readers, whether undergraduate students of classics, literature, philosophy and ancient history or generalists interested in the classical world. Each volume – written by leading figures internationally – will examine the historical significance of the writer or writers in question; their social, political and cultural contexts; their use of language, literature and mythology; extracts from their major works; and their reception in later European literature, art, music and culture. *Understanding Classics* will build a library of readable, authoritative introductions offering fresh and elegant surveys of the greatest literatures, philosophies and poetries of the ancient world.

UNDERSTANDING CLASSICS

Aristophanes and Greek Comedy
JEFFREY S. RUSTEN
Cornell University

Augustine
DENNIS E. TROUT
Tufts University

Cicero
GESINE MANUWALD
University College London

Euripides
ISABELLE TORRANCE
University of Notre Dame

Eusebius
AARON P. JOHNSON
Lee University, Tennessee

Homer
JONATHAN S. BURGESS
University of Toronto

Latin Love Poetry
DENISE MCCOSKEY & ZARA TORLONE
Miami University, Ohio

Martial
LINDSAY WATSON & PATRICIA WATSON
University of Sydney

Ovid
CAROLE E. NEWLANDS
University of Wisconsin, Madison

Pindar
RICHARD STONEMAN
University of Exeter

Plutarch
MARK BECK
University of North Carolina, Chapel Hill

The Poets of Alexandria
SUSAN A. STEPHENS
Stanford University

Roman Comedy
DAVID CHRISTENSON
University of Arizona

Sappho
PAGE DUBOIS
University of California, Berkeley

Seneca
CHRISTOPHER STAR
Middlebury College

Sophocles
STEPHEN ESPOSITO
Boston University

Tacitus
VICTORIA EMMA PAGÁN
University of Florida

Virgil
ALISON KEITH
University of Toronto

HOMER

Jonathan S. Burgess

UNDERSTANDING CLASSICS SERIES EDITOR:
RICHARD STONEMAN

I.B. TAURIS
LONDON · NEW YORK

Published in 2015 by I.B.Tauris & Co Ltd
6 Salem Road, London W2 4BU
175 Fifth Avenue, New York NY 10010
www.ibtauris.com

Distributed in the United States and Canada Exclusively by Palgrave Macmillan
175 Fifth Avenue, New York NY 10010

ISBN: 978 1 84885 862 6 (HB)
          978 1 84885 863 3 (PB)
eISBN: 978 0 85773 514 0

A full CIP record for this book is available from the British Library
A full CIP record is available from the Library of Congress

Library of Congress Catalog Card Number: available

Text design, typesetting and eBook versions by Tetragon, London

Printed and bound in Great Britain by T.J. International, Padstow, Cornwall

CONTENTS

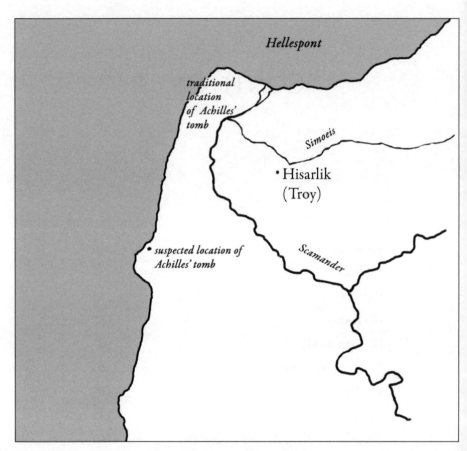

Map 1: Troy and its environs

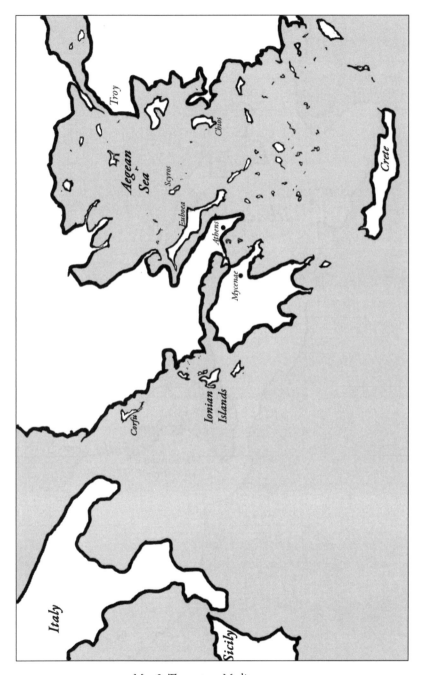

Map 2: The eastern Mediterranean

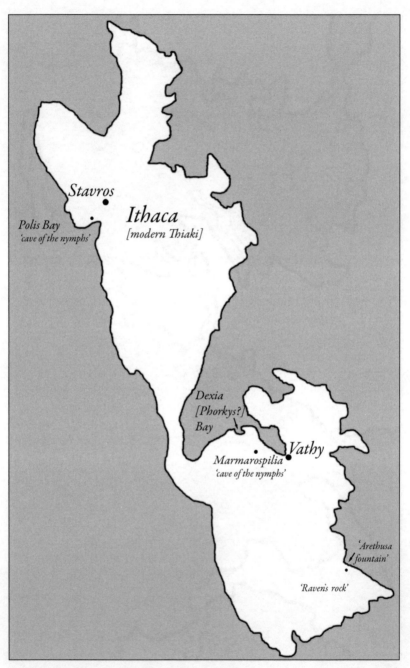

Map 3: Ithaca

For Hugh F. Burgess, Jr
poet, teacher, father

Acknowledgements

FOR SUPPORT OF RESEARCH that contributed to this project, I am grateful to the Social Sciences and Humanities Research Council of Canada, as well as for a fellowship at the Jackman Humanities Institute of the University of Toronto. Students in my Homer classes over the years, both undergraduate and graduate, deserve my thanks as well. Jogging by Lake Ontario to the beautiful Humber Bay Arch Bridge, where aboriginal routes along the lake and up the Humber constitute the *Maada-oonidiwinan Miikaansan*, the 'shared path', helped me gather my thoughts about the shared path of traditional Greek epic, as well as the millennia-long shared path of the reception of Homeric poetry.

1

MYTHS

THE WARRIOR IS about to pass out of the gates of Troy to the battlefield when his wife approaches on the run, trailed by a nurse holding their infant child. He pauses, with relief; earlier he had looked for her at home. As he smiles quietly as his son, she urges him not to fight, certain this would make her a widow and their son an orphan. Warming to her appeal, she recalls how the best Greek warrior, Achilles, had sacked her native city, killing her father and brothers. Her mother was ransomed but later died. 'Hector, you are to me father and queenly mother, you are brother, and you are my vigorous husband,' she concludes, before veering off into an implausible bit of military advice. Moved but not persuaded, the Trojan leader states his intention to fight. He's too proud to hang back, and he desires heroic *kleos* ('glory').

Yet as Hector explains himself, he affirms his tender devotion to family. The Trojan speaks of futures, inconsistently envisioned. Troy will fall, he first asserts, and Andromache will be unhappily enslaved. When he then reaches for his son, the child is terrified – not recognizing dad under a glittering, plumed helmet. Tension momentarily fades as the parents laugh; unhelmeted, the father picks up Astyanax and prays that he become a great warrior who returns victorious to a proud mother. Andromache, 'smiling through her

I

tears', receives their child, and Hector gently muses that no one knows their fate. She should return to women's work in the home, he concludes, and he to war, the 'concern of men'. She departs, turning around again and again, weeping. Once home she and her female servants lament the living Hector as if dead. Hector returns to the battlefield with his brother Paris. Later Hector will be killed by Achilles; the epic ends with his burial.

A warrior on the way home from Troy finds himself in a tight spot: he is trapped in a cave by a gigantic shepherd who makes meals out of his companions. The Greek offers the Cyclops potent wine. This pleases so much that more is requested, as well as the guest's name; a gift is promised in return. Odysseus obliges and says, 'Nobody is my name.' Polyphemus promises that 'Nobody will I eat last among his comrades [...] this shall be your gift.' But Odysseus has a plan. The cannibal cannot simply be killed – he alone has the strength to move the cave-enclosing boulder. So the Greeks plunge a giant stake into the shepherd's giant eye.

When other Cyclopes come running at his cries, Polyphemus shouts, 'It is Nobody that is slaying me.' Unimpressed, they go on their way. Odysseus and his men escape the cave by hiding under sheep. Odysseus boastfully reveals his name from his ship; Polyphemus hurls rocks and prays to his father Poseidon that Odysseus not reach home – or at least wander long. Odysseus recounts this and many other adventures to his hosts the Phaeacians. When they bring him home to Ithaca, Odysseus plots to slaughter the suitors who desired his wife in his absence.

These two memorable Homeric moments, the encounter between Hector and Andromache in Book 6 of the *Iliad*, and the blinding of Polyphemus by Odysseus in Book 9 of the *Odyssey*, demonstrate the power of Homer's poetry. Thousands of years later the *Iliad* and *Odyssey* are still read, studied and retold. The Homeric epics enchant, but also intrigue. There's much in them that makes one wonder, and certainly much that has spurred scholarly argument. The *Iliad* passage, for example, memorably portrays a family scene. Yet though the characters movingly express emotions emblematic of human experience, it is also apparent that Hector is self-involved and Andromache ineffective. Their tender feelings for each other do not break down the boundary of gender roles that divides them. The issues that they discuss are deeply rooted in the ancient world, and not necessarily familiar to our modern life. And the scene, however extraordinary, does not advance the plot of the *Iliad* in any way.

The curse of Polyphemus is central to the plot of the *Odyssey*. Yet though the episode is recounted in a sophisticated manner by Odysseus, it is essentially a folk tale, the tricking of an ogre. Here, as elsewhere, one wonders about what material preceded the composition of the Homeric epics, and what distinguishes them from their traditions. Homer's version contains fantastic elements – Polyphemus is a mythological being and the son of a god – but it also seems to reflect conflict with other cultures during a time of Greek expansion into the western Mediterranean. Then there is the episode's obsession with gift-exchange, a societal convention of ancient aristocratic culture. Enjoyable as the Homeric poems are, they raise questions great and small. Why are parts of the epics called 'Books'? is one small yet potentially puzzling question. A very large one is: who is 'Homer'?

Questions will be encouraged in this work, which aims to introduce the *Iliad* and *Odyssey*, as well as Homeric studies more generally. The epics will be celebrated, but so will the long, continuing history of their interpretation and reception. The multiplicity of perspectives on Homeric poetry, from Aristotle to *O Brother, Where Art Thou?*, is fascinating. Many readers will be Homerists and classicists, but no knowledge of Greek is assumed and jargon is avoided. My hope is that a wide range of people will be encouraged to enjoy and study Homer.

The book starts with the poems themselves, moving from the big picture of the Trojan War myth to a tighter focus on plot, characterization and poetics in subsequent chapters. The middle chapters will discuss the history of the texts, review ancient and modern scholarship, and address the so-called 'Homeric Question'. The penultimate chapter surveys theoretical approaches to Homer, and the final one discusses creative responses to the *Iliad* and the *Odyssey* down through the ages. Endnotes point the way forward to further reading.

A number of themes recur in my analysis. One is the interrelation between the Homeric poems and their epic and mythological traditions. Homeric scholars through history have sought to ascertain how the Homer poems fit into the larger stories of the Trojan War and its aftermath. In antiquity 'Homer' often seemed to mean 'heroic epics in general', even as the exceptional nature of the *Iliad* and *Odyssey* was insisted upon. Modern responses to Homeric poetry also tend to focus on the Troy story as much as the *Iliad* and *Odyssey*. Another theme of the book is the potential compatibility of different approaches to Homer. Points of contact between critical perspectives will often be noted, although Homeric studies are certainly often contentious and polemical. A final theme is the richness and variety of reactions to the *Iliad* and *Odyssey*, both interpretative and creative (the boundary between the two can be hard to draw). It is not this work's purpose to pronounce on 'what we know' about what the Homeric epics were; rather my study intends to survey inclusively the wide range of assessments of the Homeric epics, which continue to evolve as interpretation expands. Ongoing interest in the *Iliad* and *Odyssey* amply demonstrates that they endure, thanks especially to provocative interpretation and visionary creativity. While I cannot begin to claim expertise in all areas of Homeric studies and Homeric reception, I have endeavoured to sketch their outlines. The possession of a mental map of the broad reaches of the Homeric world should be useful for any foray into a particular part of its terrain.

At the end of the book I point out that everyone who experiences the epics tends to develop an image of 'Homer' in their mind. When another Homeric enthusiast's 'Homer' is not yours, it's unsettling. But even in major stand-offs about Homer in the past – for example, during the dispute over ancient and modern aesthetics in the seventeenth and eighteenth centuries, or when variant Romantic notions of Homer as Tradition or Original Genius arose in the late eighteenth century, or when polemics between Analysts and Unitarians flared up in the nineteenth and twentieth centuries – the extent of common ground is striking. Even when alternative hypotheses remain irreconcilable, the argumentation employed often blends together. Or at least there is a choice between viable perspectives on Homer. You will not want to agree with every argument in Homeric studies that you encounter, including my own, but the experience of hearing out the variety of Homeric responses will be profitable.

The Myth of the Trojan War

Hector and Andromache are in the midst of the Trojan War; Odysseus is returning from it. The *Iliad* and *Odyssey* directly narrate only very small portions of the ten-year war and Odysseus' ten-year return, but they display deep awareness of the larger cycle of myths in which they are embedded. The narrator ('Homer' by convention) and his characters talk all the time about the Trojan War and other stories of the Heroic Age. For example, in Book 6 of the *Iliad* (290–2) Homer provides a backstory for a robe that his mother Hecuba selects for dedication to Athena. Paris obtained it, the poet reports, in a meandering return to Troy from Sparta with Helen. In Book 8 of the *Odyssey* tales of the Trojan War are sung by Demodocus, bard of Odysseus' hosts the Phaeacians. His first story (73 ff.) is about a quarrel between Odysseus and Achilles; a later song (499 ff.) features the famous wooden horse that was employed to sack Troy. Demodocus can apparently perform material from the whole range of Trojan myth. It is too much to perform it all at once, but the bard seems confident that his listeners know the larger story.

Not that the story always remained the same. My examples of Trojan War material embedded in the Homeric epics are not without difficulties. Herodotus reports (*Histories* 2.117) that in a lost Trojan War epic, the *Cypria*, the return of Paris and Helen took an easy three days, with no stops. But an ancient summary of the poem reports a meandering journey, as the *Iliad* suggests. So we do not even know if the *Iliad* and *Cypria* disagree about the return of Paris and Helen. But let us suppose that the *Iliad* and the *Cypria* had different conceptions of the journey. Were poets free to tell the journey any way they preferred? Or is variance on the return of Paris allowed only because it does not change the basic outlines of the story? The Trojan War will commence no matter how Paris journeys back to Troy with Helen.

But sometimes the basic plotlines of myth *are* changed. Herodotus suspects that Homer is aware of a story in which Helen sits out the war in Egypt, while the Greeks and Trojans battle over a phantom of her! Herodotus' evidence is thin: the wandering of Paris and Helen (but not to Egypt) mentioned in *Iliad* 6, Menelaus and Helen talking of visiting Egypt *after* the war in *Odyssey* 4. But this alternative version of the Trojan War was supported by the sixth-century-BCE lyric poet Stesichorus,[1] and it is the basis of the fifth-century-BCE drama *Helen* by Euripides. Similar issues arise with Demodocus' song about the quarrel of Odysseus and Achilles. It doesn't match up very precisely with anything else we hear of the Trojan War, and the indirect, compressed and elliptical reporting of the bard's song does not assist explication. Is the 'quarrel of Odysseus and Achilles' untraditional, invented on the spot by Demodocus/Homer? If so, why does Homer report that the story's 'fame had then reached broad heaven'? In these examples we are confronted not only with our ignorance about myth outside of Homer, but also with the possibility of variance, both small and large.

These issues give scholars much to ponder. But when approaching the *Iliad* and the *Odyssey* one should assume that the myth of the Trojan War, like most ancient myths, was largely stable. Myth was not just a few epic poets jousting with each other with 'can you top this?' entertainment. Stories honed over time served the Greeks as a kind of prehistory, with serious implications about genealogical, cultural and religious matters in the contemporary world. The anti-myth of Helen staying in Egypt is designed to invert the story that everyone knows; the widespread currency of the traditional version is assumed. The literary game in later antiquity of perversely challenging Homer (see Chapter 7) similarly rested on an assumption of familiarity with the Homeric epics. Most narratives with mythological content, including the Homeric epics, worked within traditions. Myth was a kind of super-language in Greek culture, and it could not function as such if it were a chaotic mass of disjointed details. Of course, different versions might favour aspects important to local areas. The same mythological figure might be portrayed more or less sympathetically, depending on the issues involved. Certainly speakers within the Homeric poems know how to spin the details of a heroic tale in order to impress and influence their audience.

If Demodocus' song of the 'quarrel of Odysseus and Achilles' is an innovation, it is merely a detail in the larger scheme of the whole war, just as is the return of Paris and Helen to Troy. Why would Homer have Demodocus tell a non-traditional tale? It might allude to the quarrel of Achilles and

Agamemnon that occurs at the beginning of the *Iliad*, or it might reflect a thematic antithesis between Achilles (physical prowess) and Odysseus (mental agility),[2] or it might simply serve to elicit the tears of Odysseus. As for the wandering journey of Paris in Book 6, that could emphasize the importance of the robe being dedicated or remind one of the notorious elopement of Paris and Helen shortly before they appear together in Book 6. In other poems (perhaps including the *Cypria*, or a version of it), a long return home for Paris might make it possible to reference aspects in the Aegean important to various local audiences. These are all possible functions for these passages. But such effects do not necessarily depend on innovation, and one should not *expect* radical invention of myth in Homer.

Muses and Myth

Homer publicizes the traditional nature of his song when he, like other early bards, requests information from the Muses. For early Greek epic, invoking the Muses was not a poetic convention, as it was in later periods;[3] it was the means to recreate standard narratives about the distant heroic past. A single Muse is invoked at the beginning of the *Iliad* and *Odyssey*, and in the former poem Homer repeatedly calls on the Muse when hard-pressed for details (for example, the names of minor heroes). Hesiod, the other great epic poet of Homer's time, invokes Muses in the plural, as do composers of the so-called Homeric Hymns. According to Hesiod, the Muses are daughters of Mnemosyne, 'memory' (*Theogony* 53–5).

Poets looked to the Muses not just for memorized data, but also for narrative sequence. In *Odyssey* 8 the Muse directs Demodocus to sing of a quarrel of Odysseus and Achilles from the larger *oime* ('path') of Trojan War episodes. After Demodocus has finished, Odysseus states that he sang as if he had been present at Troy, or had heard about the war from someone who had been there. Since Odysseus was present at Troy, this is high praise indeed. But what Odysseus implies is that Demodocus is well trained in the singing of heroic narrative. That relatively recent events would already have been turned into traditional stories is of course ironic. Here, as elsewhere, there's tension between the Homeric characters' immediate experience of their narratives and the Homeric audience's knowledge of them as myths about the past. Sometimes characters express certainty that people of the future will know of their stories (Helen is a good example; see Chapter 3). In the *Odyssey* the ongoing transformation of the present events into future tradition becomes something of a running joke. Neoptolemus describes a song about the 'returns' of the Greek heroes from Troy by Phemius of Ithaca, another bard in the *Odyssey*, as 'newest' and therefore pleasing (1.325 ff., 351–2). This need not imply that epic poets were free to indulge in wanton innovation – the poet is playing with the paradox of traditional narrative seeming 'new' to the characters living in it. Phemius may later seem to deny tradition when he claims to be 'self-taught' in singing the 'paths' that 'the god has planted in my heart' (22.347–8), but this apparently portrays internalized expertise as divine inspiration. In Homeric poetry technical skill (and poetic composition *was* a craft) results from both training and divine favour, just as, in what is called 'double motivation', characters are driven at once by personal emotion and supernatural impulses.[4]

The general topic for Homer is the Trojan War; the *Iliad* recites one episode within it, and the *Odyssey* tells of the arrival home by a returning hero. This story of war and returning heroes is large and varied, and at times it seems infinitely expandable. The saga of Trojan War stories has no clear beginning or ending. The elopement of Paris and Helen causes the war, but one could start with earlier developments.[5] Asked to judge who among three goddesses was most beautiful, for example, Paris could not resist the promise of the most beautiful woman in the world if he chose Aphrodite, goddess of love (allusion to this story occurs at *Iliad* 24.27–30).[6] Or, going further back, one could begin with Helen's birth. When the Roman poet Horace claims in the *Art of Poetry* (147) that starting the Trojan War 'from the egg' is an aesthetic mistake, he is referring to the story of Zeus mating with Helen's mother Leda in the form of a swan.

Achilles has his own backstory. He's the product of an unhappy marriage between the Nereid (a minor sea goddess) Thetis and Peleus. Zeus fancied her, as he did so many mortal women. But after hearing that Thetis was destined to give birth to a son greater than his father, Zeus wisely forced her to marry a mortal.[7] Among the gods attending the wedding of Peleus and Thetis, the divine personification of 'strife', Eris, flung a golden apple inscribed 'for the fairest'. This was the cause of the divine beauty contest judged by Paris. Achilles did turn out to be much better than his father, especially in battle. Thetis, however, was bewildered by her son's mortality and continuously tried to prevent his death. That's the thematic impetus for the apparently post-Homeric story of 'Achilles' heel'.[8]

We can go back even further, to a 'first' Trojan War. The gods Apollo and Poseidon had been forced to build the walls of Troy, but Laomedon failed to pay them (as Poseidon recalls to Apollo at *Iliad* 21.435 ff.). Told he had to sacrifice his daughter to a sea serpent sent by an angry Poseidon, Laomedon promised Heracles his immortal horses to slay it. The monster was killed, but Laomedon failed again to deliver payment; Heracles raised an army and sacked Troy. And the Trojan saga telescopes forward in the other direction. There are multiple events between the *Iliad*'s ending and Troy's fall, to be followed by various returns home from Troy by different heroes. Agamemnon returns only to be murdered by the adulterous Clytemnestra, for example. Odysseus quite differently slays the suitors of his wife, after long wanderings at sea. Even then there were stories of further adventures *after* he reached Ithaca. Eventually a son by Odysseus and Circe, Telegonus, unwittingly kills Odysseus. Telegonus marries his father's wife Penelope, and Odysseus' son by Penelope, Telemachus, marries his father's lover Circe.

Many find some of the Trojan War stories scandalous and ridiculous (gods metamorphosing into avian rapists? humans from eggs? invulnerable heroes? post-parricide para-incestual pairings?). True, we hear nothing in Homer of Odysseus being killed by a son, for example. But the prophecy of the blind seer Tiresias in *Odyssey* 11 (119–37), which foretells that Odysseus will go on a post-return inland journey and then die at home, may allude to some such tradition. As Greek myths go, the *Telegony*'s version of unwitting parricide and marriage between family relations is not that absurd. Compare the famous myth of Oedipus, who unwittingly commits patricide and incest, then blinds himself and wanders off into exile.

Did a manifold tradition of the Trojan War and its aftermath exist when the Homeric poems were composed? Yes, as extensive allusions in the *Iliad* and *Odyssey* make clear. The *Iliad* and *Odyssey* often peer beyond their brief time spans to the whole range of events of the Trojan War and its aftermath. Besides the judgement of Paris, the *Iliad* mentions the Greek contingent gathering at Aulis, incidents on the way to Troy, and raids around Troy during the early years. The poem ends before the death of Achilles and the sack of Troy, but it foreshadows these extensively. The *Odyssey* looks back on many post-Iliadic events, including the sack of Troy (as we saw with Demodocus). Returns by heroes other than Odysseus are also narrated in the *Odyssey*, notably the one by Agamemnon that ended in his murder by his wife's lover, Aegisthus. So by prediction or retrospection, the two Homeric epics display their knowledge of the larger story of the Trojan War. Brief references suggest an assumption of audience knowledge, while lengthier remarks about earlier or later events in the Trojan War contextualize and interpret the action within the Homeric poems. We don't always know exactly how the pre-Homeric story of the Trojan War was told, and aspects of it may be modified or suppressed in Homeric epic.

And there was a lot more to myth than the Trojan War. Hesiod provides a basic frame of it all in his *Theogony* (*Lineage of the Gods*) and *Works and Days* (a poetic almanac concerning agricultural matters and much more). Together these poems trace the rise to power of the Olympian gods and their mating with mortals to produce the Heroic Age. An excursus on the 'Ages of Man' in the *Works and Days* tells of the decline of humankind from a utopian 'Golden Age' to the current degenerate 'Iron Age'. The Heroic Age is interjected rather awkwardly in the sequence of metals, but it is the time of heroic events. Hesiod specifies the Trojan War over Helen and the Theban War caused by a dispute between Oedipus' two sons. Homeric poetry is comfortably conversant with this broad scope of Greek myth also. One can find Homeric passages about the theogonic saga, Jason and the Argo, the Theban Wars (a second one started in the next generation), the Calydonian boar hunt, battles with centaurs and Amazons, and stories of Heracles, Theseus, Perseus and Bellerophon.

The Epic Cycle

The larger story of the Trojan War was narrated in the Archaic Age (*c*.800–500 BCE) by other early Greek epics, including the *Cypria* mentioned above. Unfortunately these poems, which were eventually collected into an 'Epic Cycle', have been lost. A summary of the Trojan War section of the Epic Cycle from later antiquity survives, as have a few quotations from the relevant epics.[9] The *Cypria* told the story up to the beginning of the *Iliad*, others told of events before and during the sack of Troy, and another told of the returns of heroes. The *Telegony* narrated Odysseus' post-return adventures, including his death at the hands of Telegonus. The summary reads like background material for the *Iliad* and the *Odyssey*. It points out where the two Homeric poems slot into the sequence, but they are not summarized – the reader is assumed to know them already. This summary of the Trojan War section of the Epic Cycle – probably a relatively later gathering of previously independent epics – survived in *Iliad* manuscripts precisely because of its useful contextualization of the Homeric poem.

Naturally enough, it is often assumed that the poems were composed in order to surround the Homeric epics. Near the end of the *Cypria*, according to the summary, Achilles and Agamemnon chose the captive women Briseis and Chryseis from war loot. The summary then refers to 'the plan of Zeus to aid the Trojans by removing Achilles from the Greek alliance'. This seems like a set-up for the *Iliad*, which begins with mention of a 'plan of Zeus' and tells of Achilles' withdrawal after he quarrels with Agamemnon about the concubines Chryseis and Briseis. The Cycle poem that is said to follow the *Iliad*, the *Aethiopis*, begins with the arrival of the Amazon Penthesileia 'to aid the Trojans', who surely need help after the death of their champion Hector in the *Iliad*. The subsidiary nature of this Cycle poem seems confirmed by an ancient report of an alternative ending of the *Iliad*, which changes 'Thus they busied themselves over the funeral of Hector, tamer of horses' to 'Thus they busied themselves over the funeral of Hector, and an Amazon came'. It looks like the Trojan Cycle consists of post-Homeric spin-offs.

But we need to consider carefully whether this is really so and, if it is, what it really means. First, our evidence for the Cycle poems is faulty. The poems themselves are lost; we depend on the summary, ancient reports and a few quotations. Sometimes this evidence is inconsistent. Herodotus contradicts the summary of the *Cypria*'s version of the return of Paris and Helen, and his testimony precedes the ancient summary by about a millennium. For all we know he is mistaken or misinformed, but other evidence proves that the Cycle summary is misleading, especially about the parameters of the Cycle poems. Though the summary of the *Cypria* makes it look like a lead-in to the *Iliad*, the original epic may have continued with further Trojan War episodes, including the basic story of the *Iliad*. Although in the summary the *Aethiopis* picks up the narrative thread where the *Iliad* leaves off, in its earliest forms the poem may have overlapped with the *Iliad*. It is hard for us, for whom the *Iliad* is so central, to conceive of these possibilities, but retellings of traditional material would not have seemed remarkable to the ancients. The very concept of fixed boundaries for poems was alien to traditional epic, which was orally composed and performed (see Chapter 5). Though the development of literacy in the Archaic Age led to the textual recording of early epics, it is unlikely that prequels or sequels to specific poems would arise in this period.

No one will ever know the original form of the lost Cycle epics. However, they only gained importance as recorded survivals as the tradition of early epic faded. The Epic Cycle is not equivalent to Trojan War myth; sometimes it contains variants of the usual stories. We're told that in the *Cypria*, for example, Zeus fathers Helen not with Leda but with Nemesis, the personification of 'divine punishment'. Nemesis changes into different animal forms as it tries to escape Zeus; the same themes of rape and metamorphosis are present, but the details are very different. The Cycle poems also disagree with each other at times. In the *Little Iliad* Neoptolemus kills Hector's son Astyanax, but Odysseus is the killer in the *Aethiopis*. So the Epic Cycle should not be considered exclusively or uniformly representative of Trojan War myth. It is just a very useful source for it.

What is more important is the relation between the Homeric epics and Trojan War myth in general. The seemingly subsidiary nature of the

Cycle poems has led some to conclude that the Homeric poems inspired the tradition of the Trojan War, or large portions of it. But the larger, non-Homeric scope of Trojan War myth was not invented by post-Homeric poets. Traditions about the war at Troy preceded the *Iliad* and *Odyssey* – the poems tell us so, amply. The exact content of pre-Homeric myth may not be known, but one can get the general idea from various sources. Besides the epic genre of Homer, Hesiod and the Cycle, Trojan material is found in other poetic genres, prose works and the iconography of art. And stories that are 'cyclic'[10] continue throughout Graeco-Roman antiquity. Much was expanded and changed after Homer, but cyclic myth fundamentally represents pre-Homeric traditions.

Basic differences do exist between Homeric and cyclic material. There is more action and supernatural phenomena in non-Homeric Trojan myth. The *Iliad* stresses the finality of death, whereas heroic immortality is relatively common in cyclic myth. Of course, there are plenty of gods flying about in the *Iliad* and the *Odyssey*, and fantastic things do occur. One of Achilles' horses briefly speaks of his coming death in the *Iliad*; in the *Odyssey* Odysseus tells of encounters with exotic beings (for example, Polyphemus). The difference between Homeric and cyclic material on such matters is best seen as a matter of emphasis. But in general Homeric epic seems to be more naturalistic than cyclic narrative, especially because its expansive narratives provide much space for character speech.[11]

That is enough to establish the mythological context of the *Iliad* and the *Odyssey*, as well as to suggest what is distinctive about them, even if it is impossible to distinguish the exact relationship between the Homeric epics and other lost epics. Fortunately the Homeric epics survive, and these invite close scrutiny. The following chapters will explore Homeric poetics, from plot to style and technique. What is traditional, as well as distinctive about Homeric poetry will be of interest.

II

PLOTS

COMPARED TO THE WIDE mythological context of the Trojan War, the plots of the *Iliad* and the *Odyssey* are surprisingly small. Each directly covers only a number of weeks in the ten-year war and ten-year return of Odysseus. Close attention is only given to a few days in each poem. This is a tight focus for very long poems about the size of a modern novel (about 16,000 lines for the *Iliad*, 12,000 for the *Odyssey*). The epics' generous ratio of length to content allows a leisurely pace in which the full range of Homeric poetics can be displayed.[1]

Horace praised epic that began not 'from the egg' but *in medias res*, 'in the midst of things' (*Art of Poetry* 136 ff.). It is thus that both the *Iliad* and *Odyssey* begin, after invocations of the Muse. In the *Iliad* the poet asks the goddess to sing of the *menis* ('wrath') of Achilles that follows a quarrel between him and Agamemnon in the tenth year of the war. In the *Odyssey* the Muse is requested to tell of the 'man' who wandered much after the sack of Troy (the reader quickly realizes this is Odysseus), with the topic eventually narrowed down to the end of his long journey. Both invocations speak of the Muse as the storyteller of the suggested topic; in the *Odyssey* the bard even asks the Muse to begin 'where you will' (1.10). Similarly the Phaeacian bard Demodocus, 'moved by the god', begins by 'taking up the tale' at a certain point (*Odyssey* 8.499–500). It is a cooperative effort between Demodocus and the Muse, and there is no predetermination of how to begin the song (as epic verse accompanied by lyre is conceived). Working together, the Muse and bard spontaneously decide where to start on the 'path' of mythological narrative.

Plotting the Iliad

The *Iliad* opens with vigorous concision:

> The wrath sing, goddess, of Peleus' son Achilles, the accursed wrath
> which brought countless sorrows upon the Achaeans, and sent down
> to Hades many valiant souls of warriors, and made the men themselves
> to be the spoil for dogs and birds of every kind; and thus the will of
> Zeus was brought to fulfillment. Of this sing from the time when first
> there parted in strife Atreus' son, lord of men, and noble Achilles.[2]

After the wrath of Achilles against Agamemnon is announced as the topic, Homer asks (rhetorically) what god caused the quarrel. He immediately provides the answer: Apollo, angered by the dishonouring of his priest Chryses, sent a plague. And then the proem goes further back in time to narrate this backstory. By means of quick narration interspersed with brief character speech, we are told that Chryses (of the town Chryse) comes to the Greek camp to ransom Chryseis ('daughter of Chryses'), who had been captured by the Greeks (as also reported in the *Cypria*). Chryses' plea is generally approved by the Achaeans (Homer's Greeks are variously called Achaeans, Danaans and Argives). Agamemnon refuses to release Chryseis and rudely sends her father off. The priest requests vengeance from Apollo; plague ensues. After only about fifty lines Achilles is summoning an assembly to address the disaster, and the stage is set for a quarrel between the hero and his commander. The seer Calchas is asked to explain the god's anger, and he pins it on Agamemnon's treatment of Chryses. Sure enough Agamemnon is furious, but he eventually promises to return Chryseis, so long as he gets another concubine.

There's the rub. Achilles points out there are no unclaimed concubines lying about, and he suggests that the commander will be amply recompensed after the fall of Troy. Things devolve into a heated argument, in a slow but seemingly inevitable series of exchanges. Agamemnon, accusing Achilles of deception ('Do not in this way, valiant though you are, godlike Achilles, try to deceive me by your cleverness, for you will not outstrip me nor persuade me' [131–2]), threatens to take his concubine, or another's, before pulling back with officious comments about returning Chryseis. Achilles replies hotly ('What, you clothed in shamelessness, you crafty of mind, how can any Achaean eagerly obey your words either to go on a journey or to do battle?' [149–51]), and quickly raises very large issues indeed:

> 'I did not come here to fight because of the spearmen of Troy, since they are in no way at fault toward me. Never did they drive off my cattle or my horses, nor ever in deep-soiled Phthia, nourisher of men, did they lay waste the grain, for many things lie between us – shadowy mountains and sounding sea. But you, shameless one, we followed here in order to please you, seeking to win recompense for Menelaus and for you, dog-face, from the Trojans. This you do not regard or take thought of.' (152–60)

Expressing disdain for Achilles ('Flee then, if your heart is set on it; I am not begging you to stay for my sake' [173–4]), Agamemnon now affirms that he will take his concubine Briseis (probably meaning 'daughter of Brises' [392]). Achilles' first impulse is to draw his sword and run it through Agamemnon, but Athena suddenly appears to him alone, persuading him otherwise. Achilles adds further insults ('You heavy with wine, with the face of a dog but the heart of a deer [...] People-devouring king, since you rule over nobodies!' [225, 231]), and he predicts that the Achaeans will suffer in his absence at the hands of Hector. The elder Nestor, characteristically providing advice at length, fails to resolve the dispute. After some further squabbling (Agamemnon: 'But this man is minded to be above all others; over all he is minded to hold sway and be king among all, and to all give orders' [287–9]; Achilles: 'Yes, for I should be called a coward and a nobody, if I am to yield to you in every matter whatever you say' [293–4]), Achilles only clarifies his position: he will not fight over Briseis, but will protect by force all his other possessions. The assembly breaks off and Achilles leaves with his men. The Greeks prepare an expedition to return Chryseis, and Agamemnon sends heralds to take Briseis from Achilles. Only halfway through Book 1, the Greeks are confronted by internal divisions that will not be resolved until Book 19.[3]

It is a swift and dramatic introduction to the poem. The reader is drawn *in medias res*, into the tenth year of the war, with the action unfolding as a consequence of the previous capture of Chryseis (an episode told in the *Cypria* of the Cycle and looked back on here). Horace's praise of Homeric plots (see the previous chapter) echoes an earlier analysis by Aristotle.[4] In Chapter 8 of the *Poetics* Homer is praised for centring his epics around a 'single action', as opposed to chronological rehearsal of the war and the return of Odysseus. In Chapter 23 Aristotle further describes his preferred plot as a complete single action, with a beginning, a middle and an end, as in a tragedy. Less successful, in his view, are plots that cover heroic lives, historical periods with multiple events, or even single actions with too many details. As examples of bad plotting, the *Cypria* and the *Little Iliad* of the Epic Cycle are put forward. According to the surviving ancient summary of the Cycle, the former covered the first nine years of the war, while Aristotle suggests the latter told the story of the sack of Troy. Nine years is certainly a large time span. The city's sack may sound more unified, but it involved multiple events featuring various Greek and Trojan characters.

But in what way are the plots of the Homeric poems 'single actions'? Greatly significant for the *Iliad*'s plot is an encounter in Book 1 between Achilles and his Nereid mother Thetis, who periodically emerges from the sea to visit her son (357 ff.). Achilles tells her about the quarrel and requests that she ask Zeus to help the Trojans. He expects that the Greeks, and Agamemnon in particular, will regret dishonouring him. She consents to his idea, and Zeus subsequently complies, though with hesitation, correctly guessing that pro-Greek Hera will be angry (one recalls that she was spurned by Paris in his judgement). Many since antiquity have considered Zeus' approval of Thetis' request to be the 'plan of Zeus' mentioned at the beginning of the poem (line 5). This is unlikely; Zeus' reluctant concession to Thetis is hardly a plan. As for the proem's 'plan of Zeus', it may allude to Zeus' plan to end the Heroic Age by means of the Trojan War, as told in the *Cypria*. But the phrase elsewhere is better translated as a very general 'will of Zeus' – perhaps the proem references neither the micro plot of the Homeric poem nor the macro plot of the Trojan War.[5]

In any event, it's the withdrawal of the angered Achilles that initiates the *Iliad*'s story. A more appropriate title for the *Iliad* would be *Wrath of Achilles*. *Iliad* is just a shorted form of the Greek for 'the Iliadic poem' or 'poem about Ilion/Ilios' (bynames for Troy). The titles for early epics probably originate long after their composition; it is the proems that announce, or rather decide upon, the topic. Our proem announces this as Achilles' wrath – *menis*, or 'wrath', is the first word – and it is the hero's anger that leads to his sustained withdrawal.

But if the wrath of Achilles is the plot, it loses steam in the early books of the epic. Zeus' agreement to help the Trojans is greatly delayed – it is not until the end of Book 8 that the Greeks are in enough trouble to seek help from Achilles. In Book 9 Agamemnon offers, through ambassadors, to return Briseis and to honour him with many gifts (115 ff.). Agamemnon has dishonoured the hero by reducing his stockpile (captive war-women are essentially material possessions in the heroic world), and so he offers to make amends not only by returning the concubine Briseis, but by giving much more (gold, tripods and cauldrons, horses, the promise of spoil after Troy's fall, and one of his daughters to marry upon return to Greece, with seven cities to rule over to boot). Within the economy of heroic values, that should settle the deal. Surprisingly, Achilles doesn't relent. Perhaps the amount of compensation is problematic – it could be received as an expression of power. And the offer of a daughter in marriage may be provocative; Achilles as son-in-law would be locked into a subordinate familial relationship to the commander. Anyway, Achilles' belief that he is fated to die at Troy if he fights (see below) makes the promise of postwar rewards moot. Still, when the embassy approaches Achilles it feels like the wrath plot is about to be resolved. That doesn't happen.

In his response to the embassy of Odysseus, Phoenix and Ajax, Achilles effectively questions the macro Trojan War plot by wondering why it is being waged for 'for fair-haired Helen's sake' (9.339). Ajax later turns the tables on him when he wonders why the micro wrath plot is still in play 'because of one girl only' (9.637–8). A lot happens in the *Iliad* 'because of one girl only'. The epic's plot is kick-started by Chryses' plea for his daughter Chryseis. Chryses' prayer to Apollo to afflict the Greeks with a plague is itself comparable to Achilles' request (through Thetis) of Zeus to afflict the Greeks with Trojan victories.[6] There is no indication that Achilles makes this connection, but the correspondence is there: trouble over a young woman, with resolution achieved by return of the woman. Achilles disappoints expectations by not following this pattern, at least at first.

His refusal is passionate but not strictly logical. He claims Agamemnon has taken his 'wife' (9.336), comparing this to the theft of Helen ('Do they [Menelaus and Agamemnon] then alone [...] love their wives?' [9.339–40]). But he quietly concedes that the 'wife' is 'but the captive of my spear' (9.343). Homer had briefly noted that Briseis went back to Agamemnon 'unwilling' (1.348), and Briseis later startles us by speaking of plans to wed Achilles (19.297–9). But shortly before her remarks Achilles regrets his anger 'for the sake of a girl', and goes on to wish that 'Artemis had slain her with an arrow' on the day he acquired her (19.55–60). So much for the love story that both ancient and modern audiences have been tempted to read into the plot.[7]

Achilles repeatedly toys with the poem's plot. Already in Book 1 Achilles considers running Agamemnon through with a sword (188–92), which would have immediately cut short the story of the *Iliad*. The angered hero had also threatened to return home (1.169–71). In Book 9 Achilles backs up this threat by claiming he has a choice of fates: either to return home and live long, or to die at Troy and achieve heroic *kleos*. The hero may be deceiving the embassy (or himself) about the ongoing possibility of a choice (would that not have been made when he left for war?).[8] And the replies of Achilles to his interlocutors gradually soften his position; eventually he concedes that he would return to battle if Hector attacked his Myrmidons (650–5). The wrath plot is sustained if not resolved.

In Book 16 Achilles agrees to lend Patroclus his armour (a strategy suggested to Patroclus by Nestor) as a sort of compromise. At this moment he suggests that the Greeks might offer him Briseis and gifts (85–6). This is odd – the embassy had already made that offer, yet he failed to act upon it. By his dithering Achilles has allowed the wrath plot to stretch out elastically, and it tragically snaps back at him when Patroclus is killed by Hector. Thetis points out to her grieving son that Zeus accomplished his wishes, 'as earlier you prayed' (18.74–5). His withdrawal has had consequences, but in unintended ways. Now he vows vengeance against his friend's killer. His anger towards Agamemnon means nothing to him now, and so the wrath plot jumps the track: the hero's wrath is now directed at Hector.

But this analysis of the *Iliad*'s plot so far has made it seem as if Achilles is the main character. This is true in the sense that the plot does revolve around him. But a withdrawn hero is a poor protagonist. In the long battle scenes before and after Book 9 Achilles essentially disappears from the poem. True, he speaks more than anyone else in the poem, more even than garrulous old Nestor. And in his absence the dynamic warrior Diomedes seems like his doublet, at least until he is wounded (then the Greeks hang on through the defensive efforts of Ajax). But some see a different character as central to the *Iliad*: Achilles' antagonist Hector.[9]

The Trojan leader's emotional meeting with his wife Andromache is one of the poem's most memorable scenes, as noted earlier (see also the discussion in Chapter 6). Hector is active throughout the poem on the battlefield (if sometimes cautious, and sometimes bested by the Greeks). The encounter with Achilles in Book 22 that leads to his death is the climax of the action in the poem, and in Books 22 and 24 much attention is given to the Trojan reaction to his death, notably by his wife and parents; his death is portrayed as the end of Troy's hopes. Hector is described as the 'only' defender of the city (6.403), and upon Hector's death Trojans wail 'as though all [Troy] were utterly burning with fire' (22.410–11). The Homeric epic, in its humane vision, encourages sympathy for the defeated enemies of Greeks. In this sense Hector is the tragic hero of the poem – or at least a second tragic hero, since Achilles tragically confronts his mortality as well as his guilt over the death of Patroclus.

Yet it should be noted that the Homeric poem's equation of Hector's death with Troy's sack is an illusion. After the death of Hector, other defenders will arrive from far away to defend Troy – at least in cyclic myth. In the *Aethiopis* of the Epic Cycle, the Amazon Penthesileia and the Aethiopian king Memnon arrive to defend Troy. These exotic defenders of Troy are much more powerful than Hector: each is a great warrior, with large forces behind them. After Achilles defeats Penthesileia and Memnon, and then is himself killed, the Greeks remain stymied. They discover they are required by fate to fulfil certain obligations before Troy can fall. The bow of Heracles and its current owner, Philoctetes, are fetched. And the Palladion, a small statue of Pallas Athena, is stolen from Troy. Still no sack. Neoptolemus, the son of Achilles, is brought from the island Scyros. He kills Eurypylus, *another* ally who arrives after Hector's death to defend Troy. But nothing is decided; Troy will not fall. It takes the trick of the wooden horse to sack the city.

If you learn of the Troy story from Homer first, it might seem like these cyclic episodes unnecessarily delay the story. But there's little chance that these post-Hector episodes result from post-Homeric innovation. The *Iliad* predicts that Philoctetes will be summoned (2.721–4). Achilles speaks of his son Neoptolemus at Scyros (19.326–7); Odysseus tells his shade in the underworld that he summoned his son to Troy, where he performed bravely (*Odyssey* 11.506 ff.). Penthesileia, Memnon and Eurypylus are not mentioned in the *Iliad*, but the latter two are referenced in the *Odyssey* (4.188, 11.520, 522). It is notable that Hector is *not* recalled in the *Odyssey*; in the grand scheme of things, he is a minor player. As for the wooden horse, it is absent from the *Iliad*, but it is described at length by Menelaus (4.266 ff.) and Demodocus (8.499 ff.) in the *Odyssey*, and mentioned by Odysseus (11.523–32). Of course, it is central to the cyclic story of the Trojan War, appearing in both the *Little Iliad* and the *Sack of Troy*.[10]

For some, the apparent inconsistency between the *Iliad*'s emphasis on Hector's death and the numerous episodes that follow is a 'problem'. One solution is to excise Iliadic references to cyclic material as post-Homeric intrusions and describe 'cyclic' passages in the *Odyssey* as reflections of post-Iliadic innovation. But the evidence of early Greek art, which depicts cyclic scenes earlier and more often than Homeric ones, belies that argument.[11] The earliest audiences of the *Iliad* would have known the cyclic 'extensions' of the Troy story. They also would have known that neither Hector's death nor Achilles' had any effect on the war's outcome. Not that this is a 'problem' for the poet of the *Iliad*: he is confident in his power to create a temporary impression that the city will fall soon after Hector's death. It works for this author, even though cyclic myth is not unfamiliar to him.

Just as Achilles toys with the poem's micro plot, Homer sometimes teases us by allowing the macro plot of the whole war to be threatened. In Book 2 Agamemnon clumsily tests his troops' morale by announcing Troy will never be taken – and in response the soldiers rush to the ships (109 ff.). If Odysseus hadn't stopped them, the Greeks would have returned 'beyond what was fated', we are told (155). Here 'fate' is essentially tradition. Then there is the duel between Menelaus and Paris in Book 3. Both sides agree that this duel, not further warfare, will decide who gets to keep Helen. But when Menelaus wins, or apparently does (Aphrodite whisks Paris away before he can be killed), the Trojan ally Pandarus wounds him with an arrow, breaking the agreement.

The ancient audience *knows* from tradition that Achilles will return to battle, that Hector will die, Achilles will die, and Troy will fall. Suspense might be elicited when a listener succumbs to the powerful here-and-now vividness of the poetry, but major instances of anti-tradition, like Helen never going to Troy (see Chapter 1), do not occur in Homeric poetry. So that nobody loses track of the plot, both micro and macro, the poet places signposts here and there along the way. In Book 8 Zeus authoritatively predicts the eventual return of Achilles after more Greek suffering (469 ff.), and in Book 15 he goes further, laying out the deaths of Patroclus and Hector (53 ff.). The coming sack of the city is casually mentioned here, as it often is elsewhere in the poem; Achilles' death is also predicted numerous times throughout the poem (memorably when predicted by his horse, and the dying Hector: 19.404–19; 22.358–60).[12] More indirectly, the death and funeral of Patroclus correspond to the coming death and funeral of Achilles. Achilles himself sometimes acts in a way that prefigures what we know of his death and burial. Neoanalysts have especially explored such parallelism, as discussed in Chapter 5.

Pre-Iliadic events, not just post-Iliadic, are also frequently mentioned in the poem. Characters speak of such events as Achilles' experiences at home, the beginning of the expedition at Aulis, and the plundering of towns in the vicinity of Troy. The poem also seems to enact cyclic episodes outside its story. Though Aristotle praises the *Iliad* for containing its story, he also states that the *Iliad*'s plot is diversified by events from the Trojan War in general, specifying the catalogue of Greek ships in Book 2. Presumably Aristotle means that this list of ships and their leaders indirectly reflects the gathering of ships at Aulis in the first year of the war (which is recalled directly at 2.303–4). Other passages have been thought more appropriate for the war's early years. In Book 3 (161 ff.) Priam on the walls of Troy asks Helen to point out Greek leaders to him: would this not make more sense in the initial mobilization of Greek forces? The same might be said of the subsequent duel between Menelaus and Paris. When Helen afterwards succumbs to Paris's charms in their bedroom, this is suggestive of the initial seduction. Indirect reflection of both pre- and post-Iliadic events, then, as well as direct references to the larger tradition of the Trojan War, justify the title of the *Iliad*: in a sense, it is a 'poem about Troy'.[13]

But however much the *Iliad* alludes to myth of the Trojan War, and however much its wrath plot may stray, it maintains a unified control over its own narrative. This seems apparent in its structure, whereby thematic correspondences between Book 1 and Book 24 provide a satisfying sense of circular completion. Chryses succeeds in his bid to get his daughter back from Agamemnon; Priam succeeds in recovering the corpse of his son. Whereas the first book closes with divine argument and then harmony over Zeus' intention to help the Trojans, the last book opens with divine controversy and then agreement to bring about the burial of Hector. In both situations Thetis was the intermediary between the mortal and immortal realms, relaying Achilles' request to Zeus, then in the other direction relaying the gods' wishes to Achilles.[14]

So the narrative of the *Iliad* seems to be both macro and micro. The epic assumes broad knowledge of the Trojan myth on the part of its audience, and, as Aristotle suggests, extra-Iliadic episodes from the Trojan War seem to be slotted in here and there, indirectly and anachronistically. Achilles' wrath (towards Agamemnon, then Hector) remains central to the poem, but much else happens. The pace of narration slows remarkably – between a flurry of undescribed days at the beginning of the poem (nine days of the plague, twelve days while Thetis waits for Zeus and the Olympians to return from visiting the Aethiopians) and at its end (twelve days for Achilles' mistreatment of Hector's corpse, nine days for Trojan preparation of Hector's funeral), the poem focuses mostly on three long days of battle (essentially from Book 2 to the middle of Book 7; Books 11–18; and Books 19–22). Warriors fight, characters talk, and details of human life are lovingly described. But these topics will be pursued in the next chapter; now it is time to focus on the plot of the *Odyssey*.

Plots in the Odyssey

The *Odyssey* tells the story of Odysseus' return to Ithaca after wandering at sea for many years. It opens at the hero's palace in Ithaca, where suitors who assume Odysseus to be dead harass Penelope and her son. The poem directly narrates the final stages of the return of the Ithacan, from the island of Calypso to the Phaeacians of Scheria and finally to Ithaca, where after careful planning he succeeds in slaying the suitors, thereby regaining both home and wife. As for his famous adventures at sea, the hero recounts these to the Phaeacians who finally bring him home. Odysseus' tale of exotic peoples, monsters and goddesses, who alternatingly threaten the return with violence (Polyphemus, Scylla, the Laestrygonians) or temptation (Lotus-Eaters, Circe, Sirens, Calypso), underscores certain themes later prominent at Ithaca. Odysseus has survived his wanderings more by wile than might, and he will employ disguise and deceit to overcome the suitors.[15]

The poem assumes the hero's return. It is traditional, after all, and the *Odyssey* continually signals that Odysseus will indeed arrive in Ithaca and slay the suitors. For example, in Book 2 the Ithacan seer Halitherses concludes from a bird omen that Odysseus is nearby, planning death for the suitors. Halitherses is not surprised; the seer had predicted to Odysseus at his departure that he'd return in disguise in the twentieth year after much suffering (2.161 ff.). Odysseus himself receives a somewhat ambiguous prediction about his return from Tiresias in the underworld (11.115–17). As in the

Iliad, authoritative signposting confirms the basic outlines of the plot; Zeus casually asserts in Book 5 (29 ff.) that Odysseus will get to Phaeacian Scheria and to Ithaca – though this will not happen until Book 13. And shortly before the suitors are slain, they fail to perceive supernatural portents that a seer interprets as a sign of their approaching death (20.345–57).

The *Odyssey* features a different type of hero than the *Iliad*, and it certainly contains a broader range of geography (the Mediterranean and beyond, even all the way to the underworld) and society (slaves as well as aristocrats are featured). Yet at a fundamental level the two epics are comparable. They are both about the Trojan Cycle, if different parts of it, and they share many characters (for example, Odysseus is prominent in the *Iliad*, and Achilles appears in two different underworld scenes in the *Odyssey*). That the two poems avoid duplicating material – the *Iliad* does not predict Odysseus' wandering return, for example, and the *Odyssey* never mentions Hector – suggests that they constitute a connected pair of compositions (see Chapter 5 on the question of authorship of the Homeric epics). Despite their differences, they share a fundamental structure of three basic parts: withdrawal, devastation and return. This pattern is most obvious in the *Iliad* (Achilles withdraws, the Greeks suffer, Achilles returns) but is operative in the *Odyssey* as well (Odysseus is absent, Ithaca suffers, Odysseus returns). That the poetics of the two Homeric poems are comparable will become evident in the next chapter.

The *Iliad*'s first word announces its topic: 'wrath'. The *Odyssey* is not as immediately forthcoming: the first word is *aner*, 'man'. The literal sequence of the opening words is 'man to me tell of, Muse'. In our English translation the words are rearranged a little:

> Tell me, Muse, of the man of many devices, driven far astray after he
> had sacked the sacred citadel of Troy. Many were the men whose cities
> he saw and whose minds he learned, and many the woes he suffered in
> his heart upon the sea, seeking to win his own life and the return of his
> comrades. Yet even so he did not save his comrades, for all his desire, for
> through their own blind folly they perished – fools, who devoured the
> cattle of Helios Hyperion; whereupon he took from them the day of

their returning. Of these things, goddess, daughter of Zeus, beginning
where you will, tell us in our turn. (1–10)

The poet requests that the Muse provide information about this man,
described at first only as *polytropic*. This epithet is used in reference to
Odysseus alone among heroes. It translates literally as 'much-turning', which
has the primary meaning of 'much-travelled'. The epithet thus brings the long
return of Odysseus to mind, an impression bolstered by mention of long
wandering. The specification in the second line that he wandered 'after he
had sacked the sacred citadel of Troy' (2) points directly to Odysseus, the
implementer of the wooden-horse strategy. The hero's name is not given until
line 21, perhaps prefiguring the hero's crafty reluctance to name himself later
in the poem. But by then the reader has realized that the poem's subject is
the 'return of Odysseus'. Already mentioned is the failure of the unnamed
man's companions to return (5–9), as well as his longing for *nostos* ('return')
and wife (13). Calypso detains the man, Ithaca is his goal, and Poseidon is
angry with him (14–20): this tale must be about Odysseus.

But the return of Odysseus is about ten years long; hence the Horatian
concern of the poet to negotiate with the Muse for a suitable starting point
in medias res (see Chapter 1). The poet reports that it's time for the hero to
return home, and that the gods pity him – all except for Poseidon. But since
the sea god is away visiting the exotic Aethiopians, the rest of the Olympians
can devise a plan to effect Odysseus' return. So the first scene is a gathering
of the Olympians. Zeus starts talking about Aegisthus, blaming him for
ignoring divine warning about bedding Clytemnestra and murdering her
husband Agamemnon upon his return. Even though this story is not *causally*
linked to the return of Odysseus, its early prominence alerts the reader to
its *thematic* importance. Odysseus will be urged to be more careful about
his return than Agamemnon was, and Telemachus will be urged to oppose
actively his mother's suitors, who correspond to Aegisthus.

Athena quickly changes the topic to Odysseus, whom she says Zeus
neglects. Zeus agrees that Odysseus should return to Ithaca, and with alac-
rity Athena suggests a plan: the gods' messenger Hermes is to tell Calypso
of their new resolve, and she herself will go to Ithaca to rouse Telemachus

against the suitors. In particular, she will send him off to mainland Greece for news of his missing father.

So like the *Iliad*, the *Odyssey* begins 'in the middle of things' and focuses on a single 'action' of a number of weeks. As in the *Iliad*, the plot is supported by the gods.[16] But Odysseus' return to Ithaca has a more satisfying resolution than the *Iliad*'s meandering account of Achilles' wrath. Aristotle compared Odysseus' successful return to the happy denouement of comedy, as opposed to the irresolvable complications of tragedy (*Poetics* 13). For the philosopher this was no compliment – he thought Homer was pandering to an audience unappreciative of the cathartic *frisson* of the tragic. Aristotle would presumably not be pleased to learn that the *Odyssey* has had more impact than the *Iliad* in post-antiquity (see Chapter 7). But the epic's continuing hold over readers cannot be attributed to poor taste. Employing a bold yet controlled narrative strategy, the *Odyssey* masterfully channels the sweeping expanse of the Ithacan hero's story into a climax of vengeance. And as readers have often appreciated, the subtlety of the narrative complicates the epic's seeming closure.[17]

The *Odyssey*'s tale of heroic return does seem more unified than the *Iliad*'s episode of Achilles' wrath. A wife pressured to remarry when her husband remains unaccountably absent, the husband's sudden return in the nick of time – this seems like a stand-alone story with beginning, a middle and an end. In fact it is a common folk tale.[18] Yet the return of the Ithacan hero is contextualized within the multifarious myth of the Trojan War. Before his return Odysseus has already experienced the long Trojan War, including the sack of Troy by the stratagem of the wooden horse. His return after the fall of Troy is one of many heroic returns. The Ithacan bard Phemius knows a song on the theme of the 'return [*nostos*] of the Achaeans' (1.326), a topic also covered by an Epic Cycle poem entitled *Nostoi* (*Returns*). Athena's anger at impious behaviour during the sack caused many of the Greek heroes to suffer in their returns.[19] Such stories are told by Nestor and Menelaus in Books 3 and 4. These heroes have not heard anything definite about Odysseus; his return is still to unfold in the course of the *Odyssey*. But even after Odysseus returns to Ithaca, further adventures await. Besides the mysterious 'inland journey' prophesized by Tiresias in Book 11, there are non-Homeric traditions of post-return events, such as the hero's death by the son he produced with Circe (see Chapter 1).

As Aristotle notes (*Poetics* 8), the *Odyssey* does not relate a biography of Odysseus. One might expect a 'poem about Odysseus', the title's meaning, to begin with his childhood, continue on with his Trojan War career, and end with his return and eventual death. But the Homeric poem focuses on the overcoming of the suitors at Ithaca. The *Odyssey* does not directly narrate the hero's wandering at sea; his many adventures while returning are told retroactively by Odysseus himself to the Phaeacians over the course of a long night (Books 9–12). The showdown with the suitors takes up the whole second half of the poem, and everything before Odysseus' arrival in Ithaca, including his travel stories, can be seen as the lead-up to Odysseus' recovery of wife and home.

The *Odyssey* follows a double narrative thread, as Aristotle notes with another mutter of disapproval (*Poetics* 13). Though Odysseus is the main character, at first the epic bestows its attention on his son Telemachus. The opening books describe the situation at Ithaca without Odysseus, and then the poem narrates Telemachus' visit to the heroes Nestor and Menelaus on the mainland (Books 3–4).[20] The reader does not meet Odysseus himself until Book 5, when he leaves Calypso for a perilous journey by raft to Scheria. There the Phaeacians, after hearing of his past adventures at sea, eventually agree to convey him home to Ithaca (Books 6–12). The hero arrives in Ithaca in Book 13 and slowly proceeds to weave a stratagem against the 108 suitors who desire his wife, property and power. He succeeds with the help of Telemachus, who himself returns to Ithaca in Book 15. At this point the Telemachus thread and the Odysseus thread – two travel tales – entwine at Ithaca.

Odysseus has been at Ogygia, Calypso's island, for seven years. Why this long pause in which nothing happens? It certainly ensures that Odysseus' return will be of greater duration than others, and therefore more glorious. But more importantly, it provides enough time for Telemachus to grow up in the twenty years since Odysseus left his wife and infant for Troy (cf. 2.175; 21.208). Telemachus matures just enough to serve as an important ally against improbable odds. As for the adventures recounted by Odysseus to the Phaeacians, they last only about sixteen months, including the year in which Odysseus dallied with Circe. When the shade of Odysseus' mother in the underworld speaks as if Telemachus is fully grown (11.184 ff.), she is mistaken; the boy must have been a pre-teen at this point.

It would be a mistake to become distracted by temporal considerations, however, since time in myth is elastic and often described in typologically round numbers. Though the war in the *Iliad* is described as ten years long (2.295 ff.), such a length is not required for the events of its early years – except perhaps to allow *Achilles'* son, Neoptolemus, conceived before the war, to grow up and fight at Troy after his father's death (even so, he must have matured precociously fast). Helen surprisingly claims at the end of the poem that it is the twentieth year since she left home (24.765), which seems much too long even if she's counting the preparations and initial setbacks of the expedition.

What the proem does insist on is that Odysseus has long been detained by Calypso, though he yearns for home:

> [B]ut that man alone, filled with longing for his return and for his wife,
> did the queenly nymph Calypso, that beautiful goddess, keep prisoner
> in her hollow caves, yearning that he should be her husband. (13–15)

Our first image of Odysseus in Book 5 confirms this:

> Him [Calypso] found sitting on the shore, and his eyes were never dry
> of tears, and his sweet life was ebbing away, as he grieved for his return,
> for the nymph no longer pleased him. By night indeed he would sleep
> perforce in the hollow caves, unwilling beside the willing nymph, but
> by day he would sit on the rocks and the sands, racking his heart with
> tears and groans and griefs, and he would look out over the unresting
> sea, shedding tears. (151–8)

The goddess has reluctantly agreed to Zeus' command (conveyed by Hermes) to send the hero on his way, but she cannot resist tempting him to stay by promising immortality and pointing out that she surpasses Penelope in beauty. Odysseus remains adamant, if diplomatic, in his wish to return:

'I know very well myself that wise Penelope is less impressive to look upon than you in looks and stature, for she is a mortal, while you are immortal and ageless. But even so I wish and long day in and day out to reach my home, and to see the day of my return.' (215–20)

At the beginning of Book 1 Athena expresses to Zeus her frustration at Odysseus' enforced sojourn with Calypso:

'My heart is torn for wise Odysseus, ill-fated man, who far from his friends has long been suffering woes in a sea-girt isle [...] [Calypso] keeps back that unfortunate, sorrowing man; and continually with soft and wheedling words she beguiles him that he may forget Ithaca. But Odysseus, in his longing to see were it but the smoke leaping up from his own land, yearns to die. Yet your heart does not regard it, Olympian.' (48–60)

Zeus defends himself from Athena's charge of neglect by pointing out that Poseidon, angry over the blinding of his son Polyphemus, is responsible (1.63 ff.). Polyphemus prayed to his father not to allow Odysseus to come home, or if he is fated to do so, then only 'late', without his companions, on another's ship, and finding trouble at home (9.526 ff.). These are the same circumstances of return that Tiresias prophesizes to Odysseus (11.113 ff.). So it is Poseidon's anger that is and will keep afflicting Odysseus, though the sea god is not trying to kill the hero (Zeus assures us), and apparently he cannot prevent the fated return. When Odysseus upon reaching Ithaca asks Athena why she had not helped him, she claims she was reluctant to cross Poseidon (13.341–3).

Divine intervention is needed to get Calypso to release Odysseus, but why must Athena visit Telemachus? She says her purpose is to rouse his anger against the suitors and to get him to go and ask Nestor and Menelaus about his father's whereabouts. None of this is of immediate consequence. The suitors are surprised but not impressed by the newly spirited Telemachus; Telemachus discovers little on the mainland, other than that Odysseus is being detained by Calypso, as reported by the sea divinity Proteus to

Menelaus. That his father is reportedly alive is relevant to the complicated advice given to Telemachus by Athena, disguised as the stranger Mentes, which partly hinged on whether Odysseus has perished or not. But the advice is mostly unhinged: in short, Athena/Mentes tells Telemachus to get rid of the suitors by sending Penelope to her father to wed, or if he hears on his trip that Odysseus is alive to wait a year, or if dead to give away Penelope himself – and then plot to kill the suitors (1.269 ff.).

It's not worth trying to untangle this advice (or to pin down its origins in marriage practice),[21] for it comes from a divinity who knows that Odysseus *will* return shortly. It seems as if her intention is to jolt Telemachus out of adolescence so he can later help his father. She also tells Zeus (1.95) that the little trip will give Telemachus *kleos*, a concept explored in the next chapter. But whatever the function of the Athena-inspired journey of Telemachus, the so-called *Telemachy* of the early books is wonderfully enjoyable for the reader. After the inundation of the Ithacan palace by suitors is vividly portrayed in Books 1 and 2, the subsequent focus on the Ithacan prince in Books 3 and 4 provides us with a fascinating sort of *Bildungsroman*. The journey to Pylos and Sparta also allows tales to be told of the Trojan War and heroic returns, later supplemented by the songs of Demodocus at Scheria, and the conversations of Trojan War heroes in *two* underworld scenes (Books 11 and 24). While the *Iliad* outlines the larger narrative of the Trojan War through allusion and reflective enactment, the *Odyssey* does so by direct flashback narrative provided by multiple characters.

As indicated above, the first part of Athena's plan, Hermes' mission to Calypso, does not occur until Book 5. Near the end of Book 4 Homer leaves Telemachus at Sparta and describes how the suitors, alarmed at Telemachus' travels, plan to ambush him on his return. Book 5 then starts with a *second* council of the gods, where Athena yammers on about Odysseus again, as at the first council of Book 1, and expresses outrage over the plot against Telemachus. Zeus is mildly annoyed, if less than many modern readers, at the redundancy of the 'second divine assembly'. Why was Hermes not sent out to Calypso at the same time that Athena set out for Ithaca? This is often cited as an example of the Homeric tendency to narrate simultaneous actions as consecutive. Such does not always happen, as was once thought (the so-called 'Zielinski's Law'); when it does (as here), it need not reflect 'primitive' thinking, as Homerists used to suppose.[22] It is best to accept that the poet is trying to clarify the story helpfully, not to adhere to the rule of time realistically.

In any event Hermes does succeed in getting Odysseus unstuck from Ogygia so that he may have a difficult raft trip to Scheria (Book 5). Although the Phaeacians ultimately help Odysseus, their princess, Nausicaa, represents another threat of feminine entanglement. The Phaeacian Nausicaa is a less exotic temptress than Circe or Calypso, but her initial encounter with Odysseus reminds one of the typical tale in which a princess assists a foreign hero in need (cf. Theseus and Ariadne, or Jason and Medea). At the beginning of Book 6 Athena appears in a dream and suggests that Nausicaa's marriage is nigh. This motivates the princess to wash clothes clean at the seashore, where Odysseus meets her and observes that her future husband would indeed be a happy man. Nausicaa admits to her handmaids that the stranger would be a good catch and makes a point of warning Odysseus of the gossip if they were seen together – especially by all those guys who want to marry her. And so King Alcinous offers his daughter's hand in marriage – which Odysseus politely ignores by welcoming the alternative offer to send him home (7.311 ff.). Another tantalizing Homeric marriage plot fizzles (see the previous chapter on Achilles and Briseis). As in the *Iliad*, a potential overturning of the traditional storyline arises momentarily, only to be forestalled.

After arriving at Ithaca by means of a magic Phaeacian ship (Book 13), Odysseus disguised as a beggar stays with Eumaeus the swineherd (Books 14–16). That is where he meets Telemachus, who has successfully evaded the suitors on his return from Sparta. The two strands of the plot finally merge, and now the narrative pace slows down as Odysseus takes stock of the situation in the palace and waits for an opportune time to strike. Though less travelled than his father, visitation with heroic veterans of the Trojan War has made Telemachus much more ready to assist his father in confronting the suitors. In Book 21 Penelope, still unaware of her husband's return, sets up a bridal contest in the great hall of the palace. Whoever succeeds in stringing Odysseus' old bow is to wed Penelope. In the end only Odysseus, still disguised as a beggar, can string it. With this weapon he slays the suitors (Book 22). The slaughter of over 100 opponents is remarkable, even with Telemachus, Eumaeus, a loyal cowherd, and occasionally Athena by his side (weapons that the suitors might have used had been previously removed). Disloyal servants, including the handmaids who slept with suitors, are subsequently dispatched.

Then the blood-spattered hero who had kept his identity hidden despite close calls (his dog Argus recognizes him, but dies at once [17.290 ff.]; his nurse Eurycleia recognizes his scar, but is commanded to silence [19.386 ff.]) finds his wife is unwilling to believe it's really him. Taking a bath helps. But he also has to prove himself. Penelope tests 'much-devising' Odysseus by suggesting she moved their marriage bed (23.173 ff.). With some agitation Odysseus points out that the bed could not be easily moved – he had used the trunk of a living olive tree for one of the posts. Soon the happy couple retire to this very bed, but not before Odysseus mentions the prophecy of Tiresias about a future 'inland journey' (23.248 ff.; see Chapter 1).

This mysterious tale has intrigued many: is this how he will finally appease Poseidon? What about the seer's prediction that 'death shall come to you yourself away from the sea' (11.134–5), as the statement is usually translated? Odysseus and Penelope are happy to conclude that the hero will pass away safely removed from the marine world where he suffered so much. Most Homerists complacently share this interpretation. But the words of Tiresias are misunderstood, as often with prophecies. The Greek phrase actually means that 'death will come from the sea'. It thus references stories in which the sea is the origin of Odysseus' death.[23] In the Cyclic epic *Telegony*, the hero's son by Circe, Telegonus, arrives by sea and unwittingly slays his father with a spear tipped with a stingray spine. We don't know if Tiresias alludes to this precise version of Odysseus' death, but the 'inland journey' certainly injects into the *Odyssey* a little postscript about events outside its boundaries.[24] The vague and misleading prophecy of post-return travel and death from the sea gently unsettles the conclusiveness of Odysseus' reclamation of wife and home.

The king and queen, happy in their ignorance of the prophecy's true significance, make love and then exchange pillow talk, including a tidy summary of wanderings by the hero (23.310 ff.). But the hero's story is not over. When Odysseus wakes in the morning, he immediately arms: he knows the relatives of the suitors will seek vengeance. Odysseus and his posse (Telemachus, Eumaeus and a loyal cowherd) set out to meet Odysseus' father Laertes in the country. Then in Book 24 Odysseus and a somewhat expanded set of allies face off against the suitors' relatives. After Laertes slays the father of a suitor, Athena shouts aloud to stop the fight. Odysseus wants to continue, but a lightning bolt from Zeus and a further warning from Athena stay his hand. In accordance with Zeus' previous suggestion, she establishes a truce, and the poem ends.

Many find this conclusion disappointing. They would be happier if the *Odyssey* ended with Odysseus in the arms of Penelope. What follows – besides the aborted battle, a scene of the suitors' shades going to the underworld – is considered puzzling and inelegantly narrated. Whatever the merits of the poem's ending – I find it fascinating, and so cannot recommend that you stop reading at Book 24 – one can compare it to the ending of the *Iliad*. In both, a climax in action (Hector's death; the suitors' death) is followed by the reconciliation of allies (funeral games of Patroclus; acceptance of Odysseus by Penelope) and a truce between enemies (Achilles and Priam; Odysseus' gang and the suitors' relatives). In both poems, kin of the deceased (Hector's father Priam; the families of the suitors) need to be appeased. The *Iliad* makes no pretence that the war has now finished, but if the *Odyssey* establishes a permanent truce, it is effected only by divine intervention. And with the prophecy of Tiresias (11.121–37; 23.248–84) the *Odyssey* acknowledges that Odysseus will go on a further 'inland journey'.

Although this and more general correspondences between the two Homeric poems have been demonstrated, distinctions should be noted as well. The *Odyssey* defines ethical aspects of its plot more firmly. Odysseus is praised for killing the suitors, who are consistently and steadily portrayed in an unsympathetic manner.[25] As for the comrades of Odysseus, the proem insists that their failure to return was their own fault, and Odysseus concurs in his own account of his wanderings. The gods in the *Odyssey* seem to insist on the claims of justice more than they do in the *Iliad*. This ethical dimension is not as clear in the *Iliad*, where few characters seem purely good or evil. Because of such issues, many since antiquity have believed two separate authors are responsible for the two Homeric poems (see Chapter 5).

Another major difference between the two poems is in the heroic ideology of Achilles and Odysseus. Though a passionate speaker, Achilles is superior on the battlefield. Though a respectable warrior, Odysseus is superior in cleverness. The final fates of these two heroes – death at Troy, the return home – are radically different. Achilles described his twofold fate as a choice between *nostos* and *kleos* (*Iliad* 9.410–16); the Iliadic hero chooses death on the battlefield. Odysseus has already achieved a *kleos* that 'reaches the heavens', as he boasts to the Phaeacians (*Odyssey* 9.19–20), but also achieves, in the course of the *Odyssey*, what Achilles did not: he returns. These aspects of gods, heroes and ethics, intertwined with the construction of plot in the *Iliad* and *Odyssey*, will be explored further in next chapter on Homeric poetics.

III

POETICS

HAVING CONSIDERED the broad range of Trojan War myth and explored the architectural plotting of the *Iliad* and *Odyssey*, we should delve further into the poems themselves. This chapter will survey some of the characteristics of Homeric poetics, moving from relatively larger topics to those relatively smaller, from divinities to the heroic world, from characterization to similes, and finally on to the lexical and metrical foundations of Homeric verse.

Divinities

As became apparent when we examined the plot of the two Homeric poems, the gods are very interested in the Trojan War. Sometimes they look on as enthralled spectators, sometimes they intervene – and when they do, they typically quarrel among themselves, since they variously favour or hate different heroes. For example, Athena serves as the patron of Odysseus, whose cleverness she associates with her own skills (*Odyssey* 13.287 ff.). she somewhat paradoxically afflicts the returning Greeks because of their misbehaviour at the sack of Troy (a city which she hates!).[1] No matter how beloved by the gods, heroes must continually display their respect, particularly through sacrifices – it is not just the return of Chryseis that appeases Apollo in *Iliad* 1, but also Greek sacrifice and songs in his honour (1.446 ff.).

But much of real-world ritual and local cult is neglected in Homer. The major Olympian gods are pan-Hellenic, worshipped throughout the Greek world. Even the Trojans worship the Greek Olympians – just as they speak Greek, necessarily given the story is told from a Greek perspective for Greek audiences (yet the *Iliad* is surprisingly balanced in its sympathies). Relatively minor gods, it is true, can play important roles in keeping the plot moving. The Olympian messenger god Hermes often travels back and forth between heaven and earth, but also guides Priam to the hut of Achilles (*Iliad* 24) and gives to Odysseus an antidote for the potion that the magical Circe will give him (*Odyssey* 10). The Nereid Thetis visits Achilles and relays messages between him and the gods – she is the one who gets Zeus to help the Trojans. And the river god Scamander, who does not have anthropomorphic form, almost drowns Achilles in *Iliad* 23 (he is stopped by the fire of Hephaestus, the divine smithy).

Typically, Olympians approach mortals in disguise. In Book 3 of the *Iliad*, Aphrodite, after invisibly rescuing Paris from Menelaus, summons Helen to him in the form of an aged woman (Helen eventually recognizes her, and they have a bit of a tiff, which the god of course wins). A disguised Athena orchestrates Odysseus' stay among the Phaeacians in small ways (appearing to Nausicaa in a dream, providing Odysseus with directions, acting as a herald and marking the hero's discus throw), apparently so as not to anger Poseidon. She is disguised even when she meets Odysseus alone upon his return to Ithaca (though she eventually reveals herself).

The gods often appear to be motivated by personal reasons – favouring those who honour them, harming those who have angered them. But they have larger responsibilities. Many preside over particular aspects of the human condition (Ares is practically synonymous with war, for instance, as Aphrodite with sexual love and the lame Hephaestus with craft). And divinities preserve cultural values of the heroic world. The gods protect burial rights: Hector's last words warn Achilles of the gods' anger if he refuses to return his body (22.358–60), and eventually the Olympians decide to effect its release. Zeus oversees the obligation between guests and hosts, *xenia*. It is a central theme in the *Odyssey*, notably with regard to the behaviour of the suitors as guests and Polyphemus as host. 'I will call upon the gods that are forever, in hope that Zeus will grant that deeds of requital occur,' Telemachus proclaims to the suitors at *Odyssey* 1.378–9, and this will occur, though with Athena as the active implementer of punishment.[2] Odysseus claims at *Odyssey* 9.479 that the blinding of Polyphemus is the vengeance of Zeus, although soon afterwards Zeus ignores his sacrificial offering and plans the destruction of his ships and companions – so Odysseus concludes from hindsight (9.553–5).

As noted in the last chapter, it seems to many that the *Odyssey* has a stronger sense of divine justice than the *Iliad*. Zeus' musings about Aegisthus' seduction of Clytemnestra (1.29 ff.) have been a central passage to this over-interpretation. The Olympian merely observes that Aegisthus ignored divine warnings of coming retribution by Orestes, and Athena's distracted maxim, 'let any other also be destroyed who does such deeds' (47) hardly announces a new, progressive ethical system. The Aegisthus story is repeatedly referenced throughout the epic, but flexibly, in the manner that Homeric characters typically employ myth when describing their current situation.[3] Certainly Athena insistently employs the rhetoric of justice in her eagerness to exact vengeance on the suitors, but her attitude is not morally advanced over that of Poseidon towards Odysseus. Once in a while a simile will proffer proverbial thought of gods rewarding or punishing human behaviour (*Iliad* 16.384 ff.; *Odyssey* 19.109 ff.), and in the underworld Odysseus observes the eternal punishment of a few notorious miscreants, like Sisyphus. But the tone of such passages is more characteristic of Hesiod's old-fashioned confidence that the gods oversee human morality. The Homeric gods are, instead, capricious; their disinterest in ethics represents the uncertainty of the human condition. Achilles remarks to Priam that Zeus has an urn of good things and an urn of bad things; sometimes he gives mortals a handful from each, sometimes just a double helping of bad (24.529–33).

In the *Iliad* the gods are fascinated by the momentous occasion of the Trojan War; sometimes they even participate in it. Apollo wreaks havoc on the Greeks with a plague after Agamemnon dishonours his priest, for example, and Zeus pulls strings to assist the Trojans at the request of Thetis. But Apollo comments to Poseidon, 'Shaker of the Earth, you would not call me sound of mind if I war with you for the sake of mortals, pitiful creatures, who like leaves are now full of flaming life, eating the fruit of the field, and now again waste away and perish' (21.461 ff.). This distanced philosophy suits the larger context of the Trojan War. When Zeus refrains from mating with Thetis, whose son was fated to be greater than his father, he essentially moves trouble from the immortal to the mortal realm. The Heroic Age is progressing to a close, in accordance with the cyclic 'plan of Zeus'. The Trojan War is its last hurrah, and Odysseus is the last Greek to return.

The Homeric gods are not simply constructs of literary convention, with no basis in ancient Greek religion.[4] Yet their distinctive personalities make for good poetry. The quarrels of immortals can be as diverting as heroic strife, if not as tragic. As in academia, their passion is inversely proportional to the stakes. Perhaps what surprises modern readers the most is their occasionally comic behaviour. When Hera seduces Zeus at *Iliad* 14, he blithely claims that he has never been overcome with such desire – not even with his many mortal lovers, whom he obligingly lists at length (313 ff.). In Book 21 the gods engage in a long 'battle' among themselves (383 ff.). Zeus watches with amusement as his fellow Olympians taunt each other, or just inconsequentially chat (as when Apollo waxes philosophically with Poseidon, quoted above). At one point Hera grabs Artemis' bow and smilingly beats her about the head with it; Artemis flees in tears. This *theomachy* ('god-fight') is a pale shadow of the world-shaking divine struggles narrated in Hesiod's *Theogony*. But perhaps the most striking example of divine burlesque is told by the Phaeacian bard Demodocus: Hephaestus employs a golden net to snare his wife Aphrodite as she makes love to Ares; hilarity ensues when he displays them locked in naked embrace to the rest of the gods (*Odyssey* 8.266 ff.). It is quite an entertaining show, though it also brings to mind the epic's ongoing adultery theme (Clytemnestra and Aegisthus, and, hypothetically, Penelope and the suitors).

Homeric characters live in a world filled with invisible divine forces. The psychology of heroes is often thought to be susceptible to the mysterious will of the gods. Sometimes divine influence on heroic behaviour is more explicit. When Athena grabs Achilles by the hair in order to stop him from killing Agamemnon in Book 1 (194 ff.), for example, the scene seems to be a dramatic representation of emotional self-control. In Homer such divine interference is not thought to negate the free will of humans; through 'double motivation' (see Chapter 1) heroes are motivated by divine influence and their own inclinations at the same time. Some consider this poetic conceit, some 'primitive' psychology; it is in fact more complex than either explanation.

Heroic Ideology

For Hesiod the Heroic Age consisted of 'demigods' (*hemitheoi*; *Works and Days* 160). The only major Homeric heroes with one divine parent are Achilles (Thetis) and Aeneas (Aphrodite), and there is only one reference to demigods (*Iliad* 12.23). Homeric heroes are kings or aristocrats who seek a reputation of excellence. In *Iliad* 6 the Trojan ally Glaucus says that when his father sent him to Troy he 'earnestly charged me always to be bravest and preeminent above all, and not to bring shame on the race of my fathers, who were far the best in Ephyre and in wide Lycia' (207–10). As part of the embassy to Achilles in *Iliad* 9, Phoenix claims that Achilles' father Peleus had sent him along to Troy to teach his heroic son how 'to be both a speaker of words and a doer of deeds' (443). Persuasive public speaking, especially in assemblies, is considered just as important as war prowess. Besides battle and oratory, heroes compete in athletics, like the games held in honour of Patroclus (*Iliad* 23) and presented to Odysseus by the Phoenicians (*Odyssey* 8).

In each Homeric poem heroic competition leads to disaster. At Ithaca the suitors compete among themselves to replace the seemingly dead Odysseus. At Troy quarrelling naturally erupts amid a coalition of independent kings. Agamemnon presides not only because he is the brother-in-law of the woman over whom they fight, but also because he is the most dominant king. That is the rationale Nestor uses when urging Achilles to yield to Agamemnon. True, you are 'powerful' (*karteros*; 1.280), he says to the swift-footed hero, but Agamemnon is 'mightier' (*pherteros*; 281), repeating the terms already used by Agamemnon to describe himself and his antagonist (178, 186). Later Agamemnon says he is 'kinglier' (*basileuteros*; 9.160). Yet Achilles labels himself 'best [*aristos*] of the Achaeans' (1.244). Underlying this flurry of adjectives is the nebulous and fragile system of heroic values that modern scholars call the 'heroic code'.[5]

As commander of the Greek army, Agamemnon has the right to distribute war loot, including enslaved women. Agamemnon refers to his political status when demanding another concubine to replace Chryseis. And within the heroic code, distributed loot symbolizes status. When Achilles in Book 9 complains that he has acquired much loot but little distributed property, he is not concerned so much with wealth (or sex, or love) as much as he is with *time* ('honour'). His investment in the heroic code tempts him to return home in anger, but that would mean losing *kleos*, 'fame', the ultimate heroic goal.[6] The etymological root of *kleos* is 'hearing', and Odyssean *kleos* can simply be 'rumour'. So when Telemachus travels for *kleos* of his father, it's information he's seeking. But heroes obtain everlasting *kleos* when bards sing of *klea andron*, 'famous deeds of men' (*Iliad* 9.189; *Odyssey* 8.73).

Another aspect of heroic ideology is *aidos* ('shame'). When Andromache begs Hector to stay inside the walls of Troy, he replies, 'I dreadfully feel shame before the Trojans, and the Trojans' wives with trailing robes, if like a coward I skulk apart from the battle' (6.441–3). When Hector eventually decides to await Achilles outside the walls, he fears 'some other, baser than I' might criticize him (22.106 ff.). The Trojan desires the positive *time* of his peers but fears the negative opinion of his society. A hero's relation with his people is memorably defined by Sarpedon, an ally of Troy, who asks of his companion Glaucus: '[W]hy is it that we two are most held in honor, with a seat of honor and meats and full cups, in Lycia and all men gaze on us as gods?' (*Iliad* 12.310 ff.). The land they own reflects their status, he concludes, earned by fighting at the front ranks. The soldiers of the Lycian army approve the arrangement, he's sure, and he goes on to say that mortality impels heroes to enter battle 'where men win glory' (325). Sarpedon provides a collective or typical statement by his soldiers, and that's all one ever hears of the massed ranks in Homer. A possible exception is the abusive criticism of Agamemnon by Thersites (2.211 ff.), reminiscent of Achilles' complaints. Odysseus tells Thersites that nobody is baser (*chereioteros*; 248) and beats him, much to the amusement of the soldiers. Although Thersites has aristocratic status in non-Homeric stories, Homer goes out of his way to describe him as ugly, and Odysseus tells him not to quarrel with 'kings'.

Heroic Characterization

Homer does not omnisciently divulge the inner thoughts of his characters, as in modern novels. Nor is there much effort spent on character development, although some claim Achilles learns how to be merciful and Odysseus cautious. Tradition supplies major characters with their essential characteristics, often denoted by heroic epithets that belong to them exclusively, or almost so. Achilles, you read repeatedly, is 'swift-footed' (*podokes*); poly-qualified Odysseus is 'much-resourceful' (*polymetis*), 'of many wiles' (*polymechanos*), 'much-enduring' (*polytlas*) and 'much-travelled' (*polytropos*).

Though artefacts are lovingly detailed, Homer is not generous with description of the appearance of characters. We are not told how the most beautiful woman in the world looks; it is more effective when Trojan elders express awe at Helen's appearance (*Iliad* 3.156–60). Unusual is the detail provided for the ugliness of Thersites:

> Ugly was he beyond all men who came to Ilios: he was bandy-legged and lame in one foot, and his shoulders were rounded, hunching together over his chest, and above them his head was pointed, and a scant stubble grew on it. (*Iliad* 2.216–19)

Since the rabble-rouser Thersites is subsequently beaten by Odysseus and mocked by his comrades, it seems that his physical appearance marks his inner qualities. Achilles is apparently attractive, though he is never described in any comprehensive fashion. Perhaps unsurprisingly, Odysseus is shorter than usual, if sturdy (*Iliad* 3.193–4, 210–11). But some bestowed with good looks do not have corresponding virtues. Nireus is a 'weakling' in command of few men, though 'the handsomest man' of the Greeks, Achilles excepted

(*Iliad* 2.671–5). Showy attire can even be a negative marker of character. The Trojan ally Nastes, leader of the Carians ('barbarous of speech', the only people in Homer specified to not speak Greek), is 'decked with gold, like a girl, fool that he was'. He loses his life as well as his gold to Achilles (*Iliad* 2.867–75). Paris is handsome, judging by his effect on women, but not coincidentally he is sporting a panther skin when he panics at the sight of Menelaus (3.17).

The poet is fond of giving hints of characterization without spelling out the implications. For example, Briseis leaves 'unwilling' when taken from Achilles (1.348). But characterization is for the most part accomplished through character speech.[7] Homeric epic contains an extraordinary amount of character speech: almost half of the *Iliad* and two-thirds of the *Odyssey* (including Odysseus' flashback adventures). Instead of telling the audience what the characters are like, Homer, like a dramatist, stands aside and lets them do that, as Plato (*Republic* 607a) and Aristotle (*Poetics* 24) discerned.

I now turn to the characterization of major figures in the *Iliad* and then the *Odyssey* (some appear in both). Striking aspects of their characterization will be explored, especially qualities of their speech. Though like many I will indulge in rounding out how the characters strike me, it is important to realize that these are not real people with a full psychology. Their portrayal is based on their actions in traditional myth, supplemented by rare description and hints by the poet, plus what others say of them and what they say themselves. When certain aspects of a character arise repeatedly, we are thereby most secure in ascertaining Homeric characterization.

ACHILLES

The fiercely proud Achilles reveals a tender side when he speaks of 'shadowy mountains and sounding sea' (1.157) between Troy and home, or complains about receiving from loot 'one small thing, yet my own', as if secretly pleased with it (167). To the embassy he compares himself to 'a bird [who] brings to her unfledged chicks any morsel she may find, but with herself it goes ill' (9.323–4). He compares an entreating Patroclus to 'a girl, a mere babe, who runs by her mother's side and asks her to pick her up, and clutches at her gown, and hinders her in her going, and tearfully looks up at her till the mother picks her up' (16.7–10). And this 'speaker of words' can turn philosophical as well as poetic. In his three replies to the embassy in Book 9, he searchingly explores the 'heroic code' and his own fate.[8]

If poetic and philosophical, Achilles is certainly also ferocious. The term for his 'wrath', *menis*, is usually reserved for *divine* anger.[9] When asking Achilles to return his body, the dying Hector says: 'Take thought now lest perhaps I become a cause of the god's wrath [*menima*, 'that which causes *menis*'] against you on the day when Paris and Phoebus Apollo slay you, valiant though you are, at the Scaean gates' (22.358–60). When Achilles turns his godlike wrath against the Trojans, its intensity is frightening. After capturing the Trojan Lycaon, whom he had once captured and ransomed before, he speaks chillingly of the Trojan's death – and his own:

> 'Fool, propose not ransom to me, nor make speeches [...] now there is not one who will escape death, whomever before the walls of Ilios a god delivers into my hands – not one of all the Trojans, and least of all one of the sons of Priam. No, friend, you too die; why lament you thus? Patroclus also died, and he was better far than you. And do you not see what manner of man I am, how fair and how tall? A good man was my father, and a goddess the mother that bore me; yet over me too hang death and resistless fate. There will come a dawn or evening or midday, when my life too will some man take in battle, whether he strike me with cast of the spear, or with an arrow from the string.'
> (*Iliad* 21.99–113)

The climax of his murderous rage is the slaughter of twelve Trojan youths (at the funeral mound of Patroclus; 23.175–6). He also dishonours the corpse of Hector by dragging it about behind his chariot. Yet when the gods send Thetis to demand the return of the corpse, the hero readily agrees. Achilles normally exhibits respect for societal norms; arguably his dispute with Agamemnon results from dismay at his antagonist's disregard for the 'heroic code'. As he recalls to Lycaon, he had ransomed many captured Trojans in the past; Andromache tells Hector the story of Achilles' ransoming her captured mother and burying her father in full armour – after slaying him and all seven of her brothers (6.414–27).

Many dislike him. Agamemnon says to him, 'Most hateful to me are you of the kings, nurtured by Zeus, for always is strife dear to you, and wars and battles' (1.176–7). Hecuba, Hector's mother, calls him 'savage and faithless' (24.207) and 'a violent man, in whose inmost heart I wish I could fix my teeth and feed on it' (24.212–13). But perhaps Achilles' worst critic is himself. After Patroclus' death he ruefully admits that he, 'a profitless burden on the earth', was not 'in any way a light of deliverance to Patroclus or to my other comrades' (18.102–4). And when responding to Priam's comparison of his love for his dead son to Achilles' enduring worry over his father, Achilles regrets he cannot protect Peleus, 'since far, far from my own country I sit around in the land of Troy, causing pain to you and your children' (24.540–2).

Achilles seems to achieve some equilibrium towards the end of the poem, calmly settling disputes at the funeral games (Book 23) and gently hosting Priam. But he still remains a temperamental and fearsome warrior. When Priam becomes insistent, Achilles replies:

> 'Do not provoke me further [...] lest, old sir, I spare not even you inside the huts, my suppliant though you are, and so transgress the charge of Zeus.' So he spoke, and the old man was seized with fear, and obeyed his words. (24.559 ff.)

Achilles eventually agrees to a truce so that Hector's body can be buried, but after the truce he will kill many more, all with full awareness of his approaching death and everlasting *kleos*. But in the *Odyssey*, when Odysseus tries to flatter Achilles' shade in the underworld, Achilles replies: 'I should choose, so I might live on the earth, to serve as the hireling of another, some landless man with hardly enough to live on, rather than to be lord over all of the dead that have perished' (*Odyssey* 11.489–91). Does the hero now regret his 'choice' to die young and receive glory?[10] Not exactly, since he doesn't reject *kleos*. Perhaps because the hero has experienced much death, of both friends and enemies, he is in death very aware of life's preciousness. Or maybe he is just being a rhetorical blow-hard once again. There is something contrarian about his personality; he is the type that wants to be a respected member of a community, whether on or below earth, but is ever disillusioned.

AGAMEMNON

Agamemnon makes a bad impression at the start of the *Iliad*. The leader seems crass when he tells Chryses that his daughter will share his bed back home (29–31) and publicly states how much he prefers her to his wife (the adulterous Clytemnestra who will kill him upon return; 112–15). One remembers these first impressions when Agamemnon later mishandles his testing of the troops (2.110 ff.), gets prematurely overwrought when his brother is slightly wounded (4.148 ff.), angers instead of rouses fellow commanders (4.240 ff.), brutally overrides Menelaus' inclination to spare a supplicant ('Of them let not one escape sheer destruction and our hands, not even the boy whom his mother carries in her womb'; 6.51 ff.), has to be talked out of defeatism (9.13 ff., 14.64 ff.) and makes amends to Achilles with embarrassed awkwardness (19.78 ff.). But Priam admires Agamemnon from afar (3.167–70), and he is a warrior to be reckoned with, as demonstrated in Book 11 with his *aristeia* (an ancient critical term for extended 'excellence' in Homeric battle).

MENELAUS

Cuckolded by the woman who is the cause of the war, Menelaus has a prominent mythological role. Yet in the *Iliad* he fades in importance after a star turn, duelling against Paris (*Iliad* 3). *Odyssey* 4, however, presents a very interesting portrayal of Menelaus back at home with Helen after the war. He may not be as agile in social situations as his wife, but he's quite a storyteller. First there is his tale of Helen trying to coax hidden Greeks out of the wooden horse, told straight-faced except for a brief supposition that she acted out of divine impulse (274–5). Especially memorable, however, is his account of his return. Menelaus' *nostos* resembles both Odysseus' tale of adventures and his later lying tales. Like the lying tales, it features an exotic but geographically known land (Egypt), yet it resembles the wanderings of Odysseus in other aspects. Menelaus is stuck on an island where a helpful sea nymph Eidothea coaches him on how to catch her metamorphosing, mantic father, the sea divinity Proteus. Almost as bard-like as Odysseus, Menelaus begins with a long simile and quotes both Eidothea and Proteus, the 'characters' in his story. Proteus tells the story of Agamemnon's death (complementing different perspectives by Nestor in Book 3 and the shade of Agamemnon in Book 11), and then he relates the death of Locrian Ajax at sea, predicts a remarkable afterlife for Menelaus at Elysium, and lets on that Odysseus is alive but detained by Calypso. The last bit of information is of key importance to Telemachus (though he does not seem to be much affected by it). All of this is riveting for the audience. The motifs of this *nostos* resemble those of Odysseus (detainment on an island, an assisting female deity, metamorphosis, prophecy), and Menelaus' skill at tale-telling approaches that of the master storyteller Odysseus himself.

HECTOR

Hector may be an alternative protagonist of the *Iliad*, as suggested in Chapter 2, but he often seems a lesser warrior than the best Greek soldiers. Ajax gets the better of him before their duel is stopped (7.206 ff.), and again later (14.409 ff.). He is knocked unconscious by Diomedes (11.349 ff.) and initially flees from Achilles before their climactic duel ('In front a good man fled, but one far better pursued him swiftly', observes the poet; 22.158). Eventually he takes his stand against Achilles, in a duel made unfair by Athena's interference. He is also largely responsible for his own tragic death. In Book 16 Hector doubts the dying Patroclus' prophecy of his approaching death. When Hector puts on the armour of Achilles that Patroclus had worn, Zeus comments that it is 'improper' and confirms that the Trojan's death is imminent (17.198 ff.). If it is reasonable for him to refuse Andromache's request that he not return to battle, he repeatedly rejects wise advice for caution from Polydamas in Books 11–18, even after Achilles has shown himself. The consequences are disastrous for the Trojans, as Hector later admits (22.99–103), even as he stubbornly rejects the pleas of his parents to withdraw inside the wall.

Hector is given to illusion. He tends to imagine other people making comments about him, a habit that is self-centred but endearingly self-revealing. When telling Andromache that he would especially regret her becoming a slave after the fall of Troy, Hector imagines someone saying: 'This is the wife of Hector, who was preeminent in fight above all the horse-taming Trojans when men were fighting around Ilios' (6.460–1). It's as if Andromache will be a living memorial of Hector. Comparable is what he imagines a sailor will say about a funeral mound of a vanquished foe: 'This is the mound of a man who died long ago, whom once in his prowess glorious Hector slew' (7.89–90). It is all about him. Somewhat different is the soliloquy Hector speaks while awaiting Achilles before the walls of Troy (22.98 ff.). After supposing that Polydamas would reproach him if he went inside the city, he imagines an anonymous onlooker ('baser than I') saying, 'Hector, trusting his own might, brought ruin on the army' (107). Then in a remarkable fantasy, Hector wonders if he might lay down his arms, approach Achilles, and cut a deal to return Helen and end the war. But he suddenly pulls himself up short:

> 'But why does my heart debate these things with me: Let it not be that I approach him as a suppliant, and he not pity me nor have respect for me, but slay me out of hand unarmed, as if I were a woman, when I have taken off my armour. There is no way now I may from oak tree or from rock have a lovers' chat with him, just as youth and maiden – youth and maiden! – chat the one with the other.' (122–8)

Hector realizes the improbability of this imagined scenario, even mocking it as a 'lover's chat'. Yet remarkably he twice imagines himself in the role of a woman: naked victim and romantic maiden. Recall that the Greek hero who will shortly kill him had compared himself to a female bird and a mother.

ANDROMACHE

Andromache also has a way with words, and on one occasion also creatively envisions a future scene, complete with quotation of an anonymous figure.

After running to the walls at the sound of wailing, she discovers the sight of Hector's corpse being dragged by Achilles across the plain and launches into a plaintive address to her husband (22.477–514). Like Hector, Andromache here becomes self-referential, though that is typical of the genre of funeral lament that this speech resembles. She notes that she is now a widow, but quickly turns her attention to Astyanax, whose social status – if he survives the war – will suffer without Hector around. She imagines a scene in which he begs as a needy orphan until a more fortunate child says: 'Off with you, quick! No father of yours feasts in our company' (498). Later, in her official lament over the recovered corpse of Achilles, she again returns to the subject of Astyanax. Addressing him directly, she imagines his enslavement with her when Troy falls: 'or else some Achaean will seize you by the arm and hurl you from the wall' (24.732–8). Astyanax *is* thrown from the city walls in Trojan War myth. Andromache does not know this. That is why she can alternatively imagine him as a surviving beggar or enslaved. But the ancient audience well knew the story. In Book 6 Hector had imagined the future of Astyanax as warrior of great repute, though he also has forebodings of the future. Astyanax's fright at the sight of an armoured man reaching for him alludes to his future death. Neither parent has any real knowledge of the future, and Hector and Andromache laugh at their child's fright at his own father. But for the audience informed by traditional myth, the scene ominously foreshadows what will come.

It is Andromache who runs up to Hector in Book 6 as he is about to pass out through the city gates to the battlefield. It is after her account of how Achilles sacked her home city, slaying her brothers and father, that she memorably equates him to father, mother, brother as well as husband (429–30). She then advises him where at the walls to mass his forces, which scholars have found very odd, as it certainly is in terms of ancient Greek gender roles. But Andromache with some desperation is trying different strategies of persuasion on a listener who is not about to be persuaded, just as Odysseus takes different rhetorical tacks when trying to persuade Achilles to return in Book 9.

PARIS

Paris, who also has the name 'Alexander', is visited by Hector in Book 6, after his ignominious duel with Menelaus. When the elder brother urges him to battle, Paris readily agrees. Deflection of criticism through facile concurrence is characteristic of him. When the two brothers subsequently meet up to return to battle, Paris immediately reproaches himself before Hector can even speak. One recalls the first Homeric description of the two brothers in Book 3. After Paris skulks back into the ranks upon the sight of Menelaus, Hector rounds on him vociferously: 'Evil Paris, most fair to look on, you who are mad after women, you deceiver, I wish that you had never been born and had died unwed' (39–40); compare Diomedes on Paris: 'Bowman, reviler, glorious with your curling locks, you ogler of girls!' (11.385). Hector then urges him, tauntingly, to duel with Menelaus: 'Then you would learn what kind of man he is whose lovely wife you have. The lyre will not help you, nor the gifts of Aphrodite, your locks and your appearance, when you lie low in the dust' (52–5). But sibling relationships are complex, and at the end of Book 6 Hector concedes that Paris can be a valiant warrior; he is only grieved to hear others reproach him (520 ff.). And it is true that Paris often fights well on the battlefield. Despite criticism behind his back (3.320–2, 451–4; 7.389–93) and to his face (from Hector and Helen), he is steadfast in insisting that he keep Helen (7.347 ff.). Ultimately this depends on his father. It is a sign of Priam's indulgence that he shudders when he hears of his intended duel (3.259) and publicly backs him (7.365–78).

HELEN

The woman who ran off with Paris is defended by Penelope (*Odyssey* 23.218), who argues that she was deluded by the gods and unsuspecting of consequences. Her Homeric appearances suggest a rather more self-aware and perceptive personality. Her sense of self-importance is indicated when she is first described in the *Iliad* 'weaving a great purple web of double fold on which she was embroidering many battles of the horse-taming Trojans and the bronze-clad Achaeans, which for her sake they had endured at the hand of Ares' (3.125–8). But self-reproach is intertwined with her pride. Summoned to the walls to view Paris duel Menelaus, Helen rejects Priam's assurances that she is not to blame for the war: 'I wish that evil death had been pleasing to me when I followed your son here' (173–4). She describes Agamemnon as the brother-in-law 'to shameless [lit. 'dog-eyed'] me, if ever there was such a one' (180). When she ends her words by supposing that her twin brothers Castor and Polydeuces are avoiding jibes about her, Homer, in a seeming note of pathos, adds: 'but the life-giving earth already held them fast' (243).

Returning to Paris after the duel, she states that she wishes he had been killed by Menelaus and suggests he would be killed if he fought him again. After Paris responds with his usual blithe equanimity, she silently complies with his suggestion that they make love. It's with some surprise that one hears Paris later tell Hector in Book 6 that Helen has been urging him to fight 'with gentle words' (6.337). When Hector responds with silence, Helen addresses *him* 'with gentle words' (6.343). Again she employs suicidal self-reproach:

> 'O brother of me that am a dog, a contriver of mischief and abhorred
> by all, I wish that on the day when first my mother gave me birth an
> evil blast of wind had carried me away to some mountain or to the wave
> of the loud-resounding sea, where the wave would have swept me away
> before these things came to pass.' (344–8)

Some think her play for sympathy turns flirtatious when she wishes she had a more sensible husband and invites Hector to sit by her. She hints that Paris will get his comeuppance, but blames the war on both him and herself, and calls herself a 'dog' (356). Nonetheless she predicts 'in days to come we may be a song for men that are yet to be.' Hector is not to be detained, but Helen will memorialize his kindness in the last speech of the *Iliad*, the third lament over his corpse after Andromache and Hecuba. On that occasion she again wishes she had died before reaching Troy, before confessing that she is mourning for herself as well as Hector.

When we meet her again in the *Odyssey*'s Sparta, she is still self-loathing ('for the sake of shameless [lit. 'dog-eyed'] me you Achaeans came up under the walls of Troy'; 4.145–6), self-referential and charismatically poised. There she hosts Telemachus with aplomb, guessing his identity before her husband (4.138 ff.), spiking the wine with Egyptian drugs when the conversation turns weepy (4.219 ff.) and interpreting a bird omen (15.169 ff.). She also tells a tale: how she helped Odysseus on a spying mission inside Troy (4.235 ff.). This self-serving story is seemingly countered by Menelaus' subsequent wooden-horse story. But Homer leaves judgement to the audience; the poet's characterization is never simplistically moralistic.

PATROCLUS AND BRISEIS

The plot of the *Iliad* turns on Patroclus; it is his death that turns the wrath of Achilles from Agamemnon to Hector. But though his battlefield *aristeia* is impressive, he is not a major character. He passionately admonishes Achilles in Book 16 (20 ff.) and later, as he dies, responds with dignity to a taunting Hector (843 ff.). His appearance to Achilles as a shade imploring burial is certainly impressive (23.65 ff.). But mostly he seems to be hanging around in a helpful kind of way. When the embassy visits Achilles, Patroclus is in charge of the barbecue. Sent by Achilles to get a report on the wounded in Book 11, he patiently listens to one of Nestor's typically long-winded speeches and then stops to tend the wounds of a comrade despite being eager to report back to Achilles. The most memorable description of his niceness occurs after his death. As the slave women mourn over his corpse, Briseis speaks. We had not heard from this enslaved concubine while Agamemnon and Achilles were squabbling over her. It is all the more remarkable, then, when she gives a haunting lament over the corpse of Patroclus (19.287–300).[11] In the self-referential manner of the lament genre, she speaks of seeing her husband and brothers slain and her hometown sacked – by Achilles, although she praises Patroclus for comforting her with talk of her marriage to the hero. A window has suddenly opened onto the past troubles and future hopes of a minor character whose story is not unusual for the war (compare Chryseis and Andromache). Typically Homeric is the abrupt and brief insight into the psychology of the other slave women who 'added their laments; Patroclus indeed they mourned, but each one her own sorrows' (301–2). Also Homeric is the willingness to repeat this striking conceit shortly thereafter when the Greek elders mourn Patroclus (338–9).

ODYSSEUS

It should first be noted that the *Odyssey*'s protagonist plays an important role in the *Iliad*. It is he who leads the expedition to return Chryseis (Book 1), prevents retreat back to Greece by beating up Thersites (2.243 ff.), assists Diomedes in slaying the newly arrived Trojan ally Rhesus on a night raid (Book 10), rebukes a despondent Agamemnon (14.82 ff.), and insists Agamemnon and Achilles conclude their rift with proper ceremony (19.154 ff.). Odysseus almost never disgraces himself on the battlefield (8.92–8 is a notable exception), but clever speaking is his strength. A Trojan elder recalls that Odysseus spoke 'words like snowflakes on a winter's day' (3.222) on a diplomatic mission to Troy. As one of the embassy, his speech to Achilles is masterful, weaving together his father Peleus' past enjoinders, his rival Hector's taunts and the promises of Agamemnon (with the general's bluster tactfully left out). 'Much-devising' (*polymetis*) applies to the Odysseus of the *Iliad* as well as the *Odyssey*. The reader wonders a bit when Odysseus starts speaking to Achilles after Ajax nods to Phoenix, whom Nestor had declared the embassy's leader (9.223 ff.). And Achilles may be referencing Odysseus when he comments in response that 'hateful in my eyes as the gates of Hades is that man who hides one thing in his mind and says another' (9.312–13).

But Odysseus is certainly a master storyteller. His Phaeacian hosts are spellbound by his lengthy account of his past adventures, and King Alcinous compares him to a bard: 'upon you is a grace of words, and within you is a heart of wisdom, and your tale you have told with skill, as a minstrel does' (11.367–8). Like a bard, he regularly quotes the speech of 'characters' in his tale, and sometimes these characters report the speech of others. In addition, Odysseus unusually employs bard-like skill with similes.[12]

But Odysseus is not a poet. His travel tale is spontaneous speech – though necessarily conveyed by Homer in verse, since it is embedded in an epic poem. Odysseus employs hindsight and conjecture in his report, but he is not omniscient like a bard with recourse to a Muse. Should the reader suspect the truthfulness of the adventures? In Book 19 (203) Homer comments that Odysseus made the false seem true in one of his lying tales. Hesiod similarly says that the Muses can make 'many falsehoods seem like the truth' (*Theogony* 27), but when the Muses' material is traditional, it must be 'true'. The reader knows that the lying tale in Book 19 is false innovation. As for the adventures, Homer vouches for the main outlines of Odysseus' account. In the proem the poet speaks of Odysseus' long return, specifying one adventure (the cattle of the sun-god Helios; 7–9). Homer then speaks of Calypso (14), Poseidon's anger (20–1) and the murderous Cyclops (2.17–20), whose blinding the authoritative Zeus talks of in Book 1 (68 ff.). The poet also confirms the Circe episode (8.448) and narrates Odysseus' journey to and his stay with the Phaeacians. Additionally, one can probably assume Odysseus does not lie to himself when he mentions the Cyclops in a soliloquy (20.18–21).

To us it seems a paradox that the 'lying' tales feature real places (Crete, Egypt, the Greek mainland) and historical peoples (Egyptians, Phoenicians), whereas the tales with goddesses, monsters and exotic peoples are 'true'. The two sets of stories are actually not that different. There is thematic correspondence between the adventures and the lying tales (fighting in Troy, storms, conveyance by strangers, amassing of guest-gifts), and one lying tale even borrows aspects of the wanderings (the cattle of Helios, the Phaeacians; 19.275–83). Moreover, in some of his lying tales in Ithaca Odysseus asserts that 'Odysseus' will return soon. This is true, or rather, already true, although nobody believes him – previous visitors to Ithaca had routinely lied about Odysseus' imminent return.[13] Alcinous declares the hero is *not* like a lying wanderer with unverifiable information (11.362–6). His protestation acknowledges what the Phaeacians must be thinking: can we believe this rover's sea tales? Among the epic's characters, Odysseus' credibility is an issue, in both Scheria and Ithaca, but Homer expects his audience to think the adventures are true and the lying tales are false.

One might suspect that Odysseus at least 'spins' the tale. The adventures tend to feature bad hosts, whether tempting or hostile. Whatever else the adventures do, they seem to send a programmatic message to the Phaeacians:

be good hosts and do not harm me – or tempt me with Nausicaa.[14] Homeric characters often modify traditional tales when trying to persuade or dissuade the listener. Trying to get Achilles to return, Phoenix talks of Meleager withdrawing from battle and rejecting embassies – not the way the tale was usually told (9.527 ff.). In the absence of pre-Homeric texts, it may be hard to distinguish tradition from innovation (did Meleager traditionally withdraw, which Homer copied for Achilles?). But creative tweaking of traditional stories depends on a culture-wide knowledge of their basic outlines.

In the Cyclops episode, Odysseus' verbal dexterity is dazzling. Odysseus' assumed name 'Outis' would sound almost the same as *ou tis* ('no one'), so the other Cyclopes misunderstand 'Outis is slaying me' as 'No one is slaying me' (410). When the Cyclopes use the alternative form *me tis* for *ou tis* in their dismissive reply, Odysseus is ready with a further pun. The *polymetis* ('much-devising') hero tells his Phaeacian audience how proud he was of his *metis* ('cunning'). Odysseus is not so clever when he boastingly reveals his name to the vanquished Polyphemus, which allows the Cyclops to curse him (9.502 ff.). But the 'nobody' theme persists in the epic. Shipwrecked and naked on the shore of Scheria, Odysseus is a 'nobody' who has to recover his identity slowly. At home in Ithaca he disguises himself as a beggar until the right moment to reveal himself.

The lying of Odysseus is pragmatic. Is it ethical? Are his actions ethical? This is the story of a war commander returning without men or a fleet to a homeland where he wreaks havoc (besides the slaying of suitors, a dozen handmaidens who slept with suitors are hanged, and a disloyal goatherd has his hands, feet, nose, ears and genitals cut off). In Book 24 a father of a slain suitor persuasively sums up the case against Odysseus:

> 'Friends, truly a monstrous deed has this man contrived against the Achaeans. Some he led off in his ships, many men and brave ones, and he lost his hollow ships and utterly lost his men; others again he has killed on his return.' (426–9)

However, Eupeithes is the father of the worst of the suitors, Antinous. Homer thus both allows and undercuts potential criticism of Odysseus.[15] The hero does much the same in his account of the adventures. He includes biting criticism of himself by Eurylochus (10.429–48), but Eurylochus ends up looking ridiculous for cowardly behaviour.

Still, it is difficult to blame Eurylochus when he mutinously persuades the companions to eat the cattle of Helios at Thrinacia: if the choice is starvation or risking the wrath of the Helios, he says, let us stay alive for now (12.340 ff.). This is the one episode mentioned in the proem where Homer insists that Odysseus *tried* to bring his comrades home, but they perished 'through their own bind folly' (1.7). Some wonder if the poet protests too much; eleven of Odysseus' twelve ships were lost previously to the Thrinacian episode. Elsewhere in Graeco-Roman literature the character of Odysseus ranges from suspect to villainous (see Chapter 7). This is not the consequence of post-Homeric revisionism; Homer has given us an unusually supportive portrait of Odysseus.

PENELOPE

Though often praised as icon of faithfulness, Penelope is sometimes mocked for ineffectual weepiness.[16] But it is Penelope who decides that there should be an archery contest for her hand in marriage (19.570 ff.), and in Book 22 she implements the contest, even insisting that the 'beggar' get a turn (Telemachus then sends her away). And it is Penelope who holds off from accepting that the beggar is really her husband, until she cleverly elicits proof of identity from him with the bed ruse. There is also 'Penelope's web', her delaying tactic of weaving and unweaving a funeral shroud for Odysseus' father. But this motif is not as climactic as one might expect. The web story is told as something of the past (2.93 ff.; 19.137 ff.; 24.128 ff.) and nothing changes after Penelope is found out. The Homeric poem at once suppresses her activity, yet makes Ithaca revolve around her inactivity.

The fragility of her position is underscored by constant references to the adultery of Clytemnestra (1.35–6; 3.263 ff.; 11.432–4; 24.199–202). The shade of Agamemnon advises Odysseus 'never be gentle even to your wife' (11.441) and to return home in secret, 'for no longer is there faith in women' (456), even after conceding Penelope's goodness. In Book 13 Athena advises the returning Odysseus to test Penelope (336), even as she describes her as being deceptive to the suitors. Later she urges Telemachus to return to Ithaca, suggesting that a new marriage is imminent and that Penelope will transfer his rightful property to her new husband (15.10 ff.). The icon of faithfulness is much suspected within the epic, even by those closest to her.

It is interesting, then, that Penelope defends Helen as unaware of the consequences of her adultery (23.209 ff.). When in the second underworld scene the shade of Agamemnon brings up Clytemnestra, his wife who with her lover Aegisthus murdered him, it is to contrast her with Penelope. Delighted by the tale of the web and further trickery, as claimed by the suitors, he praises her faithfulness and announces her *kleos* of excellence will be everlasting in song (24.191 ff.). Penelope herself predicts that her *kleos* will become even greater if her husband successfully returns (19.127–8), which is what happens. In the value system of Homeric epic, this is unusual validation of a female character.

TELEMACHUS

Penelope's son Telemachus is often short with his mother: in Book 1 he rebukes her for asking the bard Phemius to stop singing the *nostoi*, 'returns', of the Greeks (they make her sad because one return is incomplete), and in Book 23 he reprimands his mother for her reluctance to believe that Odysseus is truly Odysseus. Whatever his age, he strikes some readers as adolescent. Urged by Athena in disguise to tell off the suitors in a public assembly, he makes a good start but then stops in tears (2.80–1; heroes do cry: cf. Achilles at *Iliad* 1.348–50). Nonetheless, he is a poised, alert guest of Nestor and Menelaus in Books 3 and 4, and a reliable co-conspirator of Odysseus in the second half of the poem (where he claims to have matured; 18.228–9). His behaviour can seem odd, what with public sneezing (17.542) and laughing (21.105), perhaps impelled by secret knowledge. But he displays decisiveness towards the end of the poem, whether for good or bad. He persuades his father to spare Phemius and the herald Medon (22.330 ff.), and it is his idea to hang the disloyal handmaidens after Odysseus directed him to use a sword (22.435 ff.).

NAUSICAA

For a time in Book 6 Nausicaa takes centre stage with her expedition to the beach with her handmaidens. She calmly stands fast while her companions run away in fright at the approach of the sea-grimed and naked Odysseus. After she hears out his bravura rhetorical performance, in which he subtly establishes his credentials, flatters her and wishes her well – including 'marriage and a home' (181) – she sensibly takes care of his immediate needs and advises him on how to approach her parents. She speaks little but effectively. When she offers to wash clothes for her father and brothers she hides her real motivation: clean clothes for her own potential marriage (as suggested by Athena). Homer points out that dad knows what she is thinking (6.57 ff.). We do not need to be told what she is thinking when she confidingly states to her companions, 'would that such a man as he [Odysseus] might be called my husband, dwelling here, and that it might please him to remain here' (239 ff.). But although her father is soon blurting out the possibility of their marriage (7.309 ff.), Nausicaa and Odysseus only speak to each other once more, pleasantly to wish each other well (8.457 ff.).

Similes

One aspect of Odysseus' initial speech to Nausicaa that must charm her is his skilled use of the simile. He compares her to a 'young shoot of a palm springing up' (*Odyssey* 6.163) after first likening her to Artemis (6.151–2). That Homer had just provided a simile comparing Nausicaa to Artemis (6.102 ff.) underscores Odysseus' likeness to a poet. Above I also described Achilles as 'poetic', noting the two similes in which he compares himself to a mother bird and a mother. Yet character similes are usually brief, and most similes are Homer's. In the poet's voice similes also can be brief ('like a lion'), not too different from some common comparative metaphors ('winged words'). And these short similes can fill out a line, like compound epithets that describe heroes.

But it is the long similes that have dazzled Homeric audiences down through the ages.[17] These often extend beyond the particular point of contact into a mini-narrative. The scene inside the extended simile might serve to emphasize what is in the main text, but often its expansion seems to ignore or contradict it. Consider the comparison of Patroclus and his troops, rushing to battle after the long withdrawal, to wolves:

> [L]ike ravening wolves in whose hearts is fury unspeakable – wolves that have slain in the hills a great horned stag, and rend him, and the jaws of all are red with gore; and in a pack they go to lap with their slender tongues the surface of the black water from a dusky spring, belching forth blood and gore, the heart in their breasts unflinching, and their bellies gorged full. (*Iliad* 16.156–63)

The point is that the Myrmidons (Achilles' people) move quickly like fierce wolves, but the simile quickly turns its attention to the rather static post-prandial activities of bloated wolves. Perhaps this generally foreshadows bloody success on the battlefield, but in this case it looks like Homer becomes distracted by images of wolfish tongues and lupine vomiting. And why not? The reader is presented with very vivid imagery from the natural world.

The narratives within similes are generic – they are not stories about particular people, least of all traditional heroes. They can be grouped into different categories of content – for example, farming, hunting, nature, weather – though the wording of each of the longer ones is usually unique. We are told about how a typical person or animal behaves in a situation, or we are presented with a natural scene familiar to any human. Predators like lions and boars hunt prey (wild or domestic animals); hunters attack predators; shepherds defend their flocks. Similes feature humans who are unremarkable, and most are not present in the heroic world of Homer. For example, women and children: Athena diverts an arrow like a woman shooing a fly off her child's face (4.130–1) and Apollo knocks down the Greek defensive wall like a child with a sand castle (15.362–5).

However far a simile may stray from what it describes, it often makes what might be difficult to visualize conceivable. Something large in scale might be compared to something small. For example, Achilles' battle with the river Scamander is compared to a farmer irrigating his garden (*Iliad* 21.257–62). Longer similes also provide variety. That is probably why the battle scenes of the *Iliad* have so many long similes, and why the *Iliad* has many more long similes than the *Odyssey*. The *Iliad* is relatively restricted in its geographical space and social classes (though the long description of Achilles' shield in Book 18, like a kind of super simile, includes scenes of ordinary people in scenes of peace, war and nature). Arguably the *Odyssey* does not require the range provided by similes, since it portrays different social classes, gives attention to animals and describes natural settings. But it is also true that the pace of Homeric narrative tends to be slow wherever there is important content. Long similes, by pausing the narrative in the midst of battle, might have functioned for emphasis, not diversion. And close analysis of similes often demonstrates that they can signal a transition in the narrative, whether in location, content or tone.

So-called 'reverse' similes in the *Odyssey* are particularly interesting.[18] Their content seems to invert the situation on which the simile elaborates. For example, in Book 8 (523–30) Odysseus' weeping in response to Demodocus' song of the wooden horse is compared to the weeping, enslaved wife of a dying husband. This seems surprising, even shocking. Odysseus is of course famed for sacking Troy – by means of the wooden horse in the tale to which he listens. The simile describes him by bringing to mind the female victims of the Trojan War (like Andromache). When in Book 23 Penelope realizes that the beggar really is Odysseus, a simile states that her husband was as welcome to her as the sight of land to a shipwrecked sailor (23.233 ff.). Of course, it is Odysseus who knows the experience of shipwreck, not Penelope. The gender inversion of these similes is striking but not really unparalleled, since both Achilles and Hector can picture themselves as feminine types (see above). Also, the reverse similes are not unlike other similes in their toleration of disjunction outside the central pivot of comparison. Yet there's arguably further significance in the reverse similes. The example in Book 8 reminds one of the general sympathy displayed in the *Iliad* for the Trojan family of Hector, and the example in *Odyssey* 23 may suggest how Odysseus and Penelope correspond in certain qualities, like perseverance.

Two passages demonstrate how a simile can interact with its context. In *Iliad* 6 Diomedes encounters the Lycian Glaucus and asks who he is, specifying that he is loath to attack divinities (amusingly, since he attacked Aphrodite and Ares in Book 5). Glaucus takes the question to be about his lineage, and he starts off his lengthy reply with, 'Just as are the generations of leaves, so are those also of men' (146). This is a proverbial kind of generalization; Apollo similarly compares humanity to plants in Book 21, as noted above. The human/leaves comparison in particular has a long history in ancient literature and beyond, often but not always resulting from the Iliad's influence.[19] What's interesting here is how Glaucus wittily links the simile's conception of 'generation' as cyclical plant/human growth to his personal 'generation' or lineage. If at first he seems dismissive of the topic, he nonetheless proceeds to give a long account of his ancestors, particularly Bellerophon, who succeeded against great odds but eventually came to a bad end.

Do the changing fortunes of Bellerophon correspond to the cycles of life and death? Does Glaucus intimate that the great success of Diomedes that day on the battlefield might end soon? Or is Glaucus taking a distanced view of his encounter with Diomedes, suggesting that the personal concerns of two warriors do not add up to a hill of beans in the bigger picture? Or does Bellerophon's mistake of challenging the gods – a detail suppressed by Glaucus/Homer in this version of the story – point to Diomedes' recent attacks on Aphrodite and Apollo in Book 5? The proper interpretation is not made explicit by the poet. Homer does comment on Glaucus' foolishness in exchanging gold weaponry for bronze after the two decide not to fight. For Diomedes realizes that their grandfathers were friends and calls off the impending duel, and so in the end Glaucus is saved by his 'generation'.

In *Odyssey* 9, the character Odysseus provides two similes at a notable moment. Odysseus and his men sharpen a stake of huge size, which they liken to a ship's mast (321–3) and use to blind Polyphemus. At the moment when Odysseus and his companions thrust it into his eye, the narrative pauses for two key similes. First, Odysseus compares his twisting of it to a carpenter who 'bores a ship's timber with a drill, while those below keep it spinning with the strap, which they lay hold of by either end, and the drill runs unceasingly' (384–6). As Odysseus then describes the blood and gore that results, he compares the hissing of the burnt-out eye to a smith who 'dips a great axe or an adze in cold water to temper it and it makes a great hissing' (391–3). The unusual scale of the blinding, with the huge stake and large eye, is too large to picture readily, but the similes make the action more comprehensible (perhaps more so than one might wish; Odysseus clearly savours his memory of the Cyclops' pain). The number of workers manning the drill suggests the cooperative effort of Odysseus and his men (though there is inversion: Odysseus twists the stake, while the carpenter's helpers move the drill). More generally, the imagery of everyday work provides variety from the immediate heroic episode. And by providing not one but two similes, Odysseus hits the 'pause button' so as to emphasize the moment.

The similes also serve apparent themes of the episode. From the start, Odysseus has emphasized the ethnographic distinctiveness of the Cyclopes. He is particularly dismayed that they do not build ships – that is why they have not colonized 'Goat Island' or visited other peoples. It is no coincidence that the narrative of Odysseus/Homer emphasizes technology. Odysseus constructs a primitive fire-hardened stake,[20] although presumably he could have blinded the Cyclopes with his sword (if less gruesomely). The stake is compared to a ship's mast, and the similes link its use to shipbuilding and metalworking. In our mind's eye the primitive weapon is advanced to metallurgy and naval engineering. Though Odysseus is fascinated by the organized craft of pastoralism (9.216 ff.), his verbal survey of civilized technology mocks its isolated, landlubber nature.

Odysseus' skill with similes, like the inclusion of dialogue in his narrative, is an aspect of his bard-like nature. The only other character in either poem who employs these techniques extensively is Menelaus, when recounting his return in *Odyssey* 4 (a prototype for Odysseus' tales of wandering). Like all characters who are not bards, Odysseus and Menelaus are depicted as speaking conversationally to their listeners. Yet necessarily, since their character speech is embedded within epic poetry, the language is poetic. You are to imagine them speaking prose, but you hear them speak like Homer sings, with the same epic vocabulary, phrases and epithets – all in the metre of verse.

Language and Metre

Since I do not assume knowledge of Greek, my explanation of Homeric language will be general, non-technical and brief. There are two essential points to make: Homeric language differs from everyday ancient Greek, and its metrical arrangement reveals the oral nature of early epic. It might be tempting to think of the *Iliad* and *Odyssey* as novels, given their complex plots, multiple characters and a leisurely pace, and some prose translations indeed can be read as such (see Chapter 7). Yet the Homeric poems use an amalgam of lexical forms in an exacting but flexible metrical pattern – all this for the purpose of public performance, not reading.[21]

Even in translation Homeric language seems different to us. The epithets, for example – 'swift-footed' Achilles, 'much-devising' Odysseus, 'swift' ships – add repetitive regularity to an otherwise naturalistic style. And Homeric diction and morphology sounded archaic even to Greeks of the Classical Age. The Homeric language is a mix of forms – from different dialects, from different time periods, and with much innovation added. The main dialect is Ionic, which in the historical period became dominant in parts of Asia Minor and the Aegean Sea. Aeolic forms, historically present in north-west Asia Minor and north-east Greece, are also relatively common in Homer. Arcado-Cypriot, descended from the Bronze Age Greek of the Mycenaeans (its name refers to its survival in Arcadia of the Peloponnese and Cyprus), is evident but less common. A little of the Attic dialect (closely related to Ionic) is discernible; Doric, in origin from north-west Greece and widespread by the classical period, is not.[22] Many have surmised on this evidence that the epic tradition developed in Asia Minor (though some now argue for Ionian Euboea, the large island off the east coast of Greece).[23] Aeolic is considered an earlier layer (as Arcado-Cyprian would seem to be), or borrowed from contingent Aeolic areas. The mix, addition and innovation of forms reflects the duration and spread of the epic tradition. It was a language of epic performance, spoken by nobody in real life. Even non-Ionic speakers would adopt the Ionic-based epic language when composing epic.

The venerable resonance of epic diction would have been appreciated by ancient Greeks. But the mix of forms is not just poetic colouring; it results from the requirements of metre. Metre is the 'measure' of verse, the system of how syllables are organized. In English poetry, this involves (or once did) the placement of accent-stressed syllables, perhaps with rhyme.[24] In Greek verse rhyme is not sought, and syllables are not marked by stress (words have accents, but this involves pitch and is not relevant to metre). It is the length of time required for vocalizing each syllable that is important. Ones that take longer to pronounce are arranged with ones that take less time. Certain arrangements form a metrical unit (a 'foot'), and several such units formed a line of verse (where a sentence need not end; grammatical units often spilt over to the next line).

The metre of epic requires six units (or feet) in a line. Each foot could either have an initial long syllable followed by two short ones, or two short ones. The first lines of the *Iliad* and *Odyssey* (transliterated into the Latin alphabet) could be represented metrically this way:

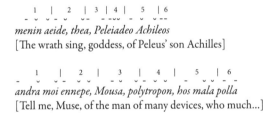

menin aeide, thea, Peleiadeo Achileos
[The wrath sing, goddess, of Peleus' son Achilles]

andra moi ennepe, Mousa, polytropon, hos mala polla
[Tell me, Muse, of the man of many devices, who much...]

Each line has six feet. The three-syllable foot is more common, and so the rhythm tends to be one of tripping momentum. There are exceptions to the rules on what constitutes a long and short syllable; for example, because of pausing at the end of the line, even a final long-short sequence (as in the examples) in effect equals the length of time of two longs.

This epic metre was called the dactylic hexameter: literally, according to the Greek roots, 'finger-like six-measure' (the digit finger has a long segment then two short ones). Each line tended to have a pause called the caesura, typically reflecting sense and syntax, between two words in the third foot. A diaeresis is a break between words that matches division between feet.

When these are noticeable, they may assist the creation of metrical sections larger than feet, and there is good reason to think that a bard and his audience would be more sensitive to three or four major units in a line of verse, rather than six 'feet'.[25] Although modern texts print out each dactylic hexameter as a distinct 'line', in what is known as enjambement meaning could push on from one line to another. This may add further information – the second line of the *Iliad* goes on to describe Achilles' wrath as 'destructive' and adds a relative clause explaining its consequences – or it might actually be necessary for syntactical completion. The dactylic hexameter thus was a highly regulated yet flexible system, offering challenges to the composer, and rhythm and variety to the listener. Early Greek epic was essentially music that poets sang. Homeric bards like Phemius of Ithaca and Demodocus of Phaeacian Scheria accompany their verse with lyre-like instruments, although performers of epic, known as 'rhapsodes', typically employed a staff instead.

It is the compositional challenges that explain much of the variation in Homeric language. Different dialectal and temporal forms provide choice in word usage. Varying morphologies sometimes exist for the same word. For example, both Achilles and Odysseus varied in spelling (*Achilleus* [˘ ¯ ¯]; *Achileus* [˘ ˘ ¯]; *Odysseus* [˘ ¯ ¯] / *Odyseus* [˘ ˘ ¯]). The presence or absence of a second consonant is the difference (this was a matter of pronunciation, not 'spelling' as it appears in our modern texts).

There is more to be said about the implications of Homeric language and metre, but it should be pursued in the next chapter, which presents the hypothesis that Homeric poetry was orally composed. Homerists now understand much better how the organization of Homeric language into verse was central to spontaneous oral composition of early Greek verse. But since oral poetics do not require texts, and since oral performance was the norm in the early Archaic Age from the eighth to the sixth centuries BCE, the time of Homer, the origins of the texts of the *Iliad* and the *Odyssey* that survive today necessarily remain a mystery.

IV

TEXTS AND PRE-TEXTS

IMPRESSED BY THE EXCELLENCE of the *Iliad* and *Odyssey*, readers throughout the ages have naturally wondered where the texts came
from and who 'Homer' is. The short answer is to both questions is that
we do not know. There are no surviving original texts of the *Iliad* and
Odyssey, or any complete ancient ones for that matter, and historical
information about Homer is absent. But Homeric research has gathered
an enormous amount of information about the historical, anthropological and archaeological contexts of the *Iliad* and the *Odyssey*. The modern
era of Homeric studies began 200 years ago, with the so-called 'Homeric
Question', which is really a bundle of related questions about the origins
of the text. In the late eighteenth century the earliest surviving complete
copy of a Homeric poem, a manuscript of the *Iliad* dating from the tenth
century CE, was published by the French classical scholar Jean-Baptiste
Gaspard d'Ansse de Villoison (commonly referred to as Villoison, for
obvious reasons).[1] Of particular interest were its marginal annotations,
called *scholia*,[2] which reported the textual scholarship (otherwise lost)
of the great Homeric critics, notably Aristarchus, associated with the
library at Alexandria in the Hellenistic Age (following Alexander the
Great's death in 323 BCE).

Excited hopes of getting closer to the 'real' Homer through Aristarchus were soon doused with cold water by F.A. Wolf, the German scholar commonly considered to be the founder of modern classical studies. In 1795 Wolf published a carefully reasoned argument that claimed the original state of the *Iliad* and *Odyssey* could never be recovered. Homer lived in an age of illiteracy, he supposed. Why would a bard write down poetry that nobody could read? That would be like building an 'inland ship' without immediate means of floating it. Homer must therefore have orally performed his works, rather smaller than our *Iliad* and *Odyssey*. What we have results from expansion and modification by subsequent singers and eventually editors.[3]

Wolf did not have much to say about the poems themselves, but his followers soon concocted myriad hypotheses about what parts of the epics were authentic and what supplemental. Other Homerists countered by arguing that the *Iliad* and *Odyssey* display a well-planned design attributable to a single, monumental author (or two poets for the two epics, as was already supposed by the *chorizontes* ['separators'] in antiquity). In the twentieth century techniques of traditional oral composition were discovered in Homeric poetry, which transformed the debate over the origin of the Homeric texts.[4]

I will return to the Homeric Question and schools of thought in Homeric studies in the next chapter. First it will be helpful to trace the history of our Homeric texts backwards, from today to antiquity.[5] Then the prehistory that led to mythological and epic traditions about the Trojan War will be considered. This survey must overleap the period when we suspect the *Iliad* and *Odyssey* were composed, without certain evidence. However, at the end of this chapter potential evidence for the dating of the Homeric epics will be examined.

Texts and Performances

The *Iliad* and *Odyssey*, like most ancient Greek texts, can now be accessed online.[6] The internet sites essentially archive modern printed editions, which reflect the judgement of editors employing the evidence of medieval manuscripts, rare scraps of ancient manuscripts and ancient quotations of Homer. The first printed editions of the Homeric texts were made in the late fifteenth century.[7] Surviving complete or almost complete manuscripts of both Homeric epics exist in the medieval period (with *Iliad* texts about twice the number of *Odyssey* texts, as in all earlier periods of textual transmission). Ancient texts are also of course manuscripts, since they were handwritten, but they are conventionally called 'papyri' even when leather parchment, not reed-derived papyrus, is used. The 'codex' of stitched leaves of parchment began to be used in the Roman period; eventually it became the dominant format. Like the modern book, it allowed a reader to flip back and forth between pages. Papyrus manuscripts, earlier in use, were glued together sheets of 'paper' rolled up into scrolls.[8]

Whereas a codex could potentially contain all of one of the Homeric poems, a scroll would usually contain only two or three books (called *rhapsoidiai* or 'performances'). This was not a user-friendly manner to read Homer, either in part or whole. The record of surviving papyri fragments suggests relatively uniform texts after the mid second century BCE, which leads to the stable 'vulgate' textual tradition of the medieval period. Many are tempted to attribute this uniformity to Alexandrian scholarship of the third and second centuries BCE. But the Homeric editor Aristarchus did not alter or delete; he merely indicated his judgement about the authenticity of variant readings, opinions often ignored by the vulgate tradition. Perhaps Alexandrian scholarship led to the uniform length of each Homeric poem through indirect influence on the contemporary book trade.[9]

The earliest Homeric papyri date back to the third century BCE. Some are deemed 'wild', because from our perspective they vary from the later vulgate, most noticeably in 'additional' passages. Since papyri are tattered remains that have resisted decomposition in the dry climate of Egypt, the extent of the variation is not comprehensively known. 'Wild' passages are usually brief and non-essential, and most Homerists view them as offshoots of an otherwise stable tradition. But they may very well have serious implications about early variety in both performance and textual transmission of Homeric poetry.[10] No physical manifestation of the *Iliad* and *Odyssey* precedes the third century CE, but it is clear that they were performed and sometimes read during the Classical Age (fifth and fourth centuries BCE). Testimony from the late fifth century BCE onwards indicates the ownership and use of a limited number of Homeric texts among the elite. As seen in earlier chapters, authors like Herodotus and Aristotle (who reportedly edited a version of Homer treasured by Alexander the Great) speak with a seemingly precise and thorough knowledge of the Homeric poems.[11] Specific lines were discussed by such scholars as the fourth-century Cynic Zoilus, who acquired the nickname 'scourge of Homer' (*Homeromastix*) for his fierce criticism of Homer's alleged inconsistency and lack of decorum.

Yet it would be a mistake to envision the Classical Age as awash with Homeric readers. The literate minority typically read aloud from hard-to-use texts in order recreate the oral performance that was the default norm in their society. The capabilities of memory in antiquity were prodigious because its culture was mostly oral in nature. Some in the Classical Age reportedly memorized all of the *Iliad* and *Odyssey* (see, for example, Xenophon, *Symposium* 3.5), perhaps with access to texts. But epic performers had long been able to memorize the poems, perhaps without texts, or at least with a much looser sense of textual fixity. Quotation of the Homeric poems, notably in the work of Plato, displays differences from 'our' texts. These may be the consequence of memorization, but multiformity in the performance and textualization of Homer may also be a cause.[12] Sometimes 'misquotations' match 'wild' papyri, which suggests that variability in Homeric transmission was not as random as many assume.

A number of brief comments by Herodotus give some insight into the state of 'Homer' at this time. He is the first surviving author to employ titles for poems. The historian quotes and discusses the *Iliad* and *Odyssey*, but he also casts doubt on the Homeric authorship of Cyclic poems like the *Cypria* and *Epigoni* (see Chapter 1). This suggests that other epics were still considered to be Homer's. Aristotle (*Poetics* 13) considers the comic poem *Margites* to be a third poem in the corpus, and Thucydides (3.104) considers the *Homeric Hymn to Apollo* to be Homer's. Some quotations of 'Homer' in lyric poetry reference content or wording that we do not find in our *Iliad* and *Odyssey*. It seems that before the late fifth century BCE 'Homer' designated epic that narrated heroic stories, not just the *Iliad* and *Odyssey*. Similarly, epic that catalogued information was attributed to 'Hesiod', even though today only the *Theogony* and *Works and Days* are usually thought to constitute this author's work.

Moving back in time, then, one has to wonder if the name 'Homer', which begins to be bandied about towards the end of the sixth century, specifies the *Iliad* and *Odyssey*. Perhaps growing appreciation of the *Iliad* and *Odyssey* fed interest in a legendary Homer. One early quotation hints at the early status of the *Iliad*. The lyric poet Simonides, active in the late sixth century, sometimes refers to 'Homer' for heroic epic in general. But this striking quotation references an Iliadic simile discussed in the previous chapter:

> One thing the Chian man said was best: 'as is the generation of leaves, so even of men.' Few mortals hearing this place it in their chests. For hope is present in each man, which grows in the breast of the young.[13]

The quotation is the same as *Iliad* 6.146, spoken by Glaucus on the battlefield when confronted by Diomedes (see previous chapter). The natural conclusion is that Simonides knows a specific verse of the *Iliad*, appreciates it, and ascribes it to a well-known author – so well-known that a name is not required. Ancient biographies of Homer, while late and more legendary than historical, often associate the poet with Chios (though other places also claimed him).[14] The narrator of the *Homeric Hymn to Apollo*, apparently subsuming the persona of Homer, refers to himself as a blind man from Chios (blindness is also characteristic of the legendary Homer). This is why Thucydides accepted the hymn as Homer's, although the modern world usually views the poet's self-reference as a manner of speaking. It may be a conventional way to claim association with traditional epic performance.

Simonides does not specify that it's the character Glaucus, not the poet, who speaks the simile.[15] And the thought of the verse is proverbial, as noted in the previous chapter. Just as Glaucus employs the simile wittily, so does Simonides, who employs the cycle of plant and human life for a pessimistic take on 'hope'. The lyric poet Mimnermus, whose heyday was a century earlier than Simonides, employs a different phraseology of the simile with no mention of Homer in order to bemoan old age. If Simonides really thinks Homer invented the simile, he is almost certainly mistaken. But Simonides is probably more interested in 'Homer' as a cultural concept than the *Iliad* specifically. His indirect invocation of the bard is typical of aristocratic gamesmanship, notably at the aristocratic *symposium* ('together-drinking'), where name-dropping, argument over what is superlative, as well as competitive wordplay were the norm. The 'fetish of Shakespeare' in popular culture, as analysed by literary critic Marjorie Garber, is comparable.[16] In the modern world Shakespeare has cultural capital as a symbol of poetic creativity. Familiarity with the actual plays varies widely; the poet's iconic portrait on a coffee cup is a sufficient marker of your enthusiasm. Tossed-off quotations of 'Shakespeare' need not stem from expertise with the plays in which they are found.

Indeed, the simile quotation of Simonides is quite similar to a Shakespeare quotation. 'Neither a borrower nor a lender be' is often passed about as good advice, but in *Hamlet* it is one of many clichés spoken by the tiresome Polonius. Like 'Every dog hath his day', spoken by the queen, it is a proverb that happens to appear in Shakespeare. If eventually *Hamlet* popularized these adages (further), this does not mean that those who quote them do so with knowledge of character or context – or even know that they are quoting Shakespeare, let alone *Hamlet*. Different is 'To be or not to be, that is the question', which is no proverb and often quoted in allusion to the play. But it may be suspected that eager quotation of this line is inversely proportional to expertise in Shakespeare.

Simonides' circle was undoubtedly well cultured in Greek poetry, but their literary games do not depend on close study of Homeric texts. Simonides imagines Homer speaking to us, not us reading Homer. Perhaps the lyric poet had heard parts or all of the *Iliad* but had no extensive knowledge of it as a text. We do not know if there were any texts of the *Iliad* or *Odyssey* at all in the Archaic Age, or even if 'Homer', or one of his admirers, recorded them in writing. Hence the Homeric Question to be explored in the next chapter.

The early Greek world was literate from the eighth century BCE onward (after losing literacy for centuries in the wake of the prehistoric Mycenaean civilization), but performance, not reading, remained dominant.[17] Whether or not the *Iliad* and *Odyssey* were recorded, we can be sure that they were publicized orally by rhapsodes.[18] One ancient etymological explanation linked the word 'rhapsode' to the staff (*rhabdos*) that was held by performers, but a more likely explanation sees the Greek words 'stitch' (*rhaptein*) and 'song' (*aoide*) as the basis of the term; rhapsodes were thereby conceived as 'stitchers of song'. Plato portrays Socrates questioning the rhapsode Ion in his characteristically probing manner in the dialogue entitled *Ion*. Other ancient testimony describes a guild of rhapsodes called Homeridae, or 'sons of Homer'. It is significant that what we call 'books' of the Homeric poems were in antiquity actually called *rhapsoidiai*, 'rhapsode performances'. In the classical period authors like Herodotus would employ phrases like 'the *aristeia* of Diomedes' (2.116), not book numbers, to specify episodes, and this practice may suggest independent performance of such passages.

A notable opportunity for performance of epic was at the Panathenaic festival at Athens, held every fourth year.[19] Some testimony from the fourth century BCE reports regulation for sequential performance of 'Homer' at this event. The testimony varies, but often a prominent public figure like Hipparchus, the son of the sixth-century tyrant Pisistratus, is credited with introducing Homeric verse to Athens. Homerists are naturally eager to suppose that all of the *Iliad* and *Odyssey* were thus performed, with the regulation perhaps based on authentic texts of them. This is optimistic; it is questionable whether there was enough time to perform both Homeric epics in a four-day festival that involved many other types of competitions and events. The *Iliad* would take longer than twenty-four hours to perform; the *Odyssey* a bit less. The Panathenaic performances may have been nothing more than rhapsodes 'stitching' together episodes of the Trojan War. Some of the sources insist that Homer's poetry was exclusively featured, but this may be based on earlier and looser definitions of 'Homer'.

Although texts were not the default means for the publication of the *Iliad* and *Odyssey* at an early date, at some point they were recorded. Various critical opinions about how this happened are surveyed in the next chapter. For now I suggest that the uncertainty about the writing-down of the *Iliad* and *Odyssey* is not necessarily a cause for dismay. What *we* possess are two excellent and fascinating epics. However that came about, we are lucky it did.

Early performance traditions possessed their own means to perpetuate their cultural product.[20] One was metre, an invisible technology of preservation. A good hexameter line (like 'just as are the generations of leaves, such are also those of men') is readily memorized, and a trained bard would not only utilize memory (the mother of the Muses) but also standard phrases and scenes (see Chapter 5). Added would be aspects of performance like gesture, voice modulation, rhythm and perhaps music. Seen from the perspective of performance culture, a text is inadequate technology; the best you can do with a manuscript is to imitate performance by reading it aloud.

A big issue for early performances of Homer, however, is the great length of the *Iliad* and *Odyssey*. The longest Homeric Hymn equals a very short book of the Homeric epics; the Hesiodic poems are each equivalent to the longest books. The *Cypria* reportedly had eleven books, while others of the Trojan Cycle contained between two to five books (so the ancient summary reports, perhaps inaccurately). The Homeric epics each have twenty-four books. How *could* performances lasting around twenty-four hours be managed? Perhaps pan-Ionian gatherings at Delos, or Mycale in Asia Minor, provided an opportunity for continuous performance.[21] Comparative fieldwork has demonstrated that major oral works around the world, some longer than the Homeric poems by multiples of ten, are capable of being performed on succeeding evenings.[22] By means of skilled performance by a bard or relay of bards, presentation of a whole Homeric epic could have been accomplished at any village. If so, it is also probable that individual episodes from both epics were performed independently.

Homeric Worlds

MYCENAEANS

Without definitive evidence of the Homer poems in the Archaic Age (indirect evidence will be considered below), we should go back further in time to the Dark Age and Bronze Age in order to consider what led to the Homeric poems.[23] The Dark Age (*c.*1100–800 BCE) that followed the fall of Mycenaean civilization of the Bronze Age was characterized by diminished population, less contact with the Mediterranean world, and illiteracy (although archaeological discoveries have lightened the 'darkness' of this period). Presumably oral traditions of myth and epic existed at this time, providing continuity of culture. These traditions may even have originated in the Bronze Age. Archaeological excavation over the last century and a half has uncovered strongly fortified 'palaces' of the late Bronze Age, like the one at Mycenae that gives the civilization its name. Surviving artefacts suggest a warlike society; the eventual decipherment of Linear B script on clay tablets revealed the redistribution of resources in palatial economies. Most importantly, the tablets proved that the Mycenaeans used Greek.[24]

What we do not find in the Linear B tablets is any poetry: the texts are mostly records of accounting, although religious material is sometimes present too. The tablets are arbitrary snapshots of moments in time, preserved only because they were baked by fire during palatial destructions. What they make clear is that the Homeric poems do not portray the Mycenaean world. Some artefacts in Homer are Mycenaean (see below), and there are remnants of the Arcado-Cypriot dialect, thought to derive from Mycenaean Greek, in Homeric language. Moreover, the tablets indicate divinities that we know of from historical sources – including Homeric poetry. So there certainly was cultural continuity from the Bronze Age to the Iron Age. Arguably an epic tradition beginning in the Bronze Age carried along vestigial elements even as it was affected by the periods through which is passed. Indeed, bronze metal is employed by Homeric characters (as well as iron). Epic tried to portray a different, distant Heroic Age as well as it could, although precise knowledge of Mycenaean civilization had been lost.[25]

THE TROJAN WAR

How about the Trojan War? Was this a historical war fought by Mycenaean Greeks? The short answer is no, with apologies if this is disappointing. There has been much interest in a real Trojan War since the German businessman Heinrich Schliemann excavated Hisarlık, a modest hill in the north-west of modern Turkey. Beginning his archaeological work in the 1870s, Schliemann was intent on proving the historicity of Homer. It was no secret that Hisarlık was the site of the historical Greek city of Ilion, later Roman Ilium, but since antiquity Priam's Troy had been thought to exist elsewhere. Frank Calvert, a British diplomat residing in the area, surmised that historical Troy was mythical Troy, and had begun exploring Hisarlık, but it took Schliemann's wealth to test the theory with many spades. The world was stunned when workers dug to the bottom of the hill and discovered hidden ruins and eventually precious artefacts.[26]

Through the on-site assistance of the archaeologically experienced Wilhelm Dörpfeld, it eventually became clear that Troy went back through seven prehistoric levels, dating to the beginning of the third millennium BCE. What Schliemann had supposed to be the treasures of Priam belonged to the second level: much too early for a war with Mycenaeans, traditionally dated around 1200 BCE.[27] The sixth level became favoured as Priam's Troy. It was destroyed about 1300 BCE and, despite the damage caused by Schliemann's digging down to bedrock, was clearly a long-lasting city with impressive walls. Imagine the disappointment when a later excavator, Carl Blegen, determined that the sixth level was destroyed by an earthquake. Historicists turned their eyes to the seventh level, apparently burnt by human agency. But this was not as impressive in its structures, and reconsideration led to the down-dating of its destruction to after 1200 BCE. This was the beginning of a period when the Mycenaean palaces themselves were destroyed. Why would threatened Greeks cross the Aegean to attack Trojans?

Texts from the Hittite kingdom of central Asia Minor may provide further evidence. Some seem to refer variously to Achaeans (*Ahhiyawa*), Troy/Ilios (*Wilusa*), and even a Trojan king called 'Alaksandu'. The last would seem to correspond, amazingly, to 'Alexander', the alternative name for Paris! But 'Alexander' is constructed from Greek roots ('defend' and 'man'). Why would a historical king of Troy have a Greek name? Arguably the non-Greek name 'Paris' stems from non-Greek legend, only to be eventually conjoined to 'Alexander'. Yet it is hard to explain why a Bronze Age ruler in Asia Minor would be a Greek, at least in name. If the document does attest to Greek interaction with prehistoric Troy, it does not support the story of the Trojan War that we know in any precise way. The Hittite evidence is too early for (disputed) archaeological evidence for the mythological Trojan War anyway. Moreover, no Trojan documents have been found, beyond a late and inconsequential seal.[28]

That need not stop one from supposing that a historical foundation underlies a gradually expanding myth of the Trojan War. The real city of Troy would have to be important enough to be memorable, and the Hittite documents do indicate that it was involved in various political and military intrigues. Troy imported some Mycenaean goods, and Mycenaeans had a presence in Asia Minor. This does not amount to a ten-year war between Greeks and Trojans. But scepticism about a 'real' Trojan War does not undermine the extremely valuable archaeological work that has been accomplished at Hisarlık. Two thousand years of a prehistoric city were uncovered – as well as another millennium of Greek and Roman ruins. The expedition led by Manfred Korfmann and Brian Rose through the 1990s has now provided the world with a sophisticated and nuanced analysis of Troy and its environs.[29] Dramatic evidence emerged of a lower city that extends beyond the modest citadel, and especially valuable is the wide geographical, chronological, environmental and economic scope of the investigation. As for Schliemann, despite harm to his reputation caused by his romantic and occasionally fibbing nature, he can be credited for excavating Mycenae as well as Troy, thus leading to the archaeological discovery of Mycenaean civilization.

NEAR EASTERN ORIGINS

It has been increasingly realized over the last few decades that ancient Near Eastern literature influenced Greek literature.[30] The anthropomorphic Near Eastern divinities resemble Greek ones, and struggles between generations of Near Eastern gods correspond rather well with those of Greek gods told in Hesiod's *Theogony*. The Near Eastern motif of gods ridding the earth of humans appears in the Greek myth of the Trojan War (as in the *Cypria*'s 'plan of Zeus'). But of greatest interest to Homerists is the *Gilgamesh Epic* of Mesopotamian origin. We know of independent Sumerian stories about the legendary king Gilgamesh towards the end of the third millennium BCE, and by the early second millennium BCE these had solidified into an

Akkadian epic (Akkadian culture succeeded and incorporated Sumerian culture). The so-called 'standard' version was composed towards the end of the second millennium and discovered in the ruins of Assyrian Nineveh.[31]

The fascinating story tells of the partly divine Gilgamesh performing many heroic deeds with his friend Enkidu, after whose death he wanders far, even under the earth and across a sea of death, to seek out Utnapishtim, who lives immortalized on a paradisiacal island. Utnapishtim convinces the hero that he cannot escape death, and so Gilgamesh returns to his home city Uruk. Some correspondences to Homeric themes are easy to spot: extended grief after the death of a close friend (compare Achilles and Patroclus), supernatural travel and return (compare Odysseus). Moreover, Gilgamesh's initial heroics are motivated by a desire for fame (compare Achilles), and the proem claims that after acquiring knowledge through his wanderings he composed his own story (compare Odysseus). Some interpret the relationship of Gilgamesh and Enkidu as homoerotic; that of Achilles and Patroclus was portrayed as sexual in the classical period (when pederasty was a norm in aristocratic circles), if not originally in the *Iliad*.[32] More generally, Gilgamesh's problematic civic role and personal behaviour are comparable to stories of Achilles and Odysseus, as well as many other Greek heroes. Although the narrative of the *Gilgamesh Epic* is not as nimble as the Homeric epic is, it does include an embedded character story (the proto-Noah Utnapishtim telling of the universal flood that he survived) and a profound meditation on mortality (compare Achilles' choice of fates, or Odysseus' declining immortality with Circe).

To many the parallels seem too strong to be coincidental.[33] But how could Homer have been influenced by the *Gilgamesh Epic*? The Gilgamesh literary tradition extends far through time, geography and language. Indirect and complex seepage into Mycenaean culture and then down through time into Greek myth is a plausible guess, although some look to Greek contact with the East in historical times. The new Greek alphabet was derived around 800 BCE from Semitic script, and the seventh century BCE is deemed the 'orientalizing period' because of the presence of Near Eastern motifs in Greek art. But Homer and his listeners would not know the *Gilgamesh Epic*, even in translation. If motifs from the *Gilgamesh Epic* crossed over the Aegean, it is hard to see how they would have been recognized as such by Homeric audiences. Exciting as the correspondences may be for academics looking into the background of Homeric poetry, this does not mean they have any significance within the epics.

INDO-EUROPEAN COMPARISONS

Greek is part of the Indo-European branch of languages, which in prehistory spread from an undocumented language ('Proto-Indo-European') originating in an unknown central location. In historical periods of antiquity Indo-European languages were spoken as far west as the British Isles and as far east as South Asia. Linguistic science has proven beyond doubt the lexical and semantic relationships between Indo-European languages. Arguments for shared mythological content can be much more speculative.[34] Apparent parallels could result from diffusion between cultures, and coincidence can be hard to rule out. Some suggestions certainly give one pause, however. For example, the concept of 'Achilles' heel' has no role in the Homeric portrayal of Achilles, but a similar story about Achilles almost certainly existed in the Archaic Age (perhaps in the Cyclic *Aethiopis*). The wounding by Paris of the foot of Diomedes (*Iliad* 11.369 ff.), who is often seen as a doublet of Achilles, might be a weak reflection of the motif. In any event, the death of Achilles by the wounding of his ankle (the actual location in antiquity, despite our modern phrase) corresponds to many Indo-European heroes (like the Ossetian Soslan) who have a uniquely vulnerable and mortal location on their body. Though certain evidence for the motif in Greek myth, including for Achilles, is not early, arguably its origins lie in the Indo-European past.[35]

The case has been made for other Indo-European elements in Trojan War myth and epic. The 'judgement of Paris' involves a choice between goddesses representing authoritative power (Hera), military might (Athena) and fertility (Aphrodite), which well matches the tripartite division of Indo-European society perceived by the mid-twentieth-century French scholar Georges Dumézil.[36] Apparent (if disputed) correspondence between the epic phrase *kleos aphthiton*, 'undying glory' (*Iliad* 9.413), and an old Indic phrase of the same meaning, *śrávas ákṣitam*, may result from independent manifestations of a common inheritance.[37] Ancient Indic literature has sometimes been seen to correspond to Homeric epic in more extensive ways. For example, Penelope's remarriage by means of a bow contest conceivably corresponds to aspects of the ancient Indic poem *Mahabharata*.[38]

As with archaeological discoveries and Near Eastern influences, Indo-European correspondences open up thrilling expanses of space and time. But what does it all mean to the reader of Homer? At the very least, exploration of the background to the Homeric epics demonstrates how naive it is to consider Homer a singular, unexplainable genius. But at times the significance of origins is circumscribed to the academic world. It is wonderful that we now know so much about the background of Greek epic tradition, but for the literary student this information is most valuable when it assists the explication of the meaning of Homeric poetry. What one really wants to know about Diomedes' foot wound, for example, is whether it alludes to some kind of 'Achilles' heel' motif current at the time of the *Iliad*'s composition. Indo-European and Near Eastern analogies, as well as Mycenaean archaeology, can potentially give one an Olympian view, but at that height the ground is too far away for precise discernment.

HOMER IN THE ARCHAIC AGE

Fascinating as such suggestions of distant influences on Homer and his tradition may be, now it is time to turn back to the Archaic Age and survey historical evidence for 'Homer'. Indeed, there is no historical evidence for the personhood of the author(s), as admitted above. There were plenty of biographies of Homer, but these are of no historical value.[39] Ancient dating of Homer is not credible; most guesses place him soon after the Trojan War or at the time of Greek migrations after the collapse of the Mycenaean civilizations. Herodotus (2.53) thought Homer and Hesiod lived around 400 years before his time (thus, in late ninth century BCE), and this approaches the upper edge of what modern scholars consider possible (essentially between the eighth and sixth centuries). But that is coincidence; Herodotus and other ancients had no real insight into the prehistory of the Iron and

Bronze Ages. Investigation should rely on two types of indirect evidence: first, indications within the Homeric poems of their time of composition; secondly, consideration of early influence of the Homeric epics.

The bardic voice of each poem provides no help. Even though there are first-person addresses to the Muses, no biographical information is given by the first-person narrator(s). Compare Hesiod: the poet of the *Theogony* and *Works and Days* not only tells us about his encounter with the Muses, but he is almost chatty in providing information about his brother, his father and his little town (Ascra, in Boeotia). Some Homeric passages suggest an Asia Minor perspective on climate and winds, but that is all. Scholarly attention therefore turns to details in the poems that might be dated. There are fundamental difficulties with such investigation: the Homeric poems portray a heroic world of the past, not their own time period, and much in them would reflect the various time periods in which traditional epic developed.[40]

There is also the internal evidence of Homeric language. Computer technology and statistics have been employed to explore the relative date of early epic poems. The most extensive study supports the conventional view that the *Iliad* precedes the *Odyssey*, which in turn precedes the *Theogony* and *Works and Days* (suggestions for some smaller epic poems are unconventional, however).[41] The author would prefer to see the Homeric poems as belonging to the eighth century, but stresses that his methodology interprets relative, not absolute, dating. Some are sceptical even about this, pointing out that the varying length and very different content of the poems compared make for a misleading database. That early Greek epics were orally composed and performed (a topic of the next chapter) raises more complicated issues. If one bard's decades-long fluid recomposition of an epic is recorded relatively early, while a contemporary bard's is recorded relatively late, is the second epic really later than the first? Recordings are not performances, which in this time period *are* the epics. Such issues only multiply if the performance tradition of an epic extends beyond a single creator.[42]

Perhaps the trick is to match up material objects and cultural practices within the poetry with what we know about Greek history. One could look for the latest historical aspects in Homer on the supposition that these belong to the time of composition, or one could argue that Homeric evidence on the whole reflects one particular time period. Both approaches are compatible: bards working within a tradition would add aspects of their contemporary world to the longstanding yet evolving portrait of the epic world that had developed over centuries. But sorting out the historical evidence in Homeric epic can be very difficult. For example, twice 'Homer' seems to allude to writing, if rather vaguely. In *Iliad* 7 (175 ff.) Greek heroes employ marked lots to determine who will duel Hector; when one pops out of a shaken helmet, Ajax somehow recognizes it as his. In Glaucus' account of his ancestor Bellerophon there is a folded tablet with 'signs many and deadly' (6.168 ff.). Do these passages suggest writing systems? If so, do the passages stem from memory of Linear B, or do they reflect the new literacy of Homer's age? Perhaps the Bellerophon passage reflects scripts in the Near East, where the story is set. In both passages, writing seems mysterious. That may be because a literate poet thinks heroes of the past were not literate. Or perhaps the poet does not quite understand the concept of a relatively new development that has not spread widely.

The supposition that Mycenaean archaeology and Linear B would be consistent with the poetic world portrayed in Homeric poetry has proven to be largely illusory. Nonetheless, some Homeric artefacts are Mycenaean, notably armour (silver-studded swords, body-sized shields, the boar's-tusk helmet worn by Odysseus in *Iliad* 10). Their presence in Homer either results from the continuation of Bronze Age poetry, cultural memory of earlier times, or the survival of treasured artefacts no longer in use. Though occasionally prominent in Homer, quantitatively they do not add up to much. More extensive are post-Bronze Age aspects of Homeric epic, like cremation, the Phoenicians and of course iron. Some passages suggest the eighth century BCE or later in their mention of pan-Hellenic sites (Delphi, Delos and Olympia); so too does apparent reflection of Greek colonization.[43] And some *realia* and practices date from the seventh century or later. For example, Agamemnon's shield has an image of a Gorgon head (*Iliad* 11.36–7); there is no historical parallel until the seventh century. Details of the extensive description of the shield of Achilles in *Iliad* 18 remind some of Mycenaean artefacts, but on the whole the described shield is analogous to Cretan and Cyprian artefacts of the early seventh century. Passages that suggest political organization of the *polis* (city) or techniques of group warfare perhaps suggest the early seventh century.

But there is also the question of external reflections of the *Iliad* and *Odyssey*. Past confidence that Homer should be dated to the eighth century (because everyone said so), coupled with the assumption that the Homeric poems were immediately influential (because we admire them so), has led to very contestable conclusions. For example, an eighth-century verse inscription on a cup found on the island of Ischia, off the west coast of Italy, refers to itself as 'Nestor's cup':

> I am Nestor's cup, good to drink from. Whoever drinks from this cup,
> him immediately the desire of Aphrodite lovely-crowned will seize.

This is often seen as a wittily parodic allusion to a big drinking vessel of Nestor's in a minor scene of the *Iliad* (11.632–7). For some, this would imply that extensive knowledge of the *Iliad* was already widespread in the late eighth century B C E Greek world (Ischia was the location of the Greek colony Pithecusae). But Nestor's cup could have existed in mythology outside of Homer; the cup inscription and the Iliadic passage may be independent manifestations of a widespread mythological item.[44]

How about the poems of the Epic Cycle? Can they not be used to date Homer? In antiquity they were considered post-Homeric, as they commonly are today. Ancient testimony sometimes dates their authors to the seventh or even the eighth century. That suggests a mid-eighth-century Homer at the very least. But ancient dating of the Cyclic epics was as confused as the ascription of their authorship (many were ascribed to Homer, as Herodotus knew). In any event, we questioned the assumption that the Cycle epics were influenced by the *Iliad* and *Odyssey* in Chapter 1. Phraseology in the Cycle can seem 'Homeric', but Homeric phraseology itself is traditional. Some Cyclic content has been thought to be post-Homeric, but non-Homeric might be a better term. For example, Cyclic immortalization of heroes has been thought to be a reflection of hero cult, yet hero cult is not post-Homeric. It is demonstrably present in Homer, if not emphasized. As for the argument that some Cyclic forms are morphologically later than Homeric ones, surviving quotations of the Cycle are vanishingly small, and measurement of linguistic development in early epic is insecure anyway, as noted above. It may very well be that some Cycle poems follow the *Iliad* and *Odyssey* in time, but this leads to little about the date of Homer.

Lyric poetry contains passages that have been judged Homeric, the earliest dated to the seventh century.[45] In fact it used to be thought that the whole lyric genre followed the epic genre; more probably both genres co-existed in prehistory. What is required is evidence that specific poems display knowledge of the Homeric poems. If one is not complacently assuming the widespread influence of Homer, many alleged parallels look formulaic in phrasing and typological in content. However, there are lyric passages in the early sixth century that seem too Homeric to be coincidental, and Simonides' attribution of the leaves/humans simile to the 'man from Chios' (discussed above) follows later in the century.

The evidence of early Greek art seems to lead us to similar conclusions. Iconography about the Trojan War is dominated by cyclic themes throughout most of the seventh century. It is only in the sixth century BCE that a few images seem to react to the Homeric poems. Consider the early-sixth-century vase fragment that depicts the 'games of Patroclus', as an inscription in the image states (compare the '*aristeia* of Diomedes' tag used by Herodotus). The details do not exactly match the *Iliad*'s version of the episode (Book 23), just as they do not in a similar scene on the famous François Vase of the same period, yet perhaps this results from the faulty memory of a Homeric performance or different creative aspirations in a different medium. Another option is to wonder whether there were variant versions of the *Iliad* at this time.

Our discussion so far has neglected the seventh-century vase images of the blinding of the Cyclops. A good number date to the first half of the century. This seems promising: the *Odyssey* (and a presumably an earlier *Iliad*) would thereby date to before 650 BCE. But do the images reflect the Homeric version of the story? Since the images vary from the Homeric account in key ways, some doubt the connection.[46] One should also wonder at the lack of other Homeric topics in early Greek art (see Chapter 1). Is it just bad luck that the only surviving Homeric representations until the end of the seventh century concern the Polyphemus episode (there are also images of the Greeks escaping under rams)? Or does this suggest that Homer's Cyclops episode was performed independently, a 'hit single' from the Homeric corpus? It may well be that the theme is popular in art because the story was popular outside of the Homeric epic. Many folk tales about the blinding of an ogre have been collected in modern times, and scholars often suppose that the tale type is pre-Homeric (see Chapter 3). The early artwork probably depicts Odysseus (though there are no inscriptions) and Polyphemus (though the artists do not or cannot depict a single eye on the blinded figure). Even so, it is myth or the epic genre in general that is more easily credited for its inspiration, not the *Odyssey* in particular. Details in the earliest representations do not necessarily encourage their being viewed as Homeric. The weapon is typically suggestive of the folk-tale spit, not Homer's wooden stake. The presence of wine vessels is more intriguing. Although wine does occur in some folk tales, it is not essential to their plot. On the other hand, the drunkenness of Polyphemus has no clear or coherent function in the *Odyssey*.

Quantitatively, evidence for the dating of the Homeric epics does not add up to much. Some evidence, both internal and external, links the *Iliad* and *Odyssey* to the first half of the seventh century. This is just an indication of the latest compositional creativity; much in the Homeric poems can be linked to earlier ages.[47] But Homer was not very influential until later in the Archaic Age. If the Homeric epics did not dominate their culture at first, this should really come as no surprise to us; publication of individual epics depended on performance. By the end of the Archaic Age the Homeric poems found some prominence at the Panathenaic festival in Athens, and this may well have involved textualization. But that is an issue for the next chapter, on the Homeric Question.

A generation ago, the eighth century was favoured for the date of 'Homer', but views have changed. Why Homerists have insisted with some strain on an earlier date is an interesting question to bear in mind, since it is relevant to the 'Homeric Question' discussed in next chapter.

V

THE HOMERIC
QUESTION

OVER TIME VARIOUS SCHOOLS of thought have arisen about the 'Homeric Question', to use the shorthand phrase for a number of questions concerning the origin of the Homeric epics.[1] Since we do not know how the Homeric poems were created, hypotheses are necessary. Speculation about origins is no substitute for critical interpretation, the topic of the next chapter, but the Homeric Question is interesting in its own right and is often relevant to analysis of the *Iliad* and *Odyssey*.

Over the last two centuries Homeric studies have focused on the genesis of the *Iliad* and *Odyssey*. Antiquity was largely content to believe that a genius named 'Homer' composed them, or at least the *Iliad*, with a second master poet given credit for the *Odyssey*.[2] Yet even back then there was concern about the integrity of the texts. Some were suspicious about the role played by sixth-century Athens, where Panathenaic performance of Homeric poetry occurred. For example, a brief passage that praises the minor Athenian leader Menestheus (2.546–56) in the catalogue of Greek ships in *Iliad* 2 raised eyebrows. Neighbouring Megara charged Athens with placing the Athenian contingent next to the Salamis one, so as to strengthen its claim on the island. Ancient sources report that a rhapsode named Cynaethus inserted passages into the Homeric poems, and even composed the *Homeric Hymn to Apollo* (considered to be Homer's composition by Thucydides, as noted in the previous chapter). Ancient sources also suggest that Book 10 was composed by Homer as an independent poem, not as part of the *Iliad*.[3]

Most relevant for our concerns, however, are ancient reports that a prominent figure, often identified as the sixth-century Athenian tyrant Pisistratus or his son Hipparchus, arranged the texts of the *Iliad* and *Odyssey* as we have them. It is at least suggested that Athens acquired texts of Homer; some late testimony also claims that the poems were arranged or at least heavily edited at this time. This account by Cicero is a concise version:

> [Pisistratus] is said to have first arranged the books of Homer, previously
> disordered, as we now have them. (*On the Orator* 3.34.137)

An original unity for the poems, at least, is apparently suggested here. Comparable is the assertion by the Hebrew historian Josephus (first century C E) that the poems required post-Homeric editorial work after being composed by an illiterate Homer and preserved by memory (*Against Apion* 1.2).[4] One is reminded of Wolf's conclusion, on the assumption that Homer's age was illiterate, that the Homeric poems were not recorded in their original form.

Wolf was not the first to express such thoughts in post-antiquity. During the so-called '*querelle des Anciens et des Modernes*' of the seventeenth and eighteenth centuries (deemed the 'battle of the books' by Jonathan Swift), the supposed illiteracy of Homer provided ammunition to those contesting the conventions of classicism.[5] In the early eighteenth century the philosopher Giambattista Vico spoke of the 'Greek people' as the real basis of Homer's works, presaging the later celebration of national literature. Passing comments by Richard Bentley pictured the Homeric poems as sequential festival songs (Iliadic for men, Odyssean for women!) later made into epics by Pisistratus. Robert Wood, travelling in the Troad a century before Schliemann, linked Homeric poetry to the topography and cultural practices that he observed. This approach flipped the 'quarrel': instead of defending Homer as an icon of neo-classicism, it praised the primitive alterity of Homer. Wood thought preservation of long epics possible, crediting illiterate societies with superior memory. Aware of stories of a Pisistratean 'recension', he was nonetheless content to judge the resulting texts both authentic and pleasing. Romantics would also embrace Homer, whether as a humble bard of transcendent genius or a transmitter of folk poetry. But Wolf's historicist focus on origins and transmission inspired a more sceptical treatment of the Homeric poems among nineteenth-century philologists.

Schools of Thought

ANALYSTS

Followers of Wolf were stimulated by the possibility of a 'Pisistratean recension'. Speculating much more extensively than Wolf, the 'Analysts' subjected the Homeric poems to close analysis, so as to pursue theories of multiple composition. One method was to argue that small lays or ballads had eventually been gathered together (as Bentley had suggested). Surging interest in the collection of folk culture in the eighteenth and nineteenth centuries encouraged such conceptions. In the second half of the eighteenth century James Macpherson claimed to have discovered medieval manuscripts of an ancient Scottish bard, 'Ossian'.[6] Though the poetry was celebrated in the Romantic movement, sceptics realized that Macpherson had imaginatively constructed Homer-like epic poems out of Scottish folklore. (Wood compared his activity to the Homeric recension.) In the nineteenth century Elias Lönnrot arranged the Finnish poetry he had collected into the unified national epic the *Kalevala*. The *Niebelungenlied* was thought to have had similar origins by Karl Lachmann, the most prominent promoter of the Homeric lay theory. One may also compare the development of the (then unknown) *Gilgamesh Epic* from independent Sumerian songs into a unified Akkadian epic. In fact a certain scribe named Sîn-lēqi-unninni was credited for the final 'standard' version. Epic development *can* happen that way. But the *Iliad* and *Odyssey* are not easily explained as strung-together ballads, even if original independence might be conjectured for parts (catalogues, heroic duels, *Iliad* 10). In the long term the 'lay' theory fell out of favour in Homeric studies.

More popular among the Analysts was the 'nucleus' approach, which looked within the Homeric poems for central cores that had become expanded and/or interpolated. The many books after *Iliad* 1 in which Zeus' plan to help the Trojans is not implemented, for example, were subject to suspicion. Achilles' wrath against Agamemnon was isolated as a kernel around which the rest of the poem was added. The exact nature of this plotline was disputed, however; Achilles' apparently inconsistent positions about returning to battle (see Chapter 2) were variously considered evidence for tampering. Homeric treatment of character, artefacts, language and style was also placed under the microscope. A notorious crux is the apparently shifting number of ambassadors to Achilles in Book 9. Three set out and later speak (Odysseus, Phoenix and Ajax), along with two heralds. But the embassy is then repeatedly described as two in its journey and welcoming. It adds to the puzzle that dual-language forms are applied to the two heralds who take Briseis away from Achilles in Book 1. Analysts saw intrusive modification of already suspect material at work – perhaps Phoenix was added to an earlier text that described an embassy of two.

As for the *Odyssey*, the so-called *Telemachy* of the first four books was usually deemed an independently composed addition. The hero's account of his travels in Books 9–12 was also often considered distinct, perhaps an originally independent poem transformed from a third-person to a first-person narrative. The doublet of divine councils in Books 1 and 5 (see Chapter 2) seemed to many like patchwork composition. Analysts also attacked the underworld episode of Book 11, deeming it insufficiently unmotivated and oddly progressing from the summoning of shades at the edge of Hades to direct encounters within. Various passages, including the catalogue of heroines, the punishment of infamous sinners and the appearance of Heracles and (the Athenian) Theseus looked additive – even to the extent that interpolations were made within interpolations. Then there is the question of the epic's ending. The Alexandrian critics reportedly thought that the *peras* ('limit') of the poem occurs towards the end of Book 23 when Odysseus and Penelope go to bed. This may be interpreted to mean that the end of Book 23 and all of Book 24 are additions, and sure enough close reading by Analysts found much to criticize in the language and the abrupt pacing of the narrative at the end of the poem.

UNITARIANS

If Analyst methodology was dominant in nineteenth-century scholarship and beyond (*Die Ilias und Homer* of 1916 by Wilamowitz-Moellendorff is often judged a high point), the Unitarian school of thought became dominant in twentieth-century Homeric studies. But it should be stressed that both methodologies were concurrent, and both existed in and outside Germany. Unitarians maintain a belief that a single, monumental poet was responsible for our *Iliad* or *Odyssey* (or one poet for each epic). Though Unitarians might be willing to jettison parts of each poem (for example, *Iliad* 10, at least some of *Odyssey* 11, or the *Odyssey*'s ending), they tend to explain away alleged inconsistencies, or at least deem them trivial. Analyst theories are criticized as tiresomely over-complicated and unconvincingly over-subjective – as well as revealingly inconsistent with one another.

At times Unitarian argument seems like mere counter-punching (occasionally animated by anti-German prejudice, especially around the time of the First World War), and Unitarians often sidestep real textual difficulties (to this day there is no widely accepted solution to *Iliad* 9's duals, for example). But at its best the school of thought employs a close reading that demonstrates unity at the macro level. Wolfgang Schadewaldt's *Iliasstudien* (1938) is still cherished for its demonstration of such intricate architectural connections within the *Iliad* that its dismemberment seems impossible. For the *Odyssey*, however, Schadewaldt proposed multiple authorship – a reminder that Homerists do not necessarily adhere to a single methodology. But the *Odyssey* as well as the *Iliad* has had plenty of Unitarian defenders.[7]

ORALISTS

It is often said that the Oralist approach made the Analyst–Unitarian stand-off irrelevant. If so, its methodology was controversial, and Oralists themselves have continuously revised it. The seminal figure is the American Milman Parry, who produced a dissertation and a number of articles before his untimely death in 1935.[8] The so-called 'oral theory' is based on Parry's close study of the interrelation between Homeric language and metrics. German scholars of the late nineteenth century preceded Parry in identifying lexical morphology and its regular usage within the hexameter line. Parry greatly systematized this type of work, concentrating initially on 'noun-epithet' phrases, comprised of a noun described by an adjective or some combination of words ('swift-footed Achilles', 'much-devising Odysseus', 'rosy-fingered dawn'). The modern reader tends to find this descriptive phraseology poetic but repetitive. What Parry makes one realize is that noun-epithet phrases are employed in the metrical scheme in a utilitarian manner.

A chart in Parry's dissertation on the subject of noun-epithet phrases indicates that 'swift-footed bright Achilles' is used from the middle of the third foot to the end of the line. For a shorter metrical space from the middle of the fourth foot onwards 'swift in feet Achilles' is almost always found. For the even shorter unit of the last two feet he is 'illustrious Achilles' thirty-four times and 'swift Achilles' only five times. Similar results occur for Odysseus with an epithet, which can be approximately graphed as follows:

two feet and part of the third foot + 'much-enduring illustrious Odysseus'
(*polutlas dios Odysseus*; 38 times)

three feet and part of the fourth foot + 'much-devising Odysseus'
(*polymetis Odysseus*; 81 times)
   or
'city-sacking Odysseus'
(*ptoliporthos Odysseus*; 4 times)

four feet + 'illustrious Odysseus'
(*dios Odysseus*; 60 times)
   or
'excellent Odysseus'
(*esthlos Odysseus*; 3 times)

'Zeus-born Odysseus' + end of the third foot and the last three feet
(*diogenes Odyseus*; 4 times)
[NB: *Odyseus* not *Odysseus*, for metrical reasons]

Though a computer program might produce a more perfected regularity, the efficiency seems more than coincidental. In the examples given above, a poet pausing mid-line could finish off with ready-set phrases about Achilles or Odysseus. Such phrases would be valued for their ability to fill up whatever metrical space was left. It does not follow that epithets are mindlessly chosen by the metre: people are not 'rosy-fingered', nor is the dawn 'much-devising', for example. And some epithets attach exclusively, or nearly so, to particular characters – Achilles is deemed swift and Odysseus wily, not vice versa. But for Parry meaning in the immediate context was not as important as metrical function. He even argued that epithets possessed a blanked-out meaning – phrases pertaining to Achilles and Odysseus would essentially register to a listener as just 'Achilles' or 'Odysseus'. Hence if they were used inappropriately for their immediate context, neither bard nor audience would care. Ruskin discerned ironic pathos in Helen's deceased brothers being covered by 'life-giving' (*phusizoos*) earth (*Iliad* 3.243), but Parry judged this analysis to be misguided sentimentality: the epithet just fills a metrical space.[9]

Parry concluded that such a complex system was too much for one bard to create, and therefore traditional. Eventually he decided it reflected an oral system of creating epic verse. This conclusion resulted from fieldwork in the former Yugoslavia, where a living tradition of illiterate bards employed formulaic phraseology in epic song. On the basis of the comparative evidence gathered there, Parry and his assistant Albert Lord hypothesized the manner in which epic verse was orally composed. What Lord called 'composition in performance' is not free improvisation but the demonstration of practised skills. Knowledge of usable phrases makes fluent production of meaning within a metrical system easier. Also characteristic of oral composition is repetition, which in Homer goes much farther than noun-epithet phrases. Whole lines are reused in certain situations, like at the beginning or end of speech. A simile or passage of some length might be found again elsewhere. For example, in *Iliad* 9 Odysseus repeats Agamemnon's earlier enumeration of gifts (with necessary grammatical modification). Analysts routinely assumed that only one instance of such a repeated passage was valid. But what Analysts attributed to the copying of pre-existing text could now be seen as intrinsic aspects of oral composition. Repetition was not unnecessary accretion, but a marker of anthropological alterity.

The 'formula' was defined by Parry as 'an expression regularly used, under the same metrical conditions, to express an essential idea'. Though formulaic efficiency (avoidance of alternatives) and extension (coverage of different metrical and syntactical needs) is best demonstrated by noun-epithet phrases, Parry argued that even phrases sharing metrical or syntactical patterns were analogous to formulas. Oralists continued to explore the nature and use of formulas throughout the twentieth century.[10] 'Soft' Parryists considered formulaic composition more flexible than Parry believed, and most Oralists became more optimistic about the possibility of contextual meaning for traditional phraseology. One might need to be cautious, but it became acceptable to interpret the extra-metrical significance of typology. For example, the phrase 'life-giving earth' occurs in the context of death in all of its three instances – perhaps the ironic pathos that Parry accused Ruskin of imposing on Homer is intrinsic to its formulaic usage. Repetition might sometimes be meaningful. The lines 'Just as he spoke these words the end of death enfolded him; and his soul fleeting from his limbs was gone to Hades, bewailing its fate, leaving manliness and youth' are only repeated when Patroclus and Hector die (16.855–7; 22.361–3); a further line, 'And to him even in his death spoke [...]' (16.858; 22.364), only varies at its ending, Hector addressing the dead Patroclus, Achilles the dead Hector. The repeated phraseology would seem to assist the poem's linkage of the two heroes' deaths.

Parry's work had little immediate impact, but Albert Lord publicized the Oralist approach in the postwar period, notably in his influential *Singer of Tales* (1960). Increasingly it was realized that Homeric poetry was marked not just by formulaic phraseology, but also by repeated motifs, typological scenes (feasting and arming, for example), and broad themes (such as the 'withdrawal, devastation, return' pattern).[11] Unitarians often welcomed the idea of an oral Homer; if an oral Homer seemed less aesthetically inclined than they would wish, at least his inconsistencies could be attributed to traditional technique and not multiple authorship. But the Homeric Question was in no way solved. The arguments of Parry and Lord persuasively demonstrated that pre-Homeric epic must have been oral, since Homer demonstrably employs long-standing techniques of oral composition. But even while acknowledging this, some continue to insist that only a literate author could succeed in achieving the level of quality in the Homeric poems. And even those who believe the Homeric poems were orally composed cannot easily explain how our Homeric texts came to be recorded.

Many have tried. One theory was that rhapsodes memorized the Homeric poems until they were eventually set in writing.[12] Lord influentially proposed that an orally composing Homer dictated his poems to a scribe (naturally enough, as he had aided Parry in recording performances by means of a scribe or a primitive recording machine).[13] Many have found this idea pleasing: the slowed-down process might arguably explain the length and quality of our Homer poems. Some prefer to imagine a transitional poet who extended the possibilities of his oral training through writing. But it has been wondered whether the Greeks of the early Archaic Age possessed adequate technology to record such long epic poems. Papyrus might conceivably have been imported, but much of it – and much time – would be required to write all that verse down. Ideological motivation is an issue as well. Nobody imagines that Homer was publicized by the passing around of multiple texts to a reading public. Why then even bother to record the Homeric epics at all? One is reminded of Wolf's mocking comparison of written Homeric epics to an inland ship waiting for future flotation. Somewhat Wolfian is the 'evolutionary' model by Gregory Nagy, which proposes that performance traditions of the Homeric poems became gradually fixed and then eventually textualized. For some, Homer as an individualized artist is perplexingly absent in Nagy's arguments. Yet like most Oralists, Nagy celebrates the poetic and cultural value of the Homeric epics.[14]

NEOANALYSTS

A fourth major school of thought, Neoanalysis, developed in the mid twentieth century. The term was coined by the Greek scholar Ioannis Kakridis, but the method was pursued primarily by German scholars, notably Schadewaldt and his student Wolfgang Kullmann.[15] Despite the name, this was a really a kind of Unitarian movement. Redeploying older arguments and techniques of the Analysts, Neoanalysts argued that a single author of the *Iliad* had used earlier poems in creating his own poem.

The *Aethiopis* of the Epic Cycle was especially an object of interest, since its contents were portrayed as pre-Homeric material that became reformulated by Homer in the *Iliad*. Neoanalysts compare the story of Memnon killing Antilochus and then being killed by Achilles to Hector killing Patroclus and then being killed by Achilles. Patroclus in his *aristeia*, death and funeral is thought to mirror the story of Achilles. Furthermore, the actions of Achilles represent later events in his story. Various inconsistencies or problems in the *Iliad* are put forward as evidence for the adaptation. One of the most influential Neoanalyst arguments, for example, focuses on the scene at the beginning of Book 18, in which Achilles learns of the death of Patroclus. He rolls on the ground in mourning and then is visited by Thetis and, unaccountably, the other Nereids. According to the influential explanation by Kakridis, Achilles is acting like a corpse and the Nereids behave as if they are attending his funeral. The Nereids did attend the funeral of Achilles, as we know from other sources, including the *Aethiopis* and *Odyssey* 24 (where the shade of Agamemnon regales the shade of Achilles with the story). The Book 18 passage is not condemned by Neoanalysts as an intrusion, but its oddities are thought to reveal its origin in non-Homeric epic.[16]

At first Neoanalyst method conceived of Homeric transformation of earlier stories as a textual process. A literate Homer was thought to be influenced by earlier texts, to the extent of reusing their wording. Neoanalysts talked somewhat vaguely of a textual prototype of the *Aethiopis* (since most considered this post-Homeric). Eventually some Neoanalysts like Kullmann began to propose that oral poems influenced Homer, even if Homer himself was literate. And some Oralists became interested in the way that Neoanalysts explored Homeric use of mythological narrative. It was posited that an orally composing Homer might naturally transform cyclic motifs from oral tradition in a general manner.[17]

Though the mixture of Neoanalyst and Oralist methodology is stimulating, much remains unresolved. The original Neoanalysts differed from Analysts in considering vestigial markers of cyclic material within Homeric poetry unproblematic: only the critic, not the audience, notices them. This confined the method's concerns to composition, not the effect on the audience. Kullmann's seminal study *Die Quellen der* Ilias (*The Sources of the* Iliad, 1960) widened the focus to all of the Epic Cycle, but the title reveals that this was a search for origins. An alternative is to think of Homeric employment of cyclic motifs as allusive, with correspondences between Homeric and cyclic stories recognizable by an audience. But whatever the hypothesis, Neoanalyst methodology is forced to replace missing evidence (the pre-Homeric epics or myth) with a bricolage of evidence: rare Cyclic fragments, ancient testimony about the Cycle, and cyclic-themed poetry and artwork. The resultant arguments typically feature lists and graphs that can be more wearisome than convincing. But the premise that the Homeric poems work within narrative traditions, and not simply with the techniques of oral epic traditions, is persuasive. Aristotle's observation that the *Iliad* incorporates the whole story of the Trojan War within its limited plot is comparable: this is what *Iliad* 18 does with the death and funeral of Achilles.

Mixed Methodology

As already indicated above, Homerists readily move in and out of various schools of thought, and different scholars employ the same methodology variously. Some issues are conducive to points of contact between apparently opposing perspectives. Consider the perceived irregularities within our texts of the *Iliad* and *Odyssey*. Some conclude that multiple authorship led to inharmonious results (Analysts); others minimalize peculiarities, finding them contained by a unified vision (Unitarians); yet others explain contextual infelicity as an organic system's consistency (Oralists), or the reformulation of extra-Homeric material by a master poet (Neoanalysts). The Analyst approach is the outlier here; Oralists and Neoanalysts tend to address Homeric 'problems' with an essentially Unitarian sensibility. But even the Analyst approach can be described as a kind of hyper-Unitarianism. A unified poem of a superior poet is desired; material thought to be in conflict with this goal is rejected.

Homerists may look for quality within the Homeric epics, but they do not expect it within the genre of Greek epic. This is surprising, since the ancients at first seemed to consider all heroic epics Homeric. Eventually the Homeric corpus was considered to be the *Iliad* and *Odyssey* exclusively – or just the *Iliad*, since some supposed the *Odyssey* to have been composed by a different poet. Modern Analysts were in the habit of portraying the *Odyssey* as a kind of mix of Homeric and Cyclic poetry. Modern Unitarians are often happy to credit a single Homer with two epics, but sometimes they suppose a second genius produced a second great epic in competitive imitation of the *Iliad*. But is it not paradoxical for two epics to be uniquely Homeric? The existence of a second Homeric epic certainly makes the very definition of what is Homeric challenging.

To separate the Homeric epics from the 'regular' genre, one might have recourse to the Aristotelian distinction between Homeric and Cyclic plotting (see Chapter 2). And then there is the eventual disappearance of the Cycle epics, which many attribute to ancient condemnation of their non-Homeric quality. For some, a 'meta-epic' or 'post-traditional' Homer planned the eventual supersession of the epic tradition in which he worked. Scripsists characterize a literate Homer as a transitional figure who employed new technology to channel oral epic in a new direction. Many Unitarians are attracted to this concept; so are classic Neoanalysts, who tend to see cyclic epic as both an influence on Homeric poetry and a casualty of it.

A different perspective would depict Homer as 'meta-cyclic', that is, self-consciously creative 'with' cyclic myth (the usual theoretical employment of the Greek root *meta*). Through a different employment of Neoanalyst method, the significance of the *Iliad* and *Odyssey* would be actively implemented by their contextualization in Trojan War myth. Homeric epic could then be distinguished from non-Homeric epic (it is '*meta*-cyclic'), but not separated from it (it is 'meta-*cyclic*'). If there is validity to this interpretation, then the fading of Homer's epic tradition would have constricted the effectiveness of the *Iliad* and *Odyssey*. But as demonstrated in the next chapters, cyclic myth remained popular – and so the Homeric poems remained meta-cyclic.

The focus of Oralist methodology on formalist technique also suggests a connection between Homeric and non-Homeric epic. The mechanics of oral composition found in Homeric epic are traditional, and thus must exist in other epics as well. One might even get the impression from Oralist argument that the *Iliad* and *Odyssey* are just two examples of a great number of very similar epics. The implication seems to be not that the Homeric poems are average, but that the whole epic tradition is excellent. Or rather, that the *Iliad* and *Odyssey* received and distilled what is excellent in centuries of traditional epic. This 'oral' Homer is as totalizing as the 'post-epic' Homer, but is celebrated for organic culmination of the past rather than break-away innovation.

Oralists, however, do much more than connect the *Iliad* and *Odyssey* to Greek traditions; they compare them to epic material from around the world. Many resisted the Parry–Lord approach by questioning whether South Slavic epic *is* comparable in terms of quality and length to the *Iliad* and *Odyssey*. That is why Avdo Međedović is a frequent topic of discussion in Oralist work, for this South Slavic poet could creatively compose poems as long as the Homeric ones. In other words, Oralists rose to the bait, though their formalist analysis of composition does not require justification by reference to size or aesthetics. In any event, those dismissive of non-Homeric bards in Greek tradition are unlikely to embrace comparative material. Many desire a unique Homer, not a typical one, whether traditional or comparative. But the apparently opposing visions – Homer the Bard and Homer the Tradition – are actually two forms of Romanticism going back two centuries. One extols the transcendence of an individual poet: the other the transcendence of the *Volk*.

If one envisions some kind of monumental poet, or two monumental poets, the question is where to place to place him/them diachronically. From an Analyst perspective, the real, authentic Homer (or Homers, as you please)[18] is usually situated at the start of the process. His work, whether brief lays or short 'wrath of Achilles' and 'return of Odysseus' epics, were subjected to later additions, interpolations and editing. Who were these post-Homer poetry-polluters? The villains vary from hypothesis to hypothesis, but they seem to comprise a small circle of bad poets, ham-fisted imitators and intrusive editors. How they got hold of the text(s), and with what authority they manipulated them is unclear. From a Unitarian perspective (which may include Neoanalysts and Oralists), a monumental Homer stands at the end of the process. He might have learnt his craft from an oral tradition (Oralists), or inherited traditional material that he then transformed (Neoanalysts), but the tradition culminates in the *Iliad* and *Odyssey* – except for *Iliad* 10, perhaps, and the end of the *Odyssey*, and bits here and there. Alexandrian editors get heroic *kleos* in this narrative for their mostly successful preservation of what Homer originated. Somehow they managed to reconstruct an authentically Homeric text from a splintering manuscript tradition that goes back to Homer himself, a literate Homer, perhaps, or a Homer with a literate friend. That's their story at least, and they're sticking to it.

But why describe typical positions of generic Homerists when three recent publications well illustrate the variety of responses to the Homeric Question? According to Martin L. West in *The Making of the* Iliad (2011), a literate Homer worked on the *Iliad* over the course of his lifetime, modifying a core poem about the wrath of Achilles. *Homer the Preclassic* by Gregory Nagy (2010) portrays the Homeric epics as performance traditions treasured for their pan-Hellenic authority – an authority contested by the Aeolic and Ionian peoples and eventually controlled by Athens through Panathenaic presentation. And Minna Skafte Jensen in *Writing Homer* (2011) finds Homeric creation in the dictation at Athens of prize-winning Panathenaic performances. These arguments – concisely and unfairly summarized here – will probably not match your mental image of Homer, but they well indicate that modern Homerists are much more complicated than the stick-figure Analysts, Unitarians, Neoanalysts and Oralists that I described above.

The hypotheses may be very different, but one finds many points of contact between these works. They all disbelieve in 'Homer' as a historical figure, although at times one is reminded of the claim by an apocryphal student that the *Iliad* and *Odyssey* were not written by Homer but by another man of the same name.[19] The ancient biographies of Homer are discussed in all three, not as historical fact but as indirect reflections of the performance or reception of Homeric poetry. The Panathenaic festival is featured in all three as well; indeed they believe that the one of 522 BCE was of particular importance. The etymology of the name 'Homer' is also explored. The name's root is suggestively explained as 'compiler' (of song) or 'gathering' (at song festivals). The ancient translation of *Homerus* as 'hostage' can be explained by the same root (hostages 'join' the enemy). Nagy takes this further by suggesting that the Homeric poems were a bond in pan-Hellenic culture. The legendary name 'Homer' thus might hint at the origin, performance and spread of Homeric poetry.

Each of these scholars applies a lifetime of expertise to their writings. West is a prolific publisher who has worked in many genres of Greek poetry, and his magisterial books on Near Eastern and Indo-European influences on Greek literature represent an enormous volume of research. In the field of early Greek epic, he has produced the standard commentaries for Hesiod (and now the Trojan Cycle), as well as the most comprehensively researched modern edition of the *Iliad*. His *Iliad* book displays a deep knowledge of Analyst scholarship, which West argues we neglect at our peril. He is also well aware that his picture of 'Homer', cutting and pasting his own text of the *Iliad*, will find little welcome in contemporary Homeric studies; presumably a post-Oralist age returning to pre-Oralist sensibilities will be more receptive.

As for Nagy, his seminal *The Best of the Achaeans* mixed Indo-European linguistics, Oralist method and attention to ritual practice; his many subsequent books expanded upon, with astonishing range, his evolutionary theory of Homeric composition and transmission. This approach is the inspiration for the ongoing group project producing a 'multitext' electronic edition of Homer as an alternative to the recreation of an 'original' text of Homer (for example, West's *Iliad*). *Homer the Preclassic* is actually just one of a pair of books; the previous *Homer the Classic* (2009) traces the fortunes of Homeric poetry down through antiquity. The two together provide a comprehensive view of the Greek and Roman civilizations through the lens of Homer. Readers will be impressed, though they may find this cleverly evolving, shape-shifting 'Homer' a curious creature.

The third scholar to whom I draw attention, Jensen, articulated her theory of Homeric dictation in the context of the Panathenaea decades ago. If it convinced few then, her masterful compilation of the evidence anticipated – and probably inspired – a revival of interest in what role the Pisistratids played in Homeric poetry. Here she returns to her theory only after providing the reader with a very helpful survey of oral performance around the world – with careful and thoughtful linkage to Homeric studies. She convincingly establishes that the *Iliad* and *Odyssey* are comparatively modest in size, although in the end she credits a dictation process for their length as well as excellence. It is a tidy solution, perhaps too tidy. Her denial of Homeric influence until well into the classical period – her *Iliad* and *Odyssey* were created over the course of a few weeks in the late sixth century BCE and then locked up, unread and unperformed for decades – will shock many. Yet it is just possible, and the shocking of Homerists out of complacency would be of value in itself. Jensen's anthropological foundation is vastly superior to an under-documented and under-theorized faith in a transcendent, immediately dominant Homer.

One is of course allowed to disagree with these original arguments, no matter how learned they are. But each mixes earlier schools of thought in interesting ways. If West practises Analysis, it is to serve a Unitarian argument as nuanced and thorough as Schadewaldt's. Nagy has always joined different methodologies together creatively, and here he moves far beyond oral poetics to the historical role of Homeric poetry in ancient culture. Jensen demands of her idiosyncratic hypothesis that it match what fieldwork reports tell her; her argument for expansive and bravura Homeric composition by means of dictation is ultimately Unitarian in nature – even if the idea of a 'Pisistratean recension' has long been anathema to Unitarians. The books are also relatively free of the polemics that are common in Homeric studies (including some of their previous work, it must be said), and they also occasionally cite each other, or at least (politely?) opt for silence over criticism (that West cites almost no contemporary is peculiar).

The above descriptions may suggest that these books have no direct engagement with the actual poetry of Homer. That is not fair; other publications by these authors do interpret poetics, and in fact the greater part of West's book is commentary on the *Iliad*, if keyed to his theory of the epic's composition. But it is also true that the Homeric Question is mostly concerned with the generation and transmission of the texts, not their meaning – even if it has implications for how one should interpret the Homeric poems. Since the Homeric Question will never be fully resolved, there is surely a point where prolonged speculation gives poor returns for the effort. These three books add up to over 1,200 pages (1,600 if we include Nagy's 'twin' book *Homer the Classic*), and although such dedicated focus in a world of distracted internet twittering is impressive, it would be a shame if the Homerist – or the author of introductory books on Homer – did not move on to other subjects. Though the Homeric Question should impact how the Homeric epics are interpreted, there is a lot more to Homeric studies. Over the last few generations, theoretical explorations of Homeric poetry have expanded, providing the field with many provocative and profound tools of interpretation. Additionally, there has been an explosion of interest in the 'reception' of Homer down through the ages. My next two chapters will turn to the very large and important topics of the interpretation and reception of the *Iliad* and *Odyssey*.

VI

THEORY

EARLIER CHAPTERS have described Homeric poetics and contextualized the Homeric epics in myth and history. This chapter provides further
perspectives, ones that explore the meaning of the *Iliad* and *Odyssey*. A survey
of theoretical interpretations of Homeric poetry should serve to unsettle
our initial impressions of Homeric poetry.[1]

Ancient Theory

Although the theoretical approaches surveyed below may be termed 'modern'
(from the last 150 years or so – modern for a classicist), there has always
been Homeric theory. Theory derives from the Greek *theoria*, 'looking', with
secondary meanings of 'pondering' or 'philosophizing'. If theory is a matter
of open-minded engagement with the poetry, then Homeric theory began
with the first performances of the *Iliad* and *Odyssey*. Though the Hellenistic
scholar Aristarchus recommended that we 'explain Homer from Homer',
an adage often used to justify literalism, it is better to 'look' at the full
complexity of Homeric poetics from a variety of theoretical perspectives.
The *Iliad* and *Odyssey* contain multitudes. In each poem a narrator ascribes

his information to a Muse, to whom he appeals; he also occasionally comments on, or directly addresses, the characters. A polyphony of character voices discuss and argue over what their actions mean. Achilles challenges the 'heroic code', his poem's plot and eventually himself; the 'polytropic' Odysseus employs clever words in order to effect his return. Characters talk about earlier myths in order to persuade or dissuade other characters in the mythological story that they are enacting.

Gods also conflict with one another, and they are interested in influencing the events of the human world. Sometimes they visit it, whether openly or in disguise. Human conflict can be explained by reference to divine abstractions: for example, the 'Prayers' (*Litai*) that settle the disputes caused by 'Blindness' (*Ate*) in Phoenix's embassy speech (*Iliad* 9.497 ff.). Phoenix is essentially telling an allegory. A common critical approach to Homeric poetry in antiquity was to explain it as allegory. Some pre-Socratic philosophers like Heraclitus and Xenophanes objected to Homeric content, but other early commentators (reportedly Theagenes of Rhegium) employed allegory to defend it. A perceived gap between an ideal of Homer and the actual poetry feeds much of this controversy: how Homer is envisioned is not always harmonious with what is in the poetry. One solution is to say that Homeric verse really means something else (etymologically allegory means 'other-speaking'). Stoics, Neoplatonists and Christians were all too happy to follow this line of interpretation.[2] When Zeus recalls in *Iliad* 15 (14 ff.) how he suspended Hera in mid-air, binding her hands and hanging anvils from her feet, it is allegorical cosmogony, not wife battery: so, reportedly, the prose mythographer Pherecydes in the sixth century BCE. The most famous example of Homeric allegory is by the Neoplatonist Porphyry (third century CE), who finds in the brief passage about Ithaca's cave of the nymphs (*Odyssey* 13.103–20) an allegory of the soul moving beyond the body and worldly possessions.

Porphyry's allegory may seem crude to us now, but all critical theory is in a sense allegorical, a way of saying *this* means *that*.[3] Some indeed fear that modern theory foists external meaning on primary text. But experimentation with new perspectives, no matter how incomplete, slanted or exaggerated, is preferable to assuming the significance of the *Iliad* and *Odyssey* is obvious and universal. Whether you prefer one theory to another, or mix different methodologies, or try out various approaches at different times, at least you're pondering meaning, just as the Homeric characters do. Theoretical practice varies greatly; some focus on text, others on context; some aim to recreate ancient meaning, others explore modern concerns. The 'reception' of Homer, surveyed in the next chapter, can involve a radically transformative vision that is not only allegorical (*this* is recreated as *that*) but often helpfully interpretative as well (*that* brings out aspects of *this*).

Modern Theory

Below you will find concise descriptions of a select number of modern theoretical approaches to Homer; following that is a rather breezy use of some to analyse the encounter between Andromache and Hector in the *Iliad* as well as the Polyphemus episode in the *Odyssey*. Space does not allow comprehensive coverage of all theories. The order of topics may seem random, but it is hoped that the clustering of approaches will bring out certain points. As above, only selective bibliography is cited, whether seminal or exemplary.

NARRATOLOGY, LINGUISTIC THEORY,
PSYCHOANALYTICAL CRITICISM

A good place to start is with narratology, which aims to describe the mechanics of narrative precisely. It has roots in formalist and structuralist theory, and in modern times has been especially influenced by the work of Gérard Genette. In Homeric studies, Irene de Jong has been the indefatigable leader of this methodology, with major studies of both the *Iliad* (*Narrators and Focalizers*, 1987) and the *Odyssey* (*A Narratological Commentary on the Odyssey*, 2001). Narratology has effected greater comprehension of how Homeric narrative works and provided Homerists with a more rigorous manner of describing it. The scientific nature of its terminology, at least in its simpler manifestations, is potentially very illuminating. Clarity results from a self-conscious eschewal of connotative significance, and the synchronic approach to the Homeric texts usually implies a Unitarian perspective. For many, this means that narratology is employed as a base for more historical or interpretive analyses.

Among its major concerns is the distinction between the *fabula* ('story' or *histoire* – narratological terminology varies) and narrative ('plot' or *récit*). The *fabula* is a chronological order of events; narrative is the arrangement of these in the text being analysed. It is also important to distinguish between the main narrator, who provides the voice responsible for the narrative, and speaking characters, who are secondary narrators (their embedded narratives may themselves have subsidiary narrators). The main narrator needs to be distinguished from the biographical author, a particularly useful concept for our ahistorical Homer. I prefer to employ the phrase 'main narrator' for 'Homer' in my work, although it has been convenient to refer to 'Homer' or the 'poet' freely above. The theoretical value of 'main narrator' is that is allows recognition of the persona-adoption inherent in narrative production. An ancient bard who begins by evoking a Muse is playing a certain conventional role; this is true even of Hesiod, who (unlike Homer) provides some biographical details about himself.

Other narratological descriptions of narrative production are helpful. The specification of an event to follow later is 'prolepsis', while reference to a prior event is 'analepsis'. Further distinction can be made as to whether the prolepsis or analepsis is within the boundaries of what the text narrates ('internal') or outside of it ('external'). The pace of narrative time varies from that of *fabula* time; for example, there is the 'pause' of static description, the brief 'summary' of previous action, or the skipping-over of 'ellipsis'. Perhaps most theoretically complex is 'focalization', which refers to the perspective of narrative. Description by the main narrator might temporarily be coloured by the subjective view of a character, for example.

The idiosyncratic nature of character speech has long fascinated Homerists. Its lexical basis can now be sliced and diced through technology, but there is a need for more than raw statistical data. *The Language of Heroes* (1989) by Richard Martin employs ethno-linguistics in its focus on the speech of Achilles (long a source of scholarly fascination; see Chapter 2). In *Poetry in Speech* (1997) Egbert Bakker employs discourse theory to discern patterns of everyday conversation in Homeric poetry, despite the restrictions of metre and epic language. Also relevant is the work of Elizabeth Minchin, which explains the production of Homeric poetry from the viewpoint of sociolinguistics and cognitive theory.[4] That communication is not accomplished by words alone is demonstrated by Donald Lateiner's *Sardonic Smile* (1995), which employs behavioural psychology and sociology to explore non-verbal behaviour in Homeric epic. The significance of physical action in Homer, like falling and overtaking, is also the focus of ongoing studies by Alex Purves.[5] Going beyond narratology, these scholars contextualize narrative by considerations of its origins in the mind and its reference to bodily actions.

The application of psychoanalytical theory to ancient literature begins with Freud, whose interest in classical antiquity is evidenced by some of his terminology ('Oedipus complex'). Psychoanalysis as literary criticism has often been seen as problematic. The assumption that characters reflect the psyche of a biographical author (elusive anyway in the case of the Homer) is long out of fashion.[6] The equation of myth to dream is debatable, and therefore so is Freudian 'dreamwork' (analysis of the symbolic meaning of dreams) as an interpretative method for myth and literature with mythological content. And subtlety is required to treat collective Greek culture as an analysand. It is also more common to use ancient myth and/or literature to illustrate psychology rather than the other way around. Though it is pleasing when Homer is found relevant to the modern world, as by Jonathan Shay in his important work on post-traumatic stress disorder,[7] the *Iliad* and *Odyssey* are not self-help books.

Nonetheless, Homeric poetry contains many passages that practically demand psychoanalytical interpretation. Take, for example, Penelope's dream of an eagle killing her geese (19.535 ff.). In the dream the eagle itself gives an allegorical analysis: the geese are the suitors and the eagle is a returning, avenging Odysseus. Penelope asks the 'beggar' what he thinks the dream means, and the disguised Odysseus is happy to confirm the eagle's interpretation of its (rather obvious) meaning. But from a psychoanalytical perspective, Penelope's admission that she wept upon finding the geese dead is of further interest: arguably a suppressed desire for the suitors is transferred onto the geese.[8] If you are looking for phallic significance, consider Odysseus' drawing of his sword from his thigh area when offered a magic potion by Circe (10.316 ff.), in response to which she immediately invites him to her bed. Odysseus, following the advice of Hermes, is careful to have her swear that she will not deprive him of his 'manhood' (341).

The *Iliad* contains passages suggestive of family psychodynamics, like Phoenix's autobiographical tale of sleeping with his father's concubine (*Iliad* 9.447 ff.), as well as his account of Meleager's mother cursing her son after he kills her brother (*Iliad* 9.566–572; the usual version in which she effects his death by throwing a totemistic log representing his life force into the fire is also promising). Then there is Patroclus as a doublet of Achilles, which might be explained in psychoanalytical – not Neoanalytical – terms (see Chapter 5). The literary trope of the *doppelganger* precedes Freud, but Polydamas, the Trojan born on the same night as Hector (18.251–2) who vainly tries to warn him, has plausibly been described as an externalization of part of Hector's psyche.[9] Achilles has also attracted psychological interpretation; it is a sign of the variety of possibilities that one study finds Achilles narcissistic because Thetis is a 'hover mother' (at Troy), while another locates his psychological dysfunction in her abandonment of him (when an infant).[10] The attraction of Freudian and post-Freudian methodologies, as with many other theoretical approaches, is the promise that it might uncover hidden layers of meaning.

STRUCTURALISM, ANTHROPOLOGY, MARXIST CRITICISM

Claude Lévi-Strauss's influential structuralist method ultimately ascribes relational patterns of semiotic meaning to universal tendencies of the human mind. Like many types of theory (for example, Lacanian), it employs Saussurean linguistic concepts of the signifier and signified, whose relation to referents of the real world are arbitrary and notional. For Greek myth, Lévi-Strauss's examination of Oedipus and his family is fascinating, if ultimately unconvincing: 'overvaluation' of family (for example, Oedipus marrying his mother) recurs in binary opposition to 'undervaluation' (for example, when his two sons kill each other).[11] Classicists have effectively contextualized structuralist method in Greek culture. A seminal study by Pierre Vidal-Naquet sees the wanderings of Odysseus as containing a conceptual exploration of the nature of Greek civilization.[12] Divine and non-human beings encountered by Odysseus are marked as non-Greek by their lack of communal organization (for example, Cyclopean society is family-based, while characters like Circe and Calypso live apart from society) and their non-agricultural diet (for example, the lotus of the Lotus-Eaters, nectar of divinities or the cannibalistic tendencies of the Cyclopes and Laestrygonians). Although the use of Homeric evidence is sometimes selective, a seemingly random sequence of supernatural adventures is startingly reinterpreted as culturally coded.

Lévi-Strauss was primarily a cultural anthropologist, basing his concepts on fieldwork among Amerindians. Comparative anthropology goes far back in classical studies; consider the proto-ethnographical work of Robert Wood, comparison of folk literature like 'Ossian' to Homer, the ritual approach to myth in the late nineteenth and early twentieth centuries, or the fieldwork of Parry and Lord.[13] In more recent times Walter Burkert, no stranger to Homeric studies, has advanced ritual-based study of Greek religion with use of sociobiological concepts. But anthropological analysis of Homer is complicated, since the epics' cultural phenomena, like their linguistic forms, stem from various time periods (see Chapter 4). Some argue the Homeric world, though nominally about the distant heroic past, primarily reflects a particular historical period. For Moses Finley (*The World of Odysseus*, 1954), this was the Dark Age of the tenth century BCE, a time of relatively undeveloped communal organization after the demise of Mycenaean palatial culture. More recently scholars have suspected that the Homeric poems largely reflect the contemporary world of the poet (whenever that is), expressing anxieties inherent in transitional period(s) of the early Archaic Age.[14] Epics about the long-ago Heroic Age can plausibly be 'imaginary gardens with real toads in them', to quote from Marianne Moore's poem 'Poetry'.

Others besides Finley have perceived a largely consistent social and economic system within the epics, whether historically or poetically constructed.[15] Central to the plot of the *Iliad* is the distribution and exchange of loot, including enslaved women. Odysseus is greatly concerned with collecting gifts from his hosts during his travels, though his lying tales feature the less aristocratic practice of trade. In Iliadic similes and in the scenes described on the shield of Achilles (18.483 ff.) one finds glimpses of a slave-based agricultural and pastoral economy, which are also present in the Ithaca of the *Odyssey*. The heroic world is hierarchical, but opinion is divided about the significance of this for historical audiences. Some conclude that the poems authenticate a contemporary elite by praise of their supposedly analogous heroic ancestors.[16] Arguably conflict among the Greek leadership at Troy and among the leaders of Ithaca reflects shifting power structures. That the Odyssean portrayal of the suitors represents unhappiness with shifting power structures is provocatively proposed in Martin Steinrück's *The Suitors in the Odyssey* (2008): the post-Heroic generation in the epic is to be associated with new social circles represented by Greek iambic poetry, sometimes called 'blame poetry' because of its irreverent content.[17]

One hears little of the lower classes in Homer. In the second book of the *Iliad* Thersites denounces Agamemnon (and Achilles for not resisting his commander more firmly), but he is beaten and ridiculed. Are new, contemporary egalitarian tendencies being thrashed into submission here, or is Thersites a voice of the future? Much depends on what status is attributed to Thersites; if he is actually a member of the elite class, then the passage reflects not class division so much as division among the elite.[18] The *Odyssey* documents the unjust treatment Odysseus experiences as a beggar, although he is ultimately able to throw off this strategic disguise instantly. The swineherd Eumaeus is a sympathetic character with a relatively major role, if of royal lineage.[19]

An intriguing example of criticism of the elite from below occurs in the Aeolus episode of *Odyssey* 10. When the companions of Odysseus open the bag of winds (28 ff.) while he is asleep, the secondary narrator, Odysseus himself (how he knows what they said is an interesting narratological question), portrays them as foolish for ruining a near-return to Ithaca. Yet we in the external audience hear the companions saying (generically, as a group):

> "'Much beautiful treasure is he carrying with him from the land of Troy
> from the booty, while we, who have accomplished the same journey as

he, are coming home bearing empty hands. And now Aeolus has given
him these gifts, granting them freely out of love." (40–4)

Odysseus thereby quotes a pithy articulation of the labour–profit disconnect
for the preferred resource acquisitions of both the *Iliad* (looting) and the
Odyssey (elite gift reciprocity). Whether our hero's tale (or the main narrative in which his words are embedded) indirectly acknowledges real-world
socio-economic issues is an open interpretative question. Although the
attention of the audience is directed to the disastrous consequences, one
might notice that the specific complaint of the companions is unanswered.

A 'double hermeneutic' in both Homeric epics – whereby ruling-class
ideology is both supported and exposed – has been provocatively explored
by Peter Rose from a Marxist perspective.[20] At times he portrays the main
narrator as a member of a middling class reluctantly rehearsing a necessary
party line (so to speak). William Thalmann's anthropological take on the
Odyssey[21] acknowledges diversity of ideological voice but is sceptical of the
epic's willingness to challenge the elite. As he points out, 'good' and 'bad'
slaves are defined by their loyalty to a monarchical system that is seemingly
benign but commandingly punitive (as when Melanthius and the handmaids
are brutally punished).

ECOCRITICISM, SPATIAL THEORY

Although the Homeric poems tend to focus on characters and action rather
than landscape, they contain many memorable descriptions of nature. In the
Iliad these mostly occur in similes and on scenes on the shield of Achilles.
More extensive description of natural phenomena is found in the *Odyssey*'s
Mediterranean and Ithacan topography. As an ecocritical approach eluci-
dates, the *Iliad* and *Odyssey* support anthropocentric exploitation of natural
resources.[22] Brief agrarian and pastoral passages perhaps hint at sustainable
environmental stewardship, but uncanny or threatening figures (for example,
Lotus-Eaters, Calypso, Sirens, Scylla) are typically used to represent nature.
Integration with the natural world is nightmarishly expressed by species
conflation – humans metamorphosed into swine by Circe, the ambiguous

status of the Cyclopes. Homeric marginalization or mythologization of the natural world reflects negative valuation of it. Ecocritical analysis can thus potentially challenge the Homeric polarity of nature–culture more than structuralism, which tends to complacently identify with the Greek bias towards culture.

Also worth noting – although this is best categorized as an example of Homeric 'reception', the next chapter's topic – is Aldo Leopold's environmental classic *A Sand County Almanac* (1949). The section entitled 'The Land Ethic' begins by referencing the hanging of the handmaidens at the end of the *Odyssey* (the key episode for Margaret Atwood's *The Penelopiad*, also discussed in the next chapter). Leopold points out that their execution is acceptable in the Homeric world that considers them property, but argues that human ethics have evolved from relations between individuals to a relation between the individual and society. The next step ('an evolutionary possibility and an ecological necessity') would be an ethics for man's relation to land and the plants and animals it supports.

Perhaps more than modern audiences realize, heroic myth largely transpires in the real world of Greek experience. The action of the *Iliad* occurs in north-west Asia Minor, between the Hellespont and Mount Ida. The epic also frequently mentions localities of the eastern Mediterranean. References to Aethiopians (1.423; 23.206), Pygmies (3.6), and 'mare-milking' people of the north (13.1–6), suggest a dim awareness of exotic cultures beyond the reach of regular Greek intercourse. The *Odyssey* features Ithaca and parts of the Greek mainland, and tales of heroic returns also involve the eastern Mediterranean (the Aethiopians, though placed at the eastern and western edges of the earth at 1.23–4, appear at 4.84 to exist somewhere in the south-east Mediterranean). Odysseus' own stories are more complicated; his 'lying' tales are mapped onto the reality of the Mediterranean world, but his 'real' adventures are paradoxically 'off the map' of Greek knowledge (though they have been localized since antiquity; see Chapter 7). And when the hero's journey extends to the edges of the earth and into the underworld, it becomes cosmographical.

Homeric geography is thus both real and conceptual, a mix open to the analysis of spatial theory.[23] Humanist or phenomenological geography explores the mental arrangement of space or the sociological creation of place from space. In the *Iliad* there is a noticeable recurrence of natural and man-made features: the rivers Scamander and Simoeis, certain trees, the defensive wall of the Greeks, the walls and gates of the city, and heroic burial mounds. Troy and its environs may be real, as Schliemann and the archaeologists have demonstrated, but the Homeric positioning of significant landmarks is poetically functional.[24] The Ithaca of the *Odyssey* may be real (although disputed: see Chapter 7), but the Homeric poem visualizes it with a notional matrix of various inhabited and wild locations (the homesteads of Eumaeus and Laertes in peripheral relation to the palace, the bay of Phorcys, 'raven's rock' and the Arethusa spring).[25] For the interpreter of Homeric poetry, the conceptual relation of such place markers should be at least as important as their geographical actuality.

The wanderings of Odysseus might also be notionally mapped, even if situated in unknown lands. Their supernatural and cosmographical nature, as well as the possible influence of Argonautic myth, complicates their overall visualization tremendously. However, simply placing them in 'Neverland' is overly pessimistic. This view is common in Unitarian scholarship, which can be curiously disdainful of the wanderings; what was commonly viewed by Analysts as an authentically original kernel tends to be perceived by Unitarians as a cordoned-off rehashing of non-Homeric material. Yet various studies have discovered patterns of repetition, parallelism and inversion in the adventures, including in their arrangement of space.[26] Even the 'inland journey' predicted for Odysseus by Tiresias, though vaguely articulated, has a spatial logic to it, as Alex Purves has impressively demonstrated as part of her exploration of Homeric spatiality in the early chapters of *Space and Time in Ancient Greek Narrative* (2010).

POST-COLONIALISM, FEMINISM, POST-STRUCTURALISM

Post-colonial theory explores the unequal power relations of modern colonialism and imperialism by analysis of their cultural representations. Outside of classical studies, post-colonial scholarship has long noticed that the *Odyssey* somehow expresses colonialist ideology.[27] The iconic passage is Odysseus' description of 'Goat Island' in Book 9 (116 ff.). Since the Cyclopes do not build ships, it is deserted. Under the Greek hero's colonial gaze, it is imaginatively transformed into plough-land, vineyards and a harbour good for ships:

> '[C]raftsmen [...] would also have made of this island a well-arranged
> settlement for them [the Cyclopes]. For the island is not at all a poor
> one, but would bear all things in season. On it are meadows by the
> shores of the gray sea, well-watered and soft, where vines would never
> fail. On it are level plowlands, from which they might reap from season
> to season very deep harvests, so rich is the soil beneath. And in it, too,
> is a harbor giving safe anchorage.'

The trope is often found in modern exploration of the New World, sometimes in tandem with portrayal of the violence of natives (cf. the cannibal Polyphemus). Why ancient epic about mythological characters should prefigure such images is not immediately clear – does the *Odyssey* coincidentally anticipate later imperialism, or are expansionist proclivities of technologically superior cultures universal?

Classicists can point to a more specific correspondence. From the eighth century onward, the Greeks created colonies in the western Mediterranean. The earliest colony, Pithecusae (modern Ischia in the Bay of Naples) – where the eighth-century-BCE 'Nestor's cup' inscription was found (see Chapter 4) – was like 'Goat Island', an island at safe remove from the mainland. Throughout the southern Italian peninsula and Sicily, 'uninhabited' land was developed, though in some cases contested by native populations who eventually became dispersed or were assimilated. Besides the colonial gaze of Odysseus, scholars have noticed the colonial nature of the Phaeacians as well. At the beginning of Book 6 the main narrator reports that they had moved away from their troublesome neighbours the Cyclopes to Scheria, where an ancestral leader apportioned plough-land and oversaw the construction of temples and walls. Such activity parallels the start-up undertakings of historical Greek colonists. It has often been concluded that the *Odyssey* reflects developments contemporary to its composition. Carol Dougherty's *The Raft of Odysseus* (2001) goes further in uncovering the Homeric poem's socio-economic ideology of expansionism.[28]

In the terminology of Michel Foucault, a major influence on New Historicists, a cultural product such as Homeric epic may very well voice certain discourses generated by historical Greek/non-Greek interaction. Whereas the structuralist method (see above) describes self-definition by the ancient Greeks in terms of notional non-Greek otherness, post-colonial theory turns the gaze back implicitly on the unsympathetic, demystified 'us' of recent centuries. This move disquietingly aligns the ancient Greeks not with comparable 'primitives' of the modern world, or with the glories of 'Western culture', but rather with European imperialists and colonizers.

Feminist theory's interest in socio-economic depictions of women necessarily applies a modern perspective on the Homeric world.[29] An impressive body of feminist interpretation of Homeric gender relations over the past few decades divides on the question of whether the *Iliad* and *Odyssey* are 'closed' or 'open' texts. The former view, well represented in a trenchant article by Sheila Murnaghan[30] and the nuanced *Siren Songs* (1995) by Lillian Doherty, finds a patriarchal authorial stance in Homeric narrative. Women are central to the plot only because they are contested through violence or distributed as material possessions. As agents they are regarded with suspicion or horror: Helen's shamelessness causes a war; Clytemnestra conspires to murder a husband. Even goddesses, though powerful, act within a patriarchal divine order and support an oppressive status quo of gender hierarchy: Athena aids Odysseus, for example, by discrediting and manipulating Penelope. What's worse, female characters like Briseis implicitly support the ideology of which they are victims. Spatiality can also be a gender issue: female activity is normally relegated to the household (as seen at Troy and Ithaca); female characters situated at the periphery of the Greek world, like Circe, Calypso and Nausicaa, are marked as doubly suspect.

A more optimistic stance, represented by studies such as *Penelope's Renown* (1991) by Marilyn Katz, *Regarding Penelope* (1994) by Nancy Felson-Rubin, and *A Penelopean Poetics* (2004) by Barbara Clayton, sees Homeric poetry as open, encompassing alternative perspectives. Certain passages seem subversive to dominant ideology, or at least make it seem problematic. Agamemnon's claim that he prefers his concubine Chryseis to Clytemnestra, for example, offers an opportunity for the audience to judge him. When told by Hermes that Zeus wants her to let Odysseus go, Calypso lets rip with an impassioned complaint of the double standard of male divinities who indulge in sexual relationships with mortals but begrudge the same for goddesses (*Odyssey* 5.116 ff.). Helen in *Iliad* 3 (383 ff.) stands up to Aphrodite's manipulative demand that she go to Paris. If she (like Circe) is ultimately powerless, she certainly displays a firm sense of subjectivity, even in her public display of self-criticism. Female character speech is given some prominence, notably in the laments.

But it is the *Odyssey*'s Penelope that has been most featured in feminist scholarship. In Chapter 3 the contradictory nature of her characterization was noted. At times she is indecisive when confronted by the suitors and her own son, and the *Odyssey* seemingly suppresses active roles emphasized elsewhere (the web trick; plotting with the husband). If we take the *Odyssey* as a closed text, Penelope might seem to be a largely passive victim. But within an open text of the *Odyssey*, other shades of characterization become visible. The interview between Penelope and the disguised Odysseus in *Odyssey* 19 is a potential site of Penelopean subjectivity. Husband and wife converse sympathetically; Penelope tells the story of her web trick; Odysseus tells a lying tale of past adventures. Eurycleia then recognizes his scar when bathing him, but is sworn to secrecy. The audience is teased by the possibility that Penelope might recognize Odysseus, but that does not happen. Critics have been fascinated by the ambiguity.[31] Perhaps an alternative, presumably pre-Homeric version in which she *does* recognize Odysseus pulls the Homeric epic into its orbit. Perhaps a secret understanding arises between Odysseus by Penelope, even if this is unspecified. Or, in the subtlest reading, perhaps there is unconscious recognition of Odysseus by Penelope. This has a psychoanalytical foundation, but also allows a feminist restoration of agency to Penelope. All of these interpretations obviously read between the lines. But perhaps it is more interesting, and ultimately more far-reaching, to view the non-recognition as an opportunity for other forms of Penelope's subjectivity to flourish. Though in the dark about Odysseus' plotting, she can thereby challenge the epic's plot with a hypothetical remarriage, as well as manage her later recognition of Odysseus in Book 23 on her own terms.

Marilyn Katz's feminist study of the *Odyssey* (1991) employs post-structuralist method to suggest a very open Odyssean text, where unity of authorial voice or character is hard to find. Post-structuralism has elsewhere played a small but effective role in Homeric studies, for instance in Pietro Pucci's deconstructive *Odysseus Polytropos* (1987) and John Peradotto's Bakhtinian *Man in the Middle Voice* (1990).[32] In such works the *Odyssey*'s self-conscious narrative sophistication, unquestionably polymorphous and polyphonous, is seen as particularly conducive to postmodern interpretation. Such studies practise the close reading typical of traditional Homeric interpretation and are not necessarily incompatible to methods long practised within the Homeric Question. Pucci gives good attention to oral poetics, for example, and Katz links the post-structuralist fascination with textual gaps to the Neoanalyst fascination with irregularities in Homeric narrative.

Despite proclamations of a 'post-theory' turn in literary criticism,[33] theoretical methodology can still usefully open a text up to socially and politically grounded readings. But if hostility to literary theory masks oblivion to one's own assumptions,[34] disregard for the historical contexts of the Homeric texts is bound to hamper interpretation. Analysis of any type should be implemented with awareness that the Homeric epics stem from orally composed and performed traditions. At times the terminology of this book refers not to the 'audience' of a 'performance' but to the 'reading' of a 'text', especially in regards to modern experience with the preserved epics. However, it is my intention to value both diachronic and synchronic studies of Homer, that is, the historical origins and transmission of the epics as well as an appreciation of how they work in and by themselves.

This chapter ends with a sketch of some possible theoretical interpretations of my two central scenes, the meeting between Andromache and Hector, and the Polyphemus episode. Space does not allow an extended implementation of any approach, all of which are proffered without judgement as to their cogency. The point of this brainstorming type of exercise is to demonstrate the multiplicity of potential interpretative strategies, which are often most effective when combined.

Andromache and Hector

As suggested above, it is a good idea to start by laying narratological foundations. At the beginning of Book 6, the main narrator portrays the Trojan setbacks on the battlefield that motivate (rather thinly) Hector's visit to Troy.[35]
Yet his encounters in Troy with Hecuba, Paris and Helen, and Andromache
are dominated by the secondary narration of these characters (some of which
were discussed in Chapter 3 for their evidence of characterization). The talky
meeting between Andromache and Hector might even give us the impression of a drama. But it also true that the main narrator intervenes to provide
key or suggestive information. For example, we hear that Andromache had
gone to the city wall with Astyanax before Hector asks after her at his house;
furthermore, the main narrator also describes the actions and gestures of
the spouses and their child. Astyanax is introduced with a brief simile: he
is 'like a fair star' (6.401). In the sense that the main narrator here channels
the perspective of the child's parents, this is 'focalization'.

One is also informed by the main narrator that Astyanax ('city-king') is
a nickname; Scamandrius is the child's real name. The narrator explains that
'only Hector guarded Ilios' (403); thus the nickname honours the father.
Non-verbal gestures are interspersed within the character speech that follows.
Hector first smiles at his son 'in silence' (404) and later reaches out to take
the child from the nurse (provoking his cries; 466 ff.). After he removes his
helmet, he is described kissing and dandling his son (474) before placing
him in the arms of Andromache, who by 'smiling through her tears' (484)
impels Hector to stroke her with his hand. As she leaves him, Andromache
repeatedly turns around (6.496). When Andromache returns to her home,
the main narrator reports that she led the handmaidens in lamentation over
Hector ('in his own house [...] while still he lived' [500] – a brief note of
pathos). Unusually, the main narrator also explains their thought: they do
not expect Hector ever to return (501–2). He will return, but the passage
serves indirectly as an internal prolepsis of the death of Hector that will
occur within the poem's boundaries. Andromache's previous recounting
of the tragic fates of her family (see Chapter 3) before the time period of

the epic is external analepsis; Hector engages in external prolepsis when he speculates variously about the future fates of his wife and child. In sum, a rather complex narratological structure girds this memorable episode, dominated by secondary narration, but subtly stage-managed and commented upon by the main narrator.

What else to interpret? Well, tightly gripped in Hector's hand is the phallic symbol of an eleven-cubit-long spear. Apparently he has it throughout his visit to Troy, though it is only mentioned when he carries it into the bedroom of Paris and Helen (318 ff.) – an excellent context for Freudian analysis. Almost too obvious is the waving horsehair crest of Hector's helmet that terrifies his infant son (469–70), but the meeting of father, mother and infant does provide a perfect scenario for familial psychodynamics. Some statements of Andromache and Hector are highly charged: for instance, when she compares him to father, mother and brother (429–30), or when he imagines her being led away as slave without voicing the sexual consequences of this fate (454 ff.).

The episode also well evokes the classic nature/culture binary of structuralism. Andromache's concerns are for the human culture of her family life with Hector and, more generally, the civilized community of the city. Hector defends his intent to return to war, which, if not exactly 'nature', represents a dissolution of civilization in the natural setting of the Trojan plain. The slotting of 'war' into the same side of the equation as 'nature' is well illustrated by the image of violence erupting amid a pastoral scene of herdsmen on the 'shield of Achilles' (18.520 ff.). Battle scenes are typically envisioned through nature similes (see Chapter 3), and fighting potentially transforms humans into food for dogs, birds and fish – an ongoing theme in the poem.[36]

Though we may focus on the individual personalities of Hector and Andromache, anthropological issues are central to their conversation. Hector's reasoning is ultimately based on the 'heroic code', that scholarly reconstruction of the value system of Homeric heroes (see Chapter 2). Hector is motivated by a sense of shame (6.441–2) concerning what the Trojans might say about him. Even after the Trojans are routed as a result of his misguidedly aggressive military strategy, he elects to stay outside the walls alone. By losing his life, he dooms the city as well his family, although his name etymologically suggests his role as a defender ('holder' or 'protector'; cf. 24.730), just as his son's nickname Astyanax ('city-lord') does. Hector talks as if he is privileging public responsibilities over private ones, yet ultimately he fails in both roles.

A socio-economic perspective underscores how different the world of Hector and Andromache is from ours. Hector belongs to the royal family that rules Troy; he and Andromache are both members of an elite social class made wealthy by a slave-based economy. Distracted by the episode's seeming expression of universal values, we might overlook the presence in the background of the silent nurse who actually does the work of raising the child. Slave women abound back in their household as well; one, in a rare moment of speech for an Iliadic slave, fills Hector in on where Andromache had gone (6.381 ff.). The others are typically engaged in weaving cloth, and it doesn't take a Marxist analysis to realize that the share of dividends from this labour is unequal. Whereas heroic conflict over the distribution of goods motors the plot of the *Iliad*, the handmaidens who belong to Andromache and Hector apparently accept their lot complacently, internalizing the ideology of slave culture to such an extent that they lament the approaching death of their owner. Compare Briseis, who once hoped to become the wife, instead of slave concubine, of the man who apparently killed her husband when he destroyed her hometown (see Chapter 3). In this passage, however, we catch the glimmer of a gap in such internalized ideology. The main narrator notes that the other slave women who join her in mourning over the corpse of Patroclus privately mourn their own misfortunes (19.301–2).

The spatiality of the encounter between Andromache and Hector is strongly marked. Arguably the city walls, which cleave the Iliadic world into military and domestic halves, serve as the main character in the scene. The main narrator describes Hector's Troy through certain topographical features. Hector first enters the city gate, by which stood an oak tree (237), then arrives at the palace of Priam, whose arrangement of bedroom chambers is described in detail (242–50). Hecuba is described entering an inner treasure chamber to fetch one of the Sidonian robes brought back by Paris (see Chapter 1), which she brings with other elder women to the temple of Athena on the acropolis (296 ff.). Hector makes his way to the house of Paris and then to his own house. Not finding Andromache there, he asks whether she is at the other places already mentioned, but is told by the house slave that his wife has gone to the wall and its tower. So he retraces his steps 'back over the same way down along the well-built streets' (390–1); when he reaches the Scaean gates again, 'by which he was about to go out to the plain' (392–3), Andromache approaches him on the run. The collocation of key landmarks allows us to create a loose conceptual map of Troy, and we experience Hector's visit not simply as a sequence of speeches but also as his movement through space.

The spatial organization that assists our comprehension of Hector's visit also has sociological dimensions. The city walls serve as a boundary between male and female social spheres, which are certainly not balanced in power.[37] After Andromache's opening speech she does not say another word. Whatever the earnestness of Hector, he dominates the conversation. Hector ignores her advice on military strategy (6.433 ff.), and feminist scholarship has certainly noticed how he puts her in her 'place': 'But go to the house and busy yourself with your own tasks, the loom and the distaff, and tell your handmaids to ply their work: and war will be the concern for men' (490–3; Penelope is told off in similar terms at *Odyssey* 1.356–9 and 21.343 ff.). Hecuba had already been charged by Hector to undertake the only public function allowed for females in the Homeric world, that of religious ritual. And Andromache plays a gender role already played by Hecuba and Helen: that of the female who delays a male's business. Hector had already refused his mother's suggestion that he drink wine and rest. Relevant is her later plea that he leave the battlefield. Standing on the city walls, she holds out the breast that once fed him to signify her moral claim on him (22.79–85). He refuses to enter the city and is killed shortly thereafter. In Book 6 (354 ff.) Helen also tries to delay Hector, with a request that he sit by her. And of course Andromache tries to convince Hector not to return to battle after happening upon him as he was about to slip out of the city.

The Polyphemus Episode

It is good to keep in mind that Odysseus addresses his sea tales to internal narratees, his hosts the Phaeacians. Odysseus is eager for them to send him on his way home, and we might suspect he spins his experiences to point out what is and what is not good hospitality (see Chapter 3). Even though the main narrator vouches for the essential truthfulness of the episode (see Chapter 2), there is much leeway for Odysseus on how the encounter with the Cyclops might be told. Polyphemus is essentially a character in Odysseus' tales (as is Odysseus himself); the words of the Cyclops are provided through the hero's narrative (when Polyphemus reports by indirect speech the former prophecy of a certain Telemus at 9.506 ff., we are four layers of narration deep: main narrator, Odysseus, Polyphemus and Telemus).

In his narration Odysseus moves back and forth between a 'real time' narration of the events as they unfold and hindsight (as when he states that it would have been better if he had listened to his companions' advice to leave without waiting for the cave's inhabitant to return; 228–9). Long before the actual arrival of Polyphemus, Odysseus proleptically tells his narratees that a huge, solitary, lawless man lived in the cave that the Greeks discover (187–92). This not only foreshadows later events, but also ethically colours the story. Odysseus also looks forward proleptically when he feels obligated to explain why he brought wine to the cave. He says that he foreboded meeting a man 'clothed in tremendous strength, a savage man that knew nothing of rights or laws' (213–15; note the ethical colouring once again). Intoxicating Polyphemus with the wine apparently helps the Greeks overcome the Cyclops (so Polyphemus in hind-blindness [454, 516], although the point is not stressed at the time). In an extended analeptic flashback Odysseus explains that Maron gave the wine to him in return for protection during the Greeks' attack on the Ciconians (196 ff.).

It is sophisticated tale-telling, but since a Muse does not inform Odysseus, his narrative sometimes strains plausibility. It is one thing for Odysseus to guess what Polyphemus was thinking (281–2, 415–19), but quite another for him to tell us that Zeus refused the sacrifice of Odysseus' rescuing ram because he was plotting the destruction of his ships and companions (551–5). This might be deduction by hindsight after he had lost his ships and companions, but it is not labelled as such. The Phaeacians, however, are certainly impressed by Odysseus' narration. When Odysseus breaks off in the midst of telling the underworld adventure, Alcinous affirms his truthfulness and compares him to a singer (see Chapter 3). Though distinctions can be found between Odysseus' style and that of the main narrator, both share epic language, formulas and poetic techniques such as character speech and similes. So although we imagine Odysseus to be speaking casually, we experience his words as Homeric epic. The distinction between main and secondary narrator is easy to forget, as Odysseus' story works its charm on us as much as the Phaeacians.

Mystery over the origins of Homeric epic is certainly relevant to our analysis of the episode. The essential story underlying the Polyphemus episode is probably pre-Homeric; a modern folk tale about a blinded ogre is so widespread that most Homerists conclude that it does not originate with the *Odyssey* (see Chapter 3). This does not mean that the Homeric poem first transformed the tale type into an episode featuring Odysseus; the crossing from folk to epic genre could have happened generations before the composition of our *Odyssey*. Whether attributed to Greek tradition or to Homer, the *Odyssey*'s ogre is unusual. A Cyclops works well for the narrative: Polyphemus is strong (the better to block a cave with a giant boulder) and one-eyed (the easier to blind). It is also narratologically convenient that there be other Cyclopes nearby: the blinding tale type needs only one bad guy, but the famous 'Nobody' gag (see Chapter 3) would be impossible without more Cyclopes to ask what all the racket is about. A different tale type in which the protagonist calls himself 'Myself', with comparable misunderstanding when the antagonist seeks help, evidently lies in the background of the Polyphemus episode here.[38]

However well these Homeric Cyclopes fit into the narrative, they are distinctly odd.[39] The parents of Polyphemus are Poseidon and the sea nymph Thoosa (*Odyssey* 1.71–3), though Uranus fathers the Cyclopes in Hesiod (*Theogony* 139 ff.). That is because the plot requires the sea god to prolong the hero's wanderings in anger at his son's blinding. There is no point in wondering how Poseidon + sea nymph = Cyclops, or about the parentage of the other Cyclopes. Odysseus' tale would work just fine with an ogre herdsman who happened to be the son of Poseidon and whose one good eye or both eyes were blinded (as in the folk tales). The slippage between an ogre and a Cyclops might be compared to an early-seventh-century Cycladic relief *pithos* on which the Medusa being decapitated by Perseus has the hind body of a horse.[40] In other words, the Gorgon is represented as a hybrid creature, like a centaur. The artist apparently relies on stock 'monster' iconography to depict a mythological Gorgon; the *Odyssey* uses a mythological Cyclops for a stock ogre. But whatever the folk, myth and epic origins of the Polyphemus episode, it is an engrossing narrative, and so the audience does not ask awkward questions.

Scholars have not hesitated to do so, however, and there are lots of wonderful aspects of the episode that can be unpacked by means of various theoretical approaches. If one is looking for phallic symbols, that stake employed to blind Polyphemus will serve the purpose, and it is notable that blinding symbolizes castration in Freudian terms. Already in antiquity Porphyry saw in the blinding an allegory for suicide, which implies Polyphemus is a potentially a symbolic projection of Odysseus' psychology.[41] Or one might prefer to think of Odysseus as infantile, eventually emerging from the 'womb' of the Cyclopean cave.[42] Post-Freudian construction of identity has also been perceived in the episode: in a Lacanian sense, Odysseus disrupts the infantile utopianism of the Cyclopes, whose construction of psychological subjectivity is enabled by the cries of Polyphemus ('much-speaking'?).[43] Such interpretations may seem to read between the lines of the text more than explicate it, but they can usefully challenge Odysseus' mesmerizing self-justifications.

Structuralists find in the Polyphemus episode excellent illustrations of the polarity of nature and culture.[44] 'Goat Island' is lush with natural resources, and the Cyclopes are described as living off a natural bounty ('wheat, and barley, and vines, which bear the rich clusters of wine' [110–111]) that is available without agriculture. Polyphemus himself is likened to 'a wooded peak of lofty mountains, which stands out to view alone, apart from the rest' in Odysseus' description (191–2). Since Odysseus in his mind's eye cultivates the island's resources, as well as employs similes of shipbuilding and metallurgy, there is much validity in seeing this as a tale of culture overcoming nature. To blind his antagonist Odysseus does not need to use a primitive stake instead of his sword (or a roasting spit, as in many folk tales), but the story thereby highlights the issue of technology, a theme that becomes insistent when Odysseus rattles off similes of technology when describing the blinding (see Chapter 3).

But one should distinguish sharply between 'Goat Island' and the Cyclopean mainland.[45] Where the former is untouched nature, abounding with wild goats, the latter is the setting for a pastoralist livelihood with domesticated livestock. Odysseus observes with interest the careful, organized craft (so culture) with which Polyphemus makes cheese, manages his livestock and diligently pastures them by day. All this belies the hero's rhetorical conflation of the Cyclopes with nature. If Polyphemus eats his victims 'like a mountain-nurtured lion' (292), guts, bones, and all, it is also true that he cuts apart their limbs and in some unspecified way prepares his cannibalistic meal (291). Interpreters employing cultural anthropology like to assume that Polyphemus eats his human flesh raw, but he probably cooks it with the firewood he brought in 'to serve him at supper time' (233–5). This is not to say that the narrative is always clear: Odysseus both implies that nature supplies the Cyclopes with wine (110–11, 357–8) and that Polyphemus can't handle it (or at least Odysseus' Maronian wine). Such nuances challenge the neatness of binary opposition, even if the theme of nature versus culture is prominent.

Also unclear is exactly how the Cyclopes practise their pastoral lifestyle. Are they nomadic, transhumant or sedentary? Odysseus seems to assume their caves are permanent homes, but here it is good to remember that the narrator has limited knowledge. Odysseus knows nothing about the other Cyclopes beyond their brief enquiry from outside the cave after the blinding. Nonetheless, he is generous with his ethically charged ethnographical description of the Cyclopes, described as a kind of exotic human tribe (not monsters, as in many translations and critical studies; cf.: 6.5; 9.187, 214). These are strange Cyclopes indeed; usually the Cyclopes are three divine beings that make lightning and thunder for Zeus, as in Hesiod (*Theogony* 139 ff.).

Odysseus begins the tale with a seemingly omniscient ethnographic description of 'an insolent and lawless folk'. Odysseus is very surprised that they do not practise agriculture (on the evidence of Hesiod's *Works and Days*, it seems the Greeks considered agriculture central to the human condition). But what really eats at Odysseus is the Cyclopean lack of political organization. With no assemblies, councils or laws, the Cyclopes are each 'lawgiver to his children and his wives, and they have no regard for one another' (112–15). This information is extraneous to the story: Polyphemus has no family. It helps to create a coherent ethnography, though, one that serves to define Greek culture by detailing the non-Greekness of the 'Other'.[46]

Anthropological issues arise often in the episode. Curiously, the hero imports aristocratic social values into a herdsman's cave, expecting the inhabitant to provide him with guest-gifts (229, 267–8).[47] Polyphemus does not play this game by heroic rules. He promises a guest-gift that turns out to be a promise to eat Odysseus last; later he deceptively offers guest-gifts and conveyance home if Odysseus returns to him (see Chapter 3). From the perspective of the heroic code, Polyphemus is a failure at cooperative values (gift-exchange) and the dupe of acceptable deception (the rustling of livestock). Odysseus' narrative also portrays a strong hierarchical division between the general and his men. With their rowing, the companions motor the hero's fleet about the sea, but though Odysseus assures his listeners that everyone receives an equal share of goods – loot from a sacked city (41–2), slain goats (159–60) and livestock rustled from Polyphemus (548–9) – an extra portion is regularly distributed to Odysseus (160, 549–51).

Just as murmuring arose over the stockpiling of guest-gifts by Odysseus in the Aeolus episode (see above), Eurylochus complains that the deaths of the companions eaten by the Cyclops was caused by Odysseus' 'folly' (10.435–7). Odysseus essentially survives the Cyclops by the attrition of companions, as he similarly survives the Scylla by the sacrifice of (the same number of) companions.[48] In the latter episode, the attrition is calculated, since he withholds his knowledge that six of them must die (12.223 ff.). Odysseus makes much in his telling of how he put on armour to defend his men, but this seems as defensive as the proem's insistence that the 'folly' of the companions doomed their return, despite Odysseus' efforts to save them (1.5–7).

Where is the land of the Cyclopes? Odysseus does not know – that is why he seeks Polyphemus' aid in returning (349–50), and so the external audience does not know either. The internal audience of the Phaeacians may know, since they used to live by the Cyclopes (6.4–6), but all Odysseus can report is that his fleet was blown south of Greece for nine days, to the Lotus-Eaters (localized in North Africa in antiquity), whence they 'sailed on' to the Cyclopes, with no indication of direction or duration of travel. In antiquity Polyphemus was placed in the vicinity of Aetna on the eastern side of Sicily, perhaps because the non-Homeric Cyclopes were eventually thought to use the volcano as a smithy to construct Zeus' lighting and thunder. Modern localization has focused on north-west Sicily, under the influence of Samuel Butler's *The Authoress of the Odyssey* (1897), which idiosyncratically argues that a young Greek woman in north-western Sicily composed the Homeric epic.[49]

In spatial terms, the episode contains two central poles: 'Goat Island', where the Greek fleet stays, and the cave of Polyphemus on the mainland, to which Odysseus travels with a ship. It is within the cave, with an entrance usually closed off by the heavy boulder, that the drama occurs. A courtyard for the livestock is outside; Polyphemus takes his flocks to a mountain for pasturage during the day. The description of nature is relatively generous for Homer throughout the passage, especially in the full portrayal of 'Goat Island', with its meadows by the shore (132–3), level fields (134) and a harbour with a spring by a cave with poplars at its head (136–41). The Cyclopes leave a relatively light ecological footprint (despite their size!) on their environment; they live in natural habitations, requiring from nature only pasturage for their flocks and what can be foraged. Odysseus is not impressed; his description of 'Goat Island' is essentially a rueful catalogue of how natural resources are not being developed.

One can move beyond Odysseus' 'colonial' description of 'Goat Island' (see above) for a post-colonial interpretation of the Polyphemus episode. A post-colonial perspective might employ an against-the-grain reading to challenge the hero's complacent ethnography. Plenty of things in the narrative give one pause. If Polyphemus is a poor host, the Greeks act poorly as guests when they enter the empty cave and help themselves to food. The companions of Odysseus even suggest that they run off with cheese and livestock, though Odysseus holds out for guest-gifts. Polyphemus assumes that the intruders are dangerous, if not merchants. When the Cyclops suggests the Greeks are pirates 'bringing evil to men of other lands', Odysseus' not-very-reassuring reply is essentially 'we sacked Troy' (259 ff.). The aggressive probing initiated by outsiders provokes a response by an indigene that justifies overwhelming violence. Comparable is the standard trope of reciprocated violence in initial contacts between Europeans and natives in the New World.

But is this line of interpretation appropriate for a story about a *cannibalistic monster*? First, if Polyphemus is a cannibal then he is not a monster but a human, as the text insists (see above). True, Polyphemus has divine parents, and, as a monocular giant, he differs physically from humans, but the species conflation is another instance of Homeric narrative having its cake and eating it too. Second, exaggerated or imagined cannibalism is a trope in accounts of culture clash. For the most part Odysseus portrays the Cyclopes as an indigenous people. This is a key difference between the Polyphemus episode and the type of ogre tale that it has cannibalized. The land of the Cyclopes may be nowhere, but the Greek/non-Greek interaction described in it well reflects the historical circumstances of Greek expansion into the western Mediterranean at the time when the Odyssey was being composed and performed.[50]

How about a feminist take on the Polyphemus episode? That would seem hard to do, given the absence of female characters. But there are female characters: the women enslaved when the Greeks sacked the Ciconian city. Odysseus reports that 'we took their wives and much treasure' (9.41). In other words, this is the fate experienced by Briseis and feared by Andromache in the *Iliad*. But whereas the *Iliad* can allow a captive female to give voice to her tragedy, here the *Odyssey* does not. The Ciconian women are never mentioned again. Probably this is because they are inconvenient to the narrative of the wanderings, but it is revealing that the epic allows their enslavement to appear momentarily as a natural consequence of war. Also, the womb-like cave, not to mention all those goat udders bursting with milk, make the episode seem obsessively marked by female signifiers. And of course the wanderings will go on to feature many prominent female characters. Circe, Calypso and Nausicaa share a role with the females of Hector's visit in *Iliad* 6: that of delayers of the male protagonist. Whether with good intentions or not, Circe, Calypso and Nausicaa are an impediment to the plot of Odysseus' return home, and so Odysseus must eventually free himself from them.

Some theoretical methods strive to explain what is really going on in Homeric poetry; some employ Homeric poetry as 'good to think with' concerning particular issues. Some simply point out that such phenomena as war, slavery, patriarchy and ethnocentrism do not need to be complacently accepted norms. That does not mean that the *Iliad* deplores the social and gender restrictions of Andromache, for example, or that the *Odyssey* views Polyphemus as a victim. But often Homeric epic seems to invite such pondering of its meaning, especially when it goes out of its way to slip in this and that interesting nugget of information, whatever the surface meaning of its narrative. In the next chapter we shall see that the reception of Homer, like theory, variously reinterprets Homeric poetry. In its most creative manifestations, reception can even rewrite the Homeric epics into what even the most radical theoretical interpretations have only imagined.

VII

RECEPTION

BY 'RECEPTION' classicists refer to modern use of antiquity. Replacing earlier terms like 'heritage' and 'influence', reception is meant to indicate a vigorously active engagement with ancient culture, as opposed to deferential passivity. It is an elastic term, ranging from intellectual history to cultural production. My focus is on inventive, challenging and transformative visions of the *Iliad* and *Odyssey* in various artistic media. This chapter will survey both ancient and modern reception of Homer, with an emphasis on Homeric retellings of the past century or so. Since no claim to comprehensiveness is made, the encounter between Andromache and Hector and the Polyphemus episode will again be favoured with particular attention. Translation of Homer is also discussed, since it is also a type of reception.[1]

Knowing allusion to Homeric poetry acknowledges its precedence. Even tacit or unwitting reuse of Homeric material – its content, technique or aesthetics – is testimony to its influence. Yet creators of reception have disparate acquaintance with the Homeric texts, as do their audiences. Artistic reception may employ Homeric epic simply as an organizational principle, or more ambitiously view it as of central significance to their work. Homeric effect depends on Homeric consciousness on the part of the audience. Modern reception theory has stressed the role of the audience in the contribution to meaning; the phrase 'horizon of expectations' by H.R. Jauss refers to the set of coded cultural understandings that any hypothetical person of a time and place brings to a received text.[2]

One key issue for Homeric reception is familiarity with the Homeric epics, for both creators and their audiences. Chapters 4 and 5 rehearsed evidence and arguments for the origins and transmission of the texts. On the basis of the limited information available, it appears that into the classical period the *Iliad* and *Odyssey*, or portions thereof, were normally performed (or fluidly recomposed in performance at an early stage). Even when the Homeric poems began to be performed at the Athenian Panathenaic festival every four years, maybe in their entirety, the audience was rather limited. Looking for early Homeric influence everywhere, as classicists tend to do, is more wishful than historical. In the Classical Age the elite might possess a text of the *Iliad* and *Odyssey*, and Homer had a widespread if not deep role in the educational systems of the Hellenistic and Roman worlds.[3] But in the Medieval Ages, when ancient Greek ceased to be studied outside of the Byzantine Empire, there were no Homeric texts in Western Europe, not even in translation. In our times the ability to read Homer in the original is not widespread, though luckily there are plenty of translations. Reception of Homer, therefore, has usually been indirect, and even tenuous. There is nothing wrong with this, certainly not when the results of creative reception have been so admirable.

A second key issue is whether apparent reception is actually coincidental or illusory. A good cautionary example is the inscription about 'Nestor's cup' on a broken eighth-century vase (see Chapter 4). It is unlikely that this is an allusion to the *Iliad*, even if the epic then existed in some form. Some concede the disappointing lack of early Homeric reception only to argue that poets and artists were unwilling, or unable, to compete with the excellence of Homer (happily, modern creators, at least, feel no such compunctions). But proclamation that Homeric influence is inestimable probably means that the evidence is lacking. In fact throughout the sixth century only a small proportion of poetry and art contains anything possibly Homeric, and this is usually the shared material of mythological tradition, proverbial thought and typological language. It is also apparent, however, that much material that seemingly avoids or even contradicts Homeric aesthetics is nonetheless consequential to the Homeric poems. Homeric reception is not simply celebratory retelling; often it challengingly interprets Homeric epic, or at least underscores its importance by the very act of rejecting it.

Another key issue is what exactly 'Homer' means. As indicated in Chapter 4, references to a bard 'Homer' began appearing by the end of the sixth century. But at that time the definition of Homeric poetry was broader than ours. We shall see that separation of the Homeric poems from the larger tradition of the Trojan War remains a problem through all ages of reception. It is a dubious approach to portray interest in non-Homeric Trojan War material as indirect reflection of Homer's prestige. Yet often reception of Homer involves a mix of both the specific Homeric poems and the larger tradition in which they are embedded.

Premodern Reception

Rhapsodes ('stitchers of song', probably) called the Homeridae ('sons of Homer') were probably active in the Archaic Age. It is reasonable to assume that impressive performances of (or from) the *Iliad* and *Odyssey* spurred an early legend of 'Homer'. Towards the end of this period Simonides quotes a line from Book 6 of the *Iliad* ('Just as are the generations of leaves, so are those also of men') as the best thing of 'the man from Chios'. This apparently indicates specific knowledge of the *Iliad*, and the specifying of Chios apparently reflects a nascent biographical tradition about 'Homer', even if the surviving biographies are much later.[4] That the *Iliad* line is seemingly proverbial, and not originally Homeric, complicates analysis (see Chapter 4). But Simonides' words at least indicate that he is reacting to Homeric poetry of some kind, and his reconfiguration of the simile thereby constitutes an early, if brief, form of Homeric reception.

Certainly in the classical period and beyond, the influence of the Homeric poems grew. Performances continue through the efforts of such rhapsodes as Ion, whom Socrates questions closely in the Platonic dialogue *Ion*. The elite were sometimes fond of quoting from the *Iliad* and *Odyssey*, although textual familiarity was never broad in ancient society. And though the Cycle epics circulated less as the *Iliad* and *Odyssey* grew in stature, the stories in them remained popular. Attic drama about the Trojan War used cyclic myth and largely ignored Homeric material. Besides some lost plays that paralleled the content of the *Iliad*, there is only the pseudo-Euripidean *Rhesus* (whose intertext, *Iliad* 10, is of disputed authenticity; see Chapter 5) and the satyr play *Cyclops* by Euripides. An anecdote about Aeschylus has the dramatist describing his work as 'slices from Homer's great banquets'.[5] If this is something Aeschylus said or plausibly said, 'Homer' must mean the traditional genre of heroic epic, through which tragedians happily rummaged. Of course, this does not mean that tragedy could not generally reflect Homeric poetics.[6]

By the Hellenistic period, 'Homer' was established both as notional ideal and as textual presence. Homeric poetry fascinated Alexander the Great, Homeric scholarship flourished in Alexandria, and youths studied Homeric texts carefully in the educational system. In art, representations of what seem to be specifically Homeric details are certain by the classical period, and faithful illustration occurs by the Hellenistic Age (notably on so-called 'Homeric' bowls, with text and images of Homeric, Cyclic and tragic literature). The growing canonicity of Homer is well illustrated by a Hellenistic relief by Archelaus of Priene that shows an enthroned Homer attended by personifications of all arts and sciences, as well as Time, the Civilized World, and the *Iliad* and *Odyssey*. This concept of Homer as the source of everything would continue to be portrayed in art and literature through various imagery – the ocean, mother's milk, and even, less decorously, vomit greedily taken up by other poets.[7]

Yet the aesthetic of Hellenistic poetry is decidedly not Homeric. Large-scale heroic narrative was derided as overblown; witty, allusive and learned poetry was praised. The *Argonautica* by Apollonius may be of Homeric size, metre and language, but the plotting and characterization are not Homeric. And the pastoral poetry of Theocritus inverts the Homeric world by placing the small and occasional pastoral moments in Homeric poetry at centre stage. Nonetheless, in its way Hellenistic practice acknowledged the centrality of Homer, and so constitutes an indirect and displaced form of Homeric reception.

Roman civilization grafted Greek culture onto its own. Aristocrats would have been well educated in canonical Greek texts like the *Iliad* and *Odyssey*. The evidence includes the frequent quotation of Homer by Cicero, praise of Homeric *in medias res* plotting by Horace (see Chapter 2), and notably the *Aeneid* by Virgil, which transforms Homer at the same time as it competes with him. The wanderings of Aeneas in the first half are Odyssean, and the fighting upon arrival in Italy Iliadic. A cyclic aspect to the intertextuality is also often discernible. Certainly the poem's interest in cyclic material is attested by the mixed cyclic and Iliadic imagery on the temple of Juno in Carthage in Book 1, as well as by the fall of Troy in Book 2. The *Aeneid* would provide the Greekless of the Medieval Age with an indirect reflection of Homer as well as a direct narration of Trojan myth.

The complexity of Homeric reception is well demonstrated by the so-called *Tabulae Iliacae*. These fragmented small marble tablets of the turn of the millennium usually display Homeric and Cyclic scenes (on some both) with extensive textual paraphrase. Like earlier 'Homeric bowls', they explicitly cite their textual sources. Some scholars have described the Iliac Tables (tablets about Troy) as crass displays by the bourgeoisie, comparable to the buffoon-ish behaviour of Trimalchio in Petronius' *Satyricon* (Chapters 27–78), who habitually botches myth (Polyphemus is said to have twisted the thumb of Odysseus with tongs, for example). But a recent study persuasively argues that the Iliac Tables would have been valued by the elite as cleverly small visualizations of the large Trojan Cycle.[8]

Trimalchio also displays artwork with Homero-cyclic themes. Comparable are large first-century-BCE wall paintings found at the Esquiline hill in Rome, as well as statuary groups found in a seaside cave at the Sperlonga resort of Emperor Tiberius. The former portrays scenes in the wanderings of Odysseus; the latter includes Polyphemus and Scylla, as well as Trojan Cycle scenes. It is notable how often the adventures of Odysseus show up in Roman art, as in the earliest Greek iconography about Odysseus. The wanderings are surely pre-Homeric, and in the *Odyssey* they are marginalized as embedded character flashback. The frescoes and statuary may be intended as public markers of the Homeric, but the inspiration for them is not exclusively Homeric. As often, ostentatious idealization of Homer is not founded on secure comprehension of what is Homeric about the Homeric epics.

'Anti-Homeric' literature arose during the Roman Empire. That is, a number of Greek works of the time challenged the validity of Homeric content. Lucian amusingly begins *True Stories* by admitting, in contra-distinction to Odysseus, the falsity of his adventures. Dio Chrysostom's *Trojan Oration* argues that Homer told the story of the Trojan War incor-rectly (actually, Hector killed Achilles; Troy won the war). In *On Heroes* by Philostratus the shade of Protesilaus, the first Greek warrior to die at Troy, tells counter-Homeric stories. This type of work perversely honours the canonicity of Homer by playing off him. If it spoke to the complexity of Greek cultural heritage within a Roman world, it also built on antecedent trends. You will recall that such earlier authors as Herodotus were willing to entertain the alternative story that Helen never reached Troy (see Chapter 1). Herodotus desires to create a plausible history out of myth, but the 'anti-Homeric' authors seem more interested in displaying their learned sophistication.[9]

Literary cleverness also appears to be the motive of two works of late antiquity that claim to be surviving first-hand accounts of the Trojan War. They are written in Latin but based on earlier Greek versions, and their pur-ported 'authors' are Dictys of Crete and Dares of Phrygia.[10] Each presents a convoluted series of incidents in a concise manner. The accounts do not harmonize with Homer, and they read something like the Epic Cycle stripped of divinities and put in a blender. The style may be plain, but as expansive prose stories with creative framing and amorous intrigue they are comparable to the ancient novel. It is their imaginative spirit, not their historical claims, that engendered a rich and broad tradition of Latin and vernacular Troy stories during the Medieval Age. The tale of Troilus and Cressida, as told by Chaucer and Shakespeare among others, derives from this development.

In a curious way, the medieval Troy tradition represents the renewed dominance of the cyclic tradition. With their macro-perspective on the Trojan War, the ancient Cycle epics were probably more representative of pre-Homeric tradition than the Homeric poems (see Chapter 1). Yet starting in antiquity some preferred to think of them as post-Homeric prequels and sequels to the *Iliad* and *Odyssey* (much like the *Post-Homerica* by Quintus of Smyrna, an epic of the fourth century CE that picks up the story at the end of the *Iliad*). If so, the Epic Cycle would represent the type of reception that expands upon generative texts. This type of subsidiary inventiveness need not be disdained,[11] although the conception of the Epic Cycle as derivative largely stems from a hyperbolic portrayal of 'Homer' as the fount of all in antiquity. In any event, since cyclic myth remained popular throughout antiquity, ancient audiences would have viewed the Homeric poems through a cyclic lens. Therefore ancient reception of Homer, no matter how prominent, cannot be easily separated from ongoing cyclic myth. In the medieval period, on the other hand, Homer was practically excluded from the reception of Trojan War myth.[12] But the Troy stories popular at the time were based on the anti-Homeric literature of antiquity that perversely acknowledged the centrality of Homeric epic. The medieval Troy stories, then, are a distant reflection of a kind of indirect reception of Homer. And idealization of Homer continued, even if separated from direct experience of the *Iliad* and the *Odyssey*. Dante deemed Homer the '*poeta sovrano*' ('sovereign poet'; *Inferno* 4.88) without knowledge of Greek.

Modern Reception

The last few centuries have found the Homeric epics endlessly stimulating, the *Odyssey* in particular. I can only touch upon a number of memorable or illustrative examples, with emphasis on recent creative responses. Organization by theme and genre, not chronology, will be necessary. Why not start with the end of the Homeric epics? One sustained thread of Homeric reception is stories of post-return travel by Odysseus.

POST-RETURNS

In the *Odyssey* Tiresias tells Odysseus that he must go on a mysterious inland journey after he reaches home (see Chapter 2). This surely alludes to a pre-Homeric tradition. The *Telegony* of the Epic Cycle also told of post-return adventures, involving mainland journeying. Without direct knowledge of the *Odyssey* or the *Telegony* Dante as well portrayed a last voyage for the hero. Unlike the ancient inland/mainland travel, Odysseus sails outside the Mediterranean and never returns home. His motive is curiosity, a pre-Homeric trait somewhat obscured in the Homeric poem (Odysseus may seek out the Cyclopes and listen to the song of the Sirens, for instance, but he is usually cautious). In the context of medieval Christianity intellectual curiosity is suspect, and so the hero's shade is found in the eighth circle of Hell (see Canto 26 of *Inferno*). But the narrator Dante and his guide to the underworld, Virgil, are clearly fascinated by the hero's tale of a journey through the Pillars of Hercules.

They were not the only ones. Tennyson's mid-nineteenth-century poem 'Ulysses' is also about one last voyage. This Odysseus is modelled on Dante's, although his restless desire to travel to a 'newer world [...] beyond the sunset' is apparently inspiring, not damnable. A close reading reveals complexities, however. Briskly non-Homeric is the hero's condescending boredom with his 'aged' wife and 'blameless' son. Even more surprising is his view of Ithaca as a kind of third-world backwater. Ulysses romanticizes adventure, but disdains imperial rule over a 'savage race' – paradoxically, the inhabitants of his homeland. Ancient and modern matrices are here superimposed; the heroic homeland of ancient Ithaca merges with the British possession of Tennyson's time.[13]

John Barth inserts a post-return story of Odysseus in his postmodern novel *The Tidewater Tales* (1987). The *Odyssey* is valued along with *Arabian Nights*, *Don Quixote*, and *Huckleberry Finn* as a model of story-telling in many of Barth's long and convoluted novels. In *The Tidewater Tales* a husband and wife encounter another pair of sailors who are very reminiscent of Odysseus and Nausicaa while sailing in the Chesapeake Bay (to the delight of my father, who messes about in boats in the same territory). After talk of mutual interest in the *Odyssey*, the Homeric couple narrates the type of Odyssean modifications that Zachary Mason would later pursue. The first tale has Odysseus and Penelope confessing their lapses in faithfulness to each other (Penelope's paramour Phemius, the Ithacan bard, is subsequently spared by Odysseus and ends up composing the *Odyssey* as 'Homer'). In the second tale Odysseus sets out with Nausicaa on one of those westward post-return journeys, eventually reaching the New World – including the tidewater of the Chesapeake.

Another vision of the post-return journeying is more extraordinary in scope and content: Kazantzakis' *The Odyssey: A Modern Sequel* (1938). The verse epic is longer that the *Iliad* and *Odyssey* combined, and presents an Odysseus insatiable in curiosity and other appetites. His megalomaniacal character moves wilfully about the aeonic pre-history of Minoan and Egyptian civilizations before fantastically travelling south through Africa, eventually to a final resting place in Antarctica. Some find in this narrative a meditation on the freedom of modern man.

A more recent Homeric epic of sorts is Derek Walcott's *Omeros* (1990). Lyric in tone and postmodern in arrangement, *Omeros* has no single, sustained narrative, let alone a post-return story. The poem centres on the Caribbean island of St Lucia (Walcott's homeland), with a point of view that shifts between native fishermen, colonial settlers and the narrator, a persona who resembles Walcott closely. 'Homer' in Modern Greek form provides the title, and the ancient bard appears in various forms. Some of the natives possess Homeric or cyclic names (Helen, Hector, 'Achille', 'Philoctete'); Polyphemus and the (non-Homeric) heel of Achilles, among other ancient topics, are referenced. An imagined journey to the African past by a sun-struck Achille is a kind of *catabasis* (journey to the underworld; cf. *Odyssey* 11, *Aeneid* 6, Dante's *Inferno*). The long poem, patterned after Dante's *terza rima* metrics, transfers Western literary tradition to our contemporary globalized world. Homeric in scope, this brilliant work is arguably the greatest example of Homeric reception in our age.

LYRIC VERSE

The epics of Dante, Kazantzakis and Walcott may be suitably Homeric in size, but lyric poetry has also produced memorable examples of Homeric reception, as Tennyson demonstrated. 'Ithaca' (1911) is an oft-quoted poem by Constantine Cavafy that exemplifies celebration of the journey of Odysseus rather than his return. '[H]ope the voyage is a long one / full of adventure, full of discovery', it advises. '[D]o not hurry the journey at all.'[14]

The reader identifies completely with Odysseus, whose wanderings symbolize an internal journey ('Laistrygonians and Cyclops, / wild Poseidon – you won't encounter them / unless you bring them along inside your soul').

Ezra Pound in his *Cantos*, mostly composed in the first half of the twentieth century, made multiple references to ancient myth and literature, notably the *Odyssey*. The first Canto starts with a translation of the Greeks sailing to Hades in Book 11 ('And then went down to the ship, / Set keel to breakers, forth on the godly sea'), before paraphrasing initial encounters in the underworld. In the eclectic manner of Pound, the poem employs Anglo-Saxon metre and syntax, but is based on a sixteenth-century Latin translation of the Homeric epic. It is a strangely effective beginning to the *Cantos*' journey to the shades of literature and history.

The hellish world of mid-twentieth-century totalitarianism is portrayed in W.H. Auden's 'The Shield of Achilles', which transforms the lively imagery of peace, war and nature on the shield of the *Iliad*'s hero (Book 18) to a world of unrelenting misery. For example:

> A ragged urchin, aimless and alone,
>> Loitered about that vacancy; a bird
> Flew up to safety from his well-aimed stone:
>> That girls are raped, that two boys knife a third,
>> Were axioms to him, who'd never heard
> Of any world where promises were kept,
> Or one could weep because another wept.

The same time period is portrayed in the recent constellation of lyric poems entitled *Bloom* (2010). Michael Lista brilliantly portrays a day's events in the life of Canadian physicist Louis Slotin, who contributed to the invention of the atomic bomb:

Louis Slotin's Sex Appeal

When our bespectacled physicist
bicycles the base, despondent past

the pandaemonic faces of his peers
    with their baby-eating smiles
and black fedoras shading
    their blackened brains
happily he thinks of his atomic bomb,
his happy Trojan horse,
his lips now breaking
    into the famous grin
that still dispatches women by the bed-load
into bedlam, into bed.

(AFTER IRVING LAYTON)

The poems fascinatingly channel Joyce's *Ulysses* (discussed below), whose protagonist's name coincides with 'bloom', the term for an accidental fission reaction. Amid the poetic cycle's intertextual whirlpool of literary antecedents (often paraphrased, as indicated at the end of poems) the *Odyssey* floats prominently. By Joycean titular referentiality to such figures as Penelope, Nausicaa, the Cyclops and the Sirens, the *Odyssey* serves as a backdrop to a study of adultery and mortality – key themes of both the *Odyssey* and *Ulysses*.

Lyric cycles, like the *Cantos* and *Bloom*, have sometimes been employed to express a feminist perspective on the *Odyssey*. Such works as 'Circe/Mud Poems' (1976) by Margaret Atwood, Linda Pastan's 'Rereading the *Odyssey* in Middle Age' (1988) and Louise Glück's *Meadowlands* (1987) give a contemporary voice to the inner thoughts of Penelope and other female characters in the *Odyssey*.[15] 'One day you simply appeared in your stupid boat,' Atwood's Circe remarks, with an irreverence that is only part of her nuanced meditation on the patterns of myth and male–female relationships. For Glück, the *Odyssey* serves as analogous illustration in a long sequence of poems about a troubled contemporary marriage. Pastan's title references a common trope in Homeric reception: the return to Homeric poetry first encountered in youth. Recollection in maturity is woven into the poetry's Penelopean retelling of the *Odyssey*'s story, even as the perspective shifts to Circe and other characters.

NOVELS

Comprehensive approximation of Homeric epic has perhaps been most successfully achieved in post-antiquity by the novel. An early example is the *Adventures of Telemachus* by François Fénelon, a prototypical *Bildungsroman* designed as ethical instruction for French royalty (1699). By the twentieth century the novel becomes a favoured means to transfer key Homeric characters and episodes to the contemporary world. The early-twentieth-century *Ulysses* by James Joyce, which narrates a day's events in Dublin, announces its Odyssean interest with its title. Leopold Bloom is an Odysseus persona; his wife Molly Bloom corresponds to Penelope (with a suitor-like lover). The young Stephen Daedalus, though not literally his son, is a type of Telemachus. An early focus on Daedalus followed by Bloom's wandering about the city and eventual return home provides the basic tripartite structure of the Homeric epic. Some scenes correlate readily to Homeric episodes; Bloom's masturbatory gazing upon a young woman at the beach matches up with the meeting of Odysseus and Nausicaa, for example. Chapter titles that refer to characters or episodes of the *Odyssey* underscore Homeric significance.[16]

These chapter titles, however, were not included in the initial publication of the completed book, and without them many connections would be obscure. A funeral scene is only loosely tied to the *catabasis* of Odysseus; the correspondence of most episodes to Homer is tenuous and abstract. But mock epithets and other allusions to Homeric epic make the source of inspiration explicit (or sources, since at least one allusion reveals the Dubliner's fascination with the Cyclic *Telegony*). Although largely Greekless, Joyce had recourse to Charles Lamb's prose summary of the *Odyssey* for children, as well as the faithful translation by Butcher and Lang.

The *Odyssey* was transposed to a Canadian setting multiple times by the classically trained Hugh MacLennan.[17] For example, *Barometer Rising* (1941) culminates in the massive explosion at Halifax in 1917 (the largest of human cause before the atomic bomb), but features a protagonist who secretly returns home to his beloved (Penelope by name) though presumed dead in the war in Europe. *Each Man's Son* (1951) has more of a Telemachean focus, as the title hints, though a returning husband is once again central to the plot. A Penelope character is torn between two men in *The Watch That Ends the Night* (1959); the sudden return of a presumed-dead husband startles her postwar suburban life; in the end the Odyssean persona proceeds into a post-return exile. Issues of Canadian identity can be rather earnestly pursued in these novels, but the contemporary world is plausibly fitted into a Homeric frame.

A more recent creative telling of the *Odyssey* reached the bestseller lists and was made into a Hollywood movie. *Cold Mountain* (1997) by Charles Frazier transplaces the heroic tale to the Appalachian mountains of the American Civil War.[18] The main character travels home from war (though as a traumatized deserter, not a victor); his beloved waits for him. That she reads from the *Odyssey* underscores the tale's obvious Homeric foundation. Frazier wisely avoids pressing correspondences, but one can find plenty of Homeric elements in various episodes and characters. The burial and then uncovering of the wounded Inman, for example, evokes the underworld scene; reminiscent of Circe is the goat woman who nurses Inman with potions and anthropomorphizes her livestock. But the novel's ending, for all that, shockingly swerves away from Odyssean plotting (and projected post-return travel).

Like *Cold Mountain*, or Auden's 'The Shield of Achilles', many modern works seek to comprehend the horrors of war through Homer. The *Odyssey* and its literary tradition arise occasionally but effectively in Primo Levi's searing memoirs of his experience as a captive of Nazi Germany. In the chapter 'The Canto of Ulysses' in *If This Is a Man* (1947), Levi recalls his attempt to remember and translate the speech of Dante's Ulysses to an appreciative fellow prisoner. This transcendent moment of literary and linguistic connection amid the suffering of a concentration camp is unforgettable. Ulysses' partially recalled and difficultly conveyed exhortation to his companions seems 'like the blast of a trumpet, like the voice of God. For a moment I forget who I am and where I am.' Odyssean referentiality also arises in Levi's *The Truce* (1963), about Levi's long and convoluted return home (the final train journey from Russia through Romania to Italy is described as 'a small railroad Odyssey within our greater Odyssey').

The travel-themed novels of W.G. Sebald also evoke the *Odyssey* in their traumatized memory of the Second World War. In *Vertigo* (1990) the protagonist wanders through the Alpine region before returning to his German homeland in a final section entitled, with some irony, '*Il ritorno in patria*' (after Monteverdi's opera based on the *Odyssey*, mentioned below). *The Emigrants* (1992), four connected stories featuring protagonists in exile from Germany, contains a number of intertextual connections with the *Odyssey*. A journey to New York's Ithaca, for instance, has obvious Homeric significance.[19]

RETELLINGS

Creative retelling of the Homeric epics can be distinguished from transformative refashioning of them or allusive intertextuality. By 'retelling' I refer to versions that largely preserve the Homeric characters and their stories, though with striking variation through anachronism, change of perspective, modulation or extension of plot, and so on. Arguably nobody has more plausibly conveyed the Homeric world in a novelistic manner than Adèle Geras in *Troy* (2002) and *Ithaca* (2007), though these are pitched as young-adult fiction. In *The Song of Achilles* (2011) by the classically trained Madeline Miller, Patroclus tells of his love for Achilles with a modern sensibility and liberal use of poetic imagery. Ancient belief in an erotic relation between Achilles and Patroclus post-dates the *Iliad*,[20] but the Homeric epic is a key source for the novel. Cyclic myth is employed in the portrayal of the two youths growing up together. The sensually evocative narrative eventually leads to the Iliadic story of Patroclus' death; after this the shade of Patroclus summarizes the rest of the Homeric epic and then Troy's fall. Comparable is the more ambitious *Achilles* (2001), a 'prose poem' of just over 100 pages that features key scenes from Achilles' cyclic and Homeric life. The work begins with Odysseus' encounter with the shade of Achilles and ends with Keats reading about Achilles at the funeral of Patroclus from Chapman's translation of the *Iliad* (discussed below).

A beautifully expansive retelling of Priam's request of the corpse of his son from Achilles can be found in *Ransom* (2009) by David Malouf. Book 24 of the *Iliad* is followed closely, but the novel movingly fills out the psychological profile of Priam and Achilles. Additionally, the invented character 'Somox',

Priam's humble muleteer, charismatically holds the tale together. It seems to be a trope of modern retellings to feature minor characters, especially those marginalized in the Homeric world. This is not absent in another recent novelistic treatment of Troy myth, *Dragonflies* (2008) by Grant Buday, told in the voice of Odysseus. The narrative centres on the story of the Trojan horse. But we hear Odysseus muse revealingly about the past, notably on his strained relationships with Palamedes and Ajax, both of whom die in the course of narrative. Odysseus is directly or indirectly responsible, but the thoughtful and nuanced voice of his narration earns the reader's sympathy (comparable is the Odysseus of Sophocles' *Ajax*). Most of the content is cyclic in nature, but the *Iliad* as visualized by the movie *Troy* (discussed below) is a discernible influence. Yet precisely where the film falls flat, in dialogue and characterization, *Dragonflies* shines brilliantly. Too often the heroic world is expressed in the ponderously trite style of professional sports heroes; these contemporary retellings contain characters that speak with the articulate verve found in Homeric poetry.

The Lost Books of the Odyssey (2010) by Zachary Mason is a series of stories that radically retell the Homeric epic. Introduced by the conceit of the discovered text (cf. Dares and Dictys), the tales display the Homeric epic's fascination with story-telling, as well as a taste for the fantastic scenarios typical of Jorge Luis Borges (whose 'The Immortal' begins with the discovered-text motif and ends with the most innovative 'Homer' of literature). The results at once entertain and force the reader to rethink the original epic. In one story Odysseus claims to have made up Polyphemus out of a 'Scythian brigand who had caught me stealing cheeses from his cave', while in another the Cyclops describes the Greeks as intrusive louts and defends his killing of a Greek as an accident. Thwarted or unsuccessful returns to Ithaca happen in other stories. A post-return voyage *retraces* the wanderings backwards to the now touristy site of Troy.

DRAMA, CINEMA, ART

Reception in other media is necessarily transformative. Opera has usually looked to cyclic and Virgilian material for Trojan War subject matter. But memorable is Monteverdi's *Il ritorno d'Ulisse in patria*, with a libretto by Giacomo Badoaro. This version of the story is centripetal in nature, focusing on the scenes in Ithaca, and not on the wanderings. The opera is not especially adventurous in its retelling of the Homeric poem, but a 2008 production by Opera Atelier in Toronto energetically showcased the work's charming musicality and spectacle. Derek Walcott's stage version of the *Odyssey* (1993) is very inventive, if more directly focused on the Homeric epic than his *Omeros*. Its story actually begins at Troy, but Walcott quickly moves through the wanderings and on to Ithaca with nifty episode rearrangements and conflations. Some characters are paired as doublets (Cyclops and Odysseus' rival-beggar Arnaeus/Irus; Ajax and the suitor Antinous; Nausicaa and the handmaiden Melantho). There are contemporizing aspects, such as the Homeric-like narrator 'Blind Billy Blue', or the London Underground as the underworld. A Caribbean flavouring, notably in the dialect of minor characters like the slave woman Eurycleia, globalizes the Mediterranean setting of the ancient Greek epic. One senses that this would all work very well on stage, though the ever-beautiful verse succeeds wonderfully by itself.

Stage production certainly adds to another creative retelling, *The Penelopiad* (2005) by Margaret Atwood, to judge by its recent production by Toronto's Nightwood Theater. The clever light verse of the handmaiden chorus blossoms as song on stage, and all-female acting ensures that the audience is shown a different kind of Odysseus. The *Odyssey*'s perspective shifts over to Penelope, who speaks as a shade in the underworld. This allows us to hear her backstory and much debunking of her legendary husband (the Polyphemus episode, she reports, was really a tavern dispute). The feminist perspective is not unreservedly supportive of Penelope. She is a royal master of slaves, after all, and *The Penelopiad* implicates her in the horrific hanging of the handmaidens who slept with the suitors. A similar socio-political dynamic is at play in Atwood's dystopian *The Handmaid's Tale* (1985), where the 'Handmaid' narrates her exploitation as a child-producer in a totalitarian theocracy. She's the concubine of a 'Commander', but also under the control of his 'Wife' (a knitter, as Penelope is a weaver), who herself is subjugated to a patriarchal society.

Homer's Odyssey (2006) by Simon Armitage might first appear to be a translation, since it follows the Homeric epic rather faithfully in content and sequence. But it was composed for a BBC broadcast, and the story emerges through voices of different characters independent of a Homeric narrator. The effect is a vigorous and insightful commentary on what is really going in the Homeric epic. Comparable is *An Iliad* by Alessandro Baricco (2006), composed for a public reading. This narrative is also told only through character voices, with content largely faithful to the model text (italics, surprisingly sparse, signal innovative content). The voices speak of the past in long, quiet monologues; when narration switches between characters, they speak to us, not to each other, as if in a documentary. Some narratological awkwardness arises; it is fascinating to have Chryseis narrate the events of Book 1, but how would she know, for instance, what Achilles and Thetis say to each other? The overall effect is a pleasingly concise retelling of the *Iliad*. A final statement by the Phaeacian bard Demodocus reports on the fall of Troy. A brief afterword by the author muses on the Homeric evocation of war's beauty in the content of the Iraq War and suggests that the prominence of female and peripheral voices in his version encourages optimism for peace.

Cinema has long looked to the ancient world, including Homer, for material.[21] The very early example of *L'Île de Calypso: Ulysse et le géant Polyphème* (1905) by Georges Méliès (the subject of the recent film *Hugo*) neatly conflates the cave of Calypso with that of Polyphemus in less than four minutes. The range of cinematic Homer to follow might be suggested by contrasting a few examples of relatively faithful and inventive films. *Troy* (2004), a Hollywood blockbuster starring Brad Pitt, focuses on the key characters and story of the *Iliad*.[22] A mishmash of prehistoric material culture buttresses a rationalistic portrayal of the war as imperialist manoeuvring (reminiscent of the war in Iraq at the time). But the most far-reaching innovation is the packaging of the *Iliad* within the whole Trojan Cycle (although the film's war is over in a number of days, not ten years). This allows the film to present emotionally poignant episodes of the *Iliad* (Andromache and Hector, Achilles and Priam), yet it also includes incidents of greater familiarity to a modern audience (the elopement of Paris and Helen, the death of Achilles by a heel wound).

Mario Camerini's *Ulisse* (1954) stars Kirk Douglas in a film that does not strain to overdo the limited special effects of its time. *Odyssey* aficionados will be surprised by the blossoming romance between Odysseus and Nausicaa, made possible by the hero's amnesia. But recovery of memory quashes her hopes and allows a relatively faithful account of the Homeric adventures. A successful return to Ithaca follows. An interesting twist is Circe and Penelope played by the same actress, the kind of doubling that is extensive in Walcott's stage version. A transformative, transplaced telling of the *Odyssey*'s tale is *O Brother, Where Art Thou?* (2000), set in the American south of the 1930s.[23] The Coen brothers delight in myriad allusions (the title references the film *Sullivan's Travels*), but the *Odyssey* provides the main framework. The protagonist 'Ulysses' travels to reach his wife 'Penny', who is engaged to a 'suitor'. Many episodes evoke the adventures of Odysseus; more abstractly, the recording by a blind man of a hit version of a traditional song ('Man of Constant Sorrow') updates the ancient epic. Godard's *Contempt* (1963) is a multi-layered evocation of the Homeric epic. The story involves a failed cinematic version of the *Odyssey*; the main characters are contemporary versions of Odysseus, Penelope and Poseidon. In one scene, Dante's Ulysses arises as a topic of discussion.

Iconographical reception of Homer of course preceded cinema.[24] Cyclic tradition, as represented by Virgil and Ovid, was the main source for representations of Trojan myth until vernacular translations of Homer arose in the sixteenth century. An early enthusiast of Homer was Francesco Primaticcio (sixteenth century), who with the assistance of his students depicted not less than fifty-eight scenes of the *Odyssey*. Not long afterwards Rubens painted images of Polyphemus and Nausicaa, as well as episodes of the Trojan Cycle and scenes from the life of Achilles. In the late eighteenth and early nineteenth centuries Jacques-Louis David's neo-classical style of painting took up such quintessential Iliadic scenes as the funeral of Patroclus, and Andromache mourning Hector. David's student Ingres carried neo-classicism into the early nineteenth century (influenced by John Flaxman's illustrations of the *Iliad* and *Odyssey*, often reproduced to this day). Ingres painted Iliadic scenes, such as Thetis imploring Zeus on behalf of her son, as well as an enthroned Homer surrounded by representative figures (the

Hellenistic relief mentioned above is the obvious model). Homeric themes continue in painting through the nineteenth and twentieth centuries, with the adventures of Odysseus dominating. Victorian artists found in Circe, Calypso and the Sirens excellent opportunities to portray sensuality in an acceptable manner. More experimental Homeric imagery followed in the twentieth century. For example, de Chirico accomplished surreal scenes featuring Odysseus, and Picasso's portrayal of Odysseus and the Sirens (1937) features a round, astounded human face amid marine colours and fish themes. But arguably the African-themed collages by the twentieth-century American artist Romare Bearden have most brilliantly visualized the wandering return of Odysseus.

COMPARANDA

Many suspected examples of Homeric reception might better be considered coincidental, even if Homeric epic can be good to think with when contemplating works of similar content. For example, the African 'epic' of Sundiata involves the exile and eventually violent return of its protagonist, a thirteenth-century founder of the Mali empire, but the correspondences are not specific enough to suggest intertextuality. Some take the film *Naked* to be an obvious reception of the *Odyssey* on the basis of some joking remarks about Homer by the protagonist. The director Mike Leigh is only willing to concede that his film is generally epic, or that it indirectly employs the *Inferno*. In the end it may be hard to see the film as a contemporary version of the *Odyssey*; the short-lived return of the protagonist to a former girlfriend is only generally comparable.[25]

Caution should also be employed concerning an Inuit legend about feud and exile that led to the film *Atanarjuat: The Fast Runner* (2001).[26] A catchy description of the film as Homer with a video camera in no way authenticates a direct relation.[27] As for the television series *Homeland*, it seems obvious to me that it is a modern take on the *Odyssey*. A soldier returns home from war to find that his wife has taken up with a lover, on the assumption that her husband is dead. He confides in his child (here a daughter), who becomes his most trusted ally, and he is an ambiguously destructive threat to his homeland. That should serve well enough for a conference paper, but I have discovered no evidence that the series' producers or audience are aware of the Odyssean parallels.

But sometimes coincidence slides into reception. A striking case of this occurred with the historical Martin Guerre, who in sixteenth-century France returned to wife from war after a long absence.[28] It turned out that he was an impostor, as the dramatic appearance of the real Martin Guerre proved during the ensuing law case. The judge noted that the case resembled the story of Odysseus, but of course that was coincidental. Yet the film *Sommersby* (1993) merges the historical incident and the *Odyssey*, setting its story in the post-Civil-War South.[29]

ANDROMACHE AND HECTOR

Both the encounter between Andromache and Hector and the Polyphemus episode have inspired memorable responses, but the Cyclops has attracted far greater attention than the tragic couple of the *Iliad*. This confirms a trend that has been amply demonstrated above: though 'Homer' is often celebrated in reception, the non-Homeric is more popular, even in 'high' art. For the Trojan War, this means memorable episodes from its ten-year duration, not the few weeks covered by the *Iliad*. For the *Odyssey*, this means a concentration on the wanderings of Odysseus, precisely what is compartmentalized through character-narrated flashback in the Homeric epic. The Polyphemus episode is full of spectacular action, while Hector and Andromache do not actually *do* anything besides talk. Yet it is also true that there have been many sensitive and sophisticated treatments of cyclic material, no matter how sensational (murder, romantic intrigue, monsters) their content. One can sometimes credit the model of Homeric poetics for this, even when the content is not strictly Homeric.

Andromache certainly received attention in antiquity.[30] In tragedy, Andromache appears in two plays by Euripides: *Trojan Women* (cf. *Trojan Women* by Seneca) and of course *Andromache*. In these plays she is in a state of servitude *after* the fall of Troy, which Hector vividly imagines in Book 6. We can also sense the intertextual pull of Homer's Andromache in

Sophocles' *Ajax* when the concubine Tecmessa begs Ajax not to leave her and their son defenceless. The comic playwright Aristophanes clearly knew the *Iliad* 6 scene, for he parodies it in the *Lysistrata* (the female lead turns Hector's claim that war is men's business on its head) and *Acharnians* (the terror of Astyanax at the sight of his father's helmet is parodied). In Book 3 of the *Aeneid* Virgil portrays an Andromache stuck in her Trojan past, as she lives in a recreated city of Troy in north-west Greece with her Trojan husband Helenos. But perhaps the most intriguing ancient reception of the *Iliad* scene occurs in Plutarch. According to his life of Brutus, the wife of Caesar's assassin could not contain her emotion upon the departure of her husband when she caught sight of a painting of the Homeric scene. Brutus later responds to a friend's quotation of the passage by stating that he does not intend to tell his wife to go weave, as Hector does to Andromache. Both here and in the *Lysistrata* resistance to the Homeric gender roles is expressed, even as the power of the Homeric scene is respected.

In post-antiquity Andromache is perhaps most prominent in Racine's tragedy *Andromaque* of the late seventeenth century, but this follows the postwar portrayals of the character found in Euripides and Virgil. More direct focus on the Homeric scene occurs in painting. Jacques Louis David's *Hector's Departure* (1812) is full of pathos, as well as an earlier image (1783) of the Trojan woman mourning her dead husband, Hector's helmet on the ground and Astyanax at her lap. More experimental representations followed in the twentieth century, notably in de Chirico's surrealist/cubist painting *Hector and Andromache* (1917). This perversely conveyed the emotional encounter with mannequin figures and served as a model for versions by Warhol and Bidlo.

The poet Michael Longley has frequently conveyed the pathos of the Irish Troubles through Homeric scenes, including two memorable versions of the meeting between Hector and Andromache. 'The Parting' (2006) is stunningly succinct:

> He: 'Leave it to the big boys, Andromache'.
> 'Hector, my darling husband, och, och,' she.

'The Helmet' (1995) is two stanzas with a devastating conclusion: Hector 'kissed the babbie and dandled him in his arms and / Prayed that his son might grow up bloodier than him'. Alice Oswald's long poem *Memorial* (discussed below) also evocatively employs the Book 6 passage.

> And an image stared at him of himself dead
> And her in Argos weaving for some foreign woman
> He blinked and went back to his work
> Hector loved Andromache
> But in the end he let her face slide from his mind
> He came back to her sightless

THE POLYPHEMUS EPISODE

The blinding of a giant is relatively popular in early Greek art, although it was noted in Chapter 4 that such images occur before the Homeric epic seems to have been influential. But once the *Odyssey* became known, it undoubtedly had some impact on versions of the Polyphemus episode in Graeco-Roman art and literature, as discussed in Chapter 4 and above. An early literary retelling of the episode occurs in Euripides' *Cyclops*, the only surviving satyr play from antiquity. The play is clearly indebted to the Homeric episode, although the conversation between Polyphemus and Odysseus reflects sophistic debate of the fifth century. Moreover, drastic changes are necessitated by the medium (the *outside* of the cave is shown on stage) and genre (shenanigans by the satyrs).

Later literature gives us a startling modification of the Homeric Cyclops: Polyphemus in love. His obsession with the sea nymph Galatea is elegantly modulated in two poems by Theocritus, the inventor of the pastoral genre (Polyphemus is a shepherd, after all, and he was commonly located in the poet's home of Sicily). Although the encounter with Odysseus is not narrated, there are plenty of intertextual allusions to the future confrontation. A further modification of the story introduces Acis as Galatea's beloved; he ends up murdered by the Cyclops (Ovid gives a memorable version in

Metamorphoses 13, the inspiration for Handel's *Acis and Galatea*). The *Aeneid* contains a belated handling of the Homeric story (Book 3). Aeneas' crew comes across a surviving but stranded companion of Odysseus who gives an account of the Homeric episode. The Trojans hastily depart with their new friend when the blinded giant appears in the distance. Lucian's dialogue between Polyphemus and his father Poseidon in *Dialogues of the Sea-Gods* allows the Cyclops to rehearse the Homeric account, with complaints that the Greeks were thieves and Odysseus was deceptive. This has been deemed 'anti-colonialist'; if so, the Homeric version is essentially 'anti-colonialist', since *Odyssey* 9 gives the same details and at least partly allows Polyphemus to articulate his point of view.[31]

As for post-antiquity, it is instructive to begin with examples where similarity may be coincidental. Folk tales about the blinding of an ogre recorded in recent centuries are so widespread that most scholars conclude they represent a pre-Homeric tale type. One might wonder, though, if the blinding of a cannibal ogre in one of the voyages of Sinbad the Sailor is derived from Homer.[32] Caliban in Shakespeare's *Tempest*, anagramically a 'cannibal', may be categorized with Polyphemus, but Shakespeare apparently had no access to Homer (Chapman's *Odyssey* was published soon after its composition). Perhaps Homeric influence was mediated through ancient authors like Virgil and Ovid, however, or contemporaries informed by the Greek original or Latin translations. Another inexplicit example of Polyphemus' correspondence occurs in Mark Twain's *The Adventures of Huckleberry Finn*. The novel is often casually spoken of as an 'American *Odyssey*', but something more precise occurs in the episode in which Huck's father locks his son in a cabin. Huck employs makeshift tools and deception to escape, much like Odysseus does to escape the cave of the Cyclops. The intertextuality is marked by the description of 'Pap' as 'blind drunk' – like Polyphemus, he is unable to handle his liquor. Twain enjoyed the *Odyssey* in translation and socialized with classicists, who he probably hoped would notice the correspondences.[33]

Modern painters have shied away from the gory topic of the blinding. But Turner's *Ulysses Deriding Polyphemus* (1829) impressively represents the (contemporary-looking) ship of Odysseus departing from the shore as the vague shape of the Cyclops looms up above. The image of Polyphemus melds with a towering mountain, apparently an allusion to Odysseus' description of him as 'like the wooded peak of lofty mountains' (9.191–2). Turner's Polyphemus-as-nature is diametrically countered by Polyphemus-as-technology in Kubrick's *2001: A Space Odyssey*. Based on a concept by Arthur C. Clarke, the movie features the computer Hal as a memorable Cyclops analogue.[34] Hal has a camera lens 'eye' and becomes increasingly dangerous until a thrusting key shuts down its system. More generally, the film explores the correlation of technology to violence. This theme is also central to the Homeric episode: Odysseus employs a stone-age weapon (see Chapter 3) that he describes with imagery of his civilization's advanced technology. The Homeric episode's sweeping survey of human technology well matches the film's famous 'match-cut' in which a bone tool spinning in the air fades into a spinning satellite. Whereas nature is negatively valued in the *Odyssey*, in the modern film it is technology, partially represented by a Cyclops figure, that is negatively valued.

In Ralph Ellison's *Invisible Man* (1952), intertextuality with the blinding of Polyphemus is marked by a glass eye that 'seemed to erupt out' of the face of 'Brother Jack'. Ellison was fascinated with Graeco-Roman mythology and the Homeric epic, and Cyclopean themes of entrapment and vision have been ascertained throughout the novel. More generally, the novel's exploration of the African-American experience within American culture evokes Odyssean themes of identity.[35] Exploration of the African-American experience has also followed Odyssean paths in the work of Toni Morrison, perhaps most clearly in the recent *Home* (2012), featuring a soldier returning home from war to rescue a loved one (here a sister).

Several of the works mentioned earlier in this chapter contain Polyphemus analogues: the 'citizen' in Joyce's *Ulysses* who throws a biscuit tin at the retreating Bloom, the shower attendant in Levi's *If This Is a Man* who reaches out 'like Polyphemus' at the exit to feel if the prisoners are wet, the totalitarian bully in Walcott's stage version of the *Odyssey*, the eye-patch wearing conman in *O Brother, Where Art Thou?*, almost blinded in his good eye by a Ku Klux Klan flagstaff, to name a few. These Cyclopean figures follow the Homeric lead in casting the Cyclops persona as a villain, but in our post-colonial world Polyphemus has also often been portrayed as a victim.[36] This revisionist perspective does not propose an alternative 'true' meaning of the episode so much as question its basic assumptions and speculate on its real-world impetus.

TRANSLATION

Translations provide the Greekless with a window into Homeric poetry, but even the most earnest attempts at faithfulness end up being interpretive.[37] Jorge Luis Borges in his essay 'The Homeric Versions' happily noted that his 'opportune ignorance of Greek' turned his Homer into 'an international bookstore of works in prose and verse'.[38] Not all have welcomed the variety of translation method in such an easy-going manner. What Borges calls 'the beautiful Newman–Arnold debate' refers to Matthew Arnold's polemics against the translation by Francis W. Newman. Arnold insisted that a translation convey what he saw as the rapid, plain, yet noble style of Homer. Newman's employment of alliterative Anglo-Saxon diction, in caesura-pausing ballad form, confronted readers with an alien, challenging Homer. His reasoning was sound, since he knew that Homeric epic mixed dialects and employed archaic diction in a way that even Classical Age Greeks often found baffling. In a sense, both Arnold and Newman shared the goal of recreating the original effect of Homeric poetry for a modern audience. The former's Homeric effect was a pleasingly articulate expression of universal values; the latter's was a jarringly antiquated survival from a different world. This is the same bipolar Homer, universal/alien in nature, that has caused so much trouble in Homeric scholarship (see Chapters 5 and 6).

The problem for translators is that no matter which Homer you envision, translating his epics from Greek to English is always very difficult (Arnold's was no more successful than Newman's). Greek's vowel-rich, polysyllabic flow is very different from the consonant-heavy ponderousness of English. And its grammar, though intricately regulated, allows much greater variation in word order; metrical necessities only intensify this aspect. How does the translator express these qualities with the instrument of English?

Then there is the matter of verse. Homeric epic follows a flexible but demanding pattern of long- and short-sounding syllables known as dactylic hexameter (see Chapter 3). Are the systems of accent stress and rhyme that are (or at least used to be) employed in English poetry analogous to this? Some translators have adapted the dactylic hexameter of Homer to English, indicating dactyls and spondees by patterns of accent. The results have generally not pleased. Here is the opening of the first complete dactylic translation in English:

> Sing, O Goddess, the wrath of Achilles, scion of Peleus,
> Ruinous wrath, that afflicted with numberless woes the Achaeans,
> hurling headlong to Hades souls many and brave ones – of heroes
> Slain – ay, gave unto dogs, unto all birds lonelily flying
> *Them* as a prey.

(W.B. SMITH AND W. MILLER, 1945)

The second line begins to suggest the downhill fluency of dactyls, but the others indicate the wooden, ay, halting nature of English shackled by measures dactylic.[39]

Nonetheless early translators assumed that some sort of metrical arrangement was necessary. The first translation of Homer was in verse, Livius Andronicus' version of the *Odyssey* in the third century BCE. This adapted Homeric poetry to its new context by employing a Roman metrical system and New World approximations (like the Italian water deity Camena for the Greek Muse). The *Ilias Latina* (*Latin Iliad*) of the early first century CE used hexameter to paraphrase concisely all of the *Iliad* in a thousand lines or so. Technically it is not a translation, since it omits so much of the original. But the goal was functionality, not aesthetics, and on those terms it was a grand success, carrying the torch for Homer well into the Medieval Ages. These two Roman versions of Homer demonstrate that faithfulness need not be the only goal of a translation.

With the Renaissance, Latin translations (like the one used by Pound) began to serve as aids to most translators of the Greek until recently. Vernacular translations began in the sixteenth century, with the first memorable one being George Chapman's *Iliad* (1598–1611), followed by his *Odyssey* (1616). These display the lively and inventive style of the Elizabethan Age, in a 'fourteener' verse pattern (think 'Mary had a little lamb...') for the *Iliad* and a decasyllabic (ten syllables) metre for the *Odyssey*. Here's Astyanax reacting to his dad's helmet:

> This said, he reacht to take his sonne, who (of his armes afraid,
> And then the horse-haire plume, with which he was so overlaid,
> Nodded so horribly) he clingd backe to his nurse and cride.
> Laughter affected his great Sire, who doft, and laid aside
> His fearfull Helme [...][40]

Chapman's translations inspired Keats' famous 'On First Looking into Chapman's Homer', which interestingly compared a mediated 'discovery' of Homer to New World exploration:

> Yet did I never breathe its pure serene
> Till I heard Chapman speak out loud and bold:
> Then felt I like some watcher of the skies
> When a new planet swims into his ken;
> Or like stout Cortez when with eagle eyes
> He star'd at the Pacific – and all his men
> look'd at each other with a wild surmise [...]

The second important English translation of Homer was by Alexander Pope in the early eighteenth century, in iambic pentameter with an AABB rhyme scheme (the 'heroic couplet'). Compare this selection with Chapman's version:

> Thus having spoke, th' illustrious Chief of Troy
> Stretch'd his fond arms to clasp the lovely Boy.
> The Babe clung crying to his Nurse's breast,
> Scar'd at the dazling helm, and nodding crest.
> With secret pleasure each fond parent smil'd,

> And Hector hasted to relieve his child,
> The glitt'ring terrors from his brows unbound,
> And plac'd the beaming helmet on the ground.

The rhyming, however admirable, continually interrupts momentum: no Arnoldian swiftness here. And if both Chapman and Pope are skilled wordsmiths, their method often leads them far from the original. The classicist Richard Bentley famously remarked: 'It is a pretty poem, Mr Pope, but you must not call it Homer.'

Rather more faithful translations of the Homeric epics were created in the second half of the twentieth century by the classicist Richmond Lattimore, in verse. Or rather, verse of a sort. Lattimore explains that each of his lines – so close to the original that they are numbered as the Greek text – has six 'beats', or stress accents, in no particular metrical arrangement. This sounds a little hazy, and Lattimore's plain, contemporary diction sometimes makes the verse seem like prose cut up into lines. But I am grateful for the translation that first allowed my Greekless undergraduate self to breathe Homer's pure serene. Lattimore's style produces a tragically profound *Iliad* (1951):

> So speaking glorious Hektor held out his arms to his baby,
> who shrank back to his fair-girdled nurse's bosom
> screaming, and frightened at the aspect of his own father,
> terrified as he saw the bronze and the crest with its horse-hair,
> nodding dreadfully, as he thought, from the peak of the helmet.

For the *Odyssey* perhaps a lighter touch is preferable, and Robert Fitzgerald's *Odyssey* (1961) is justly valued for its poetic sensitivity (he also did an *Iliad*, 1974). Here is his take on the name trick in Book 9:

> "'What ails you,
> Polyphemos? Why do you cry so sore
> in the starry night? You will not let us sleep.
> Sure no man's driving off your flock? No man
> has tricked you, ruined you?"

> Out of the cave
> the mammoth Polyphemos roared in answer:
> "Nohbdy, Nohbdy's tricked me, Nohbdy's ruined me!"'

Fitzgerald's lyric sensibility resists Homeric typology and is less than faithful to literal meaning. 'Nohbdy' is a clever transposition of the pun into English, but the translation elides Polyphemus' insistence that he was bested by a trick and *not* by force, an antithesis central to the episode. The verse is a loose iambic pentameter, unrhymed ('blank verse'), and certainly reads smoothly. But Lattimore started a metrical trend in Homeric translations. The popular versions by Robert Fagles (1990, 1996) give us admirably lively character speech in lines of six – or seven, five, who's counting? – 'beats'.[41]

English 'hexameter' translations can become wearisome, and the Homeric epics are long poems. It is therefore important to note alternative, swifter verse Homers. For example, the classicist M.L. West admirably set portions of the *Iliad* (1971) in four trochee (stress, non-stress) units:

> Sing me, goddess, of the anger
> of Achilles, son of Peleus,
> bane that brought to the Achaeans
> countless woe, and hurled to Hades
> countless mighty hero spirits,
> left to dogs and birds their carrion,
> and the will of Zeus accomplished.

Then there is the *Iliad* by Michael Reck (1994), which sticks to a decasyllabic line. The results move along at a good pace:

> Sing, Goddess, Achilles' maniac rage:
> ruinous thing! it roused a thousand sorrows
> and hurled many souls of mighty warriors
> to Hades, made their bodies food for dogs
> and carrion birds – as Zeus's will foredoomed.

But given the difficulties of verse translation, why not employ prose? Many have so concluded, often with excellent results. Such translations are arguably no more distant from the Homeric system of poetry than English verse translations. And they handle the scale of the Homeric epics well. As noted above, the modern world is comfortable with a novelistic approach to the scope of Homeric narrative. In fact the most successful translation of all time is Rieu's *Odyssey*:

> "'What on earth is wrong with you, Polyphemus? Why must you disturb the peaceful night and spoil our sleep with all this shouting? Is a robber driving off your sheep, or is somebody trying by treachery or violence to kill you?"
>
> Out of the cave came Polyphemus' great voice in reply: "O my friends, it's Nobody's treachery, no violence, that is doing me to death."[42]

This may sound rather unheroic, but it is readable, and one suspects that verse translations are more praised than read. Other prose translations have sold well: either because they spoke to their age, or because they usefully approximated the Greek to students of the original Greek. In the late nineteenth century, two collaborative efforts became standard: the *Iliad* by Lang, Leaf and Myers (1882), and the *Odyssey* by Butcher and Lang (1879). Conscious of Homeric's archaic diction, these employed the biblical phrasing of the King James Bible. Here is the name-trick passage from the latter:

> "'What hath so distressed thee, Polyphemus, that thou criest thus aloud through the immortal night, and makest us sleepless? Surely no mortal driveth off thy flocks against thy will: surely none slayeth thyself by force or craft?" And the strong Polyphemus spake to them again from out the cave: "My friends, Noman is slaying me by guile, nor at all by force."

Notable prose versions were produced by two literary celebrities. Samuel Butler, the novelist (*The Way of All Flesh* and *Erewhon*) and provocateur (*The Authoress of the* Odyssey), employed his characteristically ironic tone to effect a Homer deflated of heroic pomposity (*Iliad* in 1888; *Odyssey* in 1900).

Scandalous at the time (much to his delight), they have aged better than the King James versions. T.E. Lawrence ('Lawrence of Arabia') was judged a good match for the *Odyssey*, and many discern his adventuresome nature in his translation of that Homeric epic (1932). Both Butler and Lawrence relied on their schoolboy training in Greek. Past students of Homer undoubtedly have had recourse to the translations employed throughout this book, the revised Loebs (prose translation facing the Greek) by A.T. Murray. They are faithful and functional, which is one valid goal of translation.

But the most recent translation of the *Iliad*, by Anthony Verity (2012), succeeds admirably without verse, though like Lattimore it respects Homeric line numeration. The author promisingly states that he 'kept clear of "poeticizing" Homer at one extreme and reducing the scale of his invention to the level of a modern adventure story at the other'. Here is his Andromache in Book 6:

> So speaking illustrious Hector stretched out his arms to his son; but the boy shrank back crying into the bosom of his finely girdled nurse, terrified at the sight of his dear father and frightened by the bronze and the horsehair crest, seeing how it nodded on top of his helmet, a terrifying thing. His dear father and his revered mother laughed out loud, and at once illustrious Hector took the helmet from his head and laid it, gleaming brightly, on the ground.

At the other end of the spectrum are authors who forge translation into creative reception. The most renowned example of the past century is Christopher Logue, who since the 1960s has been producing portions of the *Iliad* in a modernist style of anachronistic, cinematic brilliancy.[43] Here is his take on the pre-embassy gathering of Greek leaders in Book 9:

> Silence.
> A ring of lights.
> Within
> Immaculate
> In boat-cloaks lined with red
> King Agamemnon's lords –

The depression of retreat,

The depression of returning to camp.

   Him at the centre of their circle

Sobbing,

Shouting:

   'We must run for it!'

   Dark glasses in parked cars.

   'King Agamemnon of Mycenae,

God called, God raised, God recognised,

You are a piece of shit,' Diomed said.

   Silence again.

A more recent example of radical translation is Alice Oswald's *Memorial* (2011), a 'translation of the *Iliad*'s atmosphere, not its story'. Leaving the plot to one side, the 'antiphonal' version handles only biographies of killed warriors ('paraphrases') and similes ('fairly irreverent' translations). Oswald's *Iliad* begins by listing the battle dead and bows out with a series of oft-praised Homeric similes (like the 'leaves of man'). In between, biographies and similes follow one another in the order of the poem. The original conception is implemented by bracingly beautiful imagery, often in swift, four-beat free verse. I read out loud one pairing of biography and simile to someone whose I judgement trust; silent weeping was the immediate effect. Penniless newcomer Othryon 'went blushing into battle and died' soon after offering to fight in exchange for the hand of Cassandra ('everyone laughed and laughed / Except Cassandra'). Following is the simile of a wounded deer 'escaping into loneliness / To the very breaking of her being' in flight from hounds; a 'huge angel' of a lion scatters their feast on her corpse. Oswald conveys the *Iliad*'s grand pathos by focusing on the peripheral: slain minor characters, anonymous everyday people, contextualizing scenes of nature.

VISIONS OF HOMER

Different types of translations present us with multiple Homers, as have scholars, interpreters and artists down through the ages. Everyone desires to envision their own Homer. There is a natural longing to develop a personal vision of the bard, his characters and the places of Homeric narrative. The ancients wanted to think of the legendary poet as a historical person, as the (conflicting and ahistorical) biographical traditions about Homer demonstrate. Chatting with Homer (or his characters) in the afterworld was a common motif (e.g. Plato *Apology* 41a–c; Lucian *True Stories* 2.20). So was the dream or vision of Homer (for example, the start of *Annales*, by the Roman poet Ennius). In the modern world, Rembrandt's so-called 'Aristotle Contemplating a Bust of Homer' (1653) shows someone, perhaps the philosopher, deep in thought, with a hand on a bust of Homer. The poet's likeness has clearly inspired deep rumination. And so images of Homer have been summoned to the mind of listeners, scholars, retellers and translators of the *Iliad* and *Odyssey*.

From antiquity onwards, many have imagined Homer travelling through the topography of his poetry. In ancient biographies of Homer, the Aegean and sometimes Ithaca provided the setting for fictional accounts of the bard's wanderings.[44] Ancient Greek myth-tellers in general placed the action of the past Heroic Age in their contemporary world. For the Trojan War, this is north-west Asia Minor, and the home to which Odysseus returns is Ithaca (modern Thiaki) of the Ionian Islands.[45] The geographical reality was certainly overlaid with a fantastic dimension, but Homer's audience lived in the lands and seas of the mythological stories.

Even when locations were inexplicit, as for the adventures of Odysseus, people wanted to authenticate their homelands with claims of heroic visitation.[46] If the *Odyssey* mentions only Libya and Sicily in the western Mediterranean, and rarely and vaguely at that, Greek and Roman traditions localized many of the adventures in the southern Italian peninsula and Sicily. Odysseus' island of the sun, Thrinacia, was linked to the historical term for Sicily, Trinacria ('three-cornered'; Thucydides 6.2). The Cyclopes and Laestrygonians were localized on Sicily. Scylla and Charybdis were placed in the Strait of Messina (plausibly enough, and reports of traders or colonizers may be their origin). Other Odyssean episodes were located in Italy, notably the association of the underworld scene with Lake Avernus, and Phaeacian Scheria was believed to be Corfu (ancient Corcyra). Inhabitants of these

Western locales, just like Greeks in Asia Minor, welcomed such connections to Homeric poetry. There may have been disputes between different claims to a myth – or even to 'Homer' – but it is pointless for ancient or modern scholars to label such tendencies 'wrong'. Linkage of story and place was always an organic part of Greek myth, and the ancient reception of Homeric poetry through localization by countless people over centuries cannot be dismissed out of hand.

From an academic perspective, however, positivistic focus on the geographical reality of the Homeric epics has often had poor returns, leading us away from the poetry. Already in antiquity scholars argued rather inconsequentially over the location of Troy and the geography of Odysseus' wanderings. In the modern times Schliemann found prehistoric Troy, but with dubious motivations and conclusions. The ancients considered low hills in the area of Troy to be the burial mounds of Homeric heroes, but which was associated with which hero is not certain today (as probably in antiquity).[47] Many still unproductively argue about the location of mythological Ithaca. Others rather optimistically identify Homeric topography in Ithaca by strolling about with the *Odyssey* open in hand, visiting the 'cave of the Nymphs' (there are two candidates), 'Raven's Rock', and the Arethusa fountain.[48] These localizing efforts may be faulted as wasted energy (at least in terms of positivistic search for Homeric truth; the archaeological discoveries of Greek prehistory are invaluable). Still, they are but an exaggeration of something inherent in the ancient conception of traditional myth, and therefore potentially enlightening. We may be separated from antiquity by a yawning gulf of time, but we can profitably visit the general areas through which Homeric heroes were said to move. Robert Wood's eighteenth-century travel in the eastern Mediterranean, for example, was essentially the study of Homeric poetry through re-enactment of Homer's travels.[49]

To be sure, localization often insists on unwarranted precision. The location of place in the wanderings of Odysseus has in particular been a Sirens' song for many, whether scholars, amateur enthusiasts or out-and-out cranks. Those who propose that Odysseus visited the Bay of Fundy or Antarctica wish to con you into thinking they are the very first to break a hidden code. Others are essentially travel writers re-enacting tropes of discovery. Influential in this field has been Samuel Butler's argument in *The Authoress of the* Odyssey (1897) that much of the *Odyssey*'s story was inspired by Sicily and its environs. His provocative thesis – at times it seems parodic – was that a young Sicilian woman composed the epic.[50] His talk of Cyclopes as Sicilian natives might sound post-colonial, but the details of his argument cannot be reconciled with historical facts. Moreover, Butler's case for a female author of the *Odyssey*, with its mockery of Penelope and out-of-date essentialism of gender, is unattractive to feminist scholarship.[51]

Apparently more mainstream are the extensive localization theories in the first half of the twentieth century by the classicist Victor Bérard (who also edited and translated the *Odyssey*). He claimed that Phoenician trade routes were the ultimate source for perceived correspondences between sites in the wanderings and specific Mediterranean locales.[52] But though there is a notable Phoenician presence in the *Odyssey*, scholars today find this thesis unconvincing. It is another example of obsession, with origins obscuring poetics.

Nonetheless, one can concede to Butler and Bérard the pleasure of pursuing their private visions of Homer. No armchair scholars, they enjoyed experiential research out and about in the Mediterranean. And whatever their negligible impact on classics, they have become influential in other ways. Joyce read them enthusiastically, and their localization theories arguably inspired Joyce's Dublin 'localization' of the *Odyssey*.[53] From this perspective, it is immaterial whether Bérard, Butler or Joyce are mistaken about the geographical basis of the wanderings.

Not all personal visions are the same, and when they are put forth as public argument not everyone will be persuaded. As students of Homer, we are part of an ongoing conversation: sometimes we convince others; sometimes they get the better of us. Disagreements will remain, and consensus will often cycle back to earlier discarded views. But the public discourse of Homeric study need not dim our personal visions of Homer. As pre-Homeric traditions of myth and epic nourished the Homeric poems, so different responses to the *Iliad* and *Odyssey* have kept Homer alive. We – classicists, students in other fields, the general public, as well as artists and writers who recreate Homeric poetry – honour the *Iliad* and *Odyssey* with our visions of Homer.

Notes

I. MYTHS

1   In his 'Palinode' Stesichorus reportedly regretted his earlier, more conventional treatment of Helen. The story is given at Plato *Phaedrus* 243a, *Republic* 9.586c; Isocrates *Helen* 64; Pausanias 3.19.11–13. See: B. Graziosi, *Inventing Homer: The Early Reception of Epic* (Cambridge, 2002), pp. 117–18; B. Sammons, 'History and *hyponoia*: Herodotus and early literary criticism', *Histos* vi (2012), pp. 52–66, on Herodotus' interpretation of Homer here; I.J.F. de Jong, 'The Helen *logos* and Herodotus' fingerprint', in E. Baragwanath and M. de Bakker (eds), *Myth, Truth, and Narrative in Herodotus* (Oxford, 2012), pp. 127–42, for Herodotus' innovative approach to the pre-existing alternative story about Helen.

2   For the song of Demodocus as the expression of a traditional polarity, see G. Nagy, *The Best of the Achaeans* (Baltimore, 1979), Part I.1.

3   For a general description of Muses in classical antiquity, see P. Murray, 'The Muses and their arts', in P. Murray and P. Wilson (eds), *Music and the Muses* (Oxford, 2004), pp. 365–89. For changing conceptions of poetic inspiration in the Hellenistic period (after the death of Alexander the Great), see P. Bing, *The Well-Read Muse* (Göttingen, 1988).

4   'Double motivation' is a key concept in E. Dodds, *The Greeks and the Irrational* (Berkeley, 1951), a classic exploration of irrationality in Greek thought.

5   There were many sources for Trojan War myth in antiquity; a key one, the Epic Cycle, is discussed below. An ancient survey of Greek myth is the *Bibliotheca* (*Library*) by Apollodorus, of uncertain date (and authorship); T. Gantz, *Early Greek Myth: A Guide to Literary and Artistic Sources* (Baltimore, 1993) is a thorough collection of our surviving textual and iconographical sources for Greek myth.

6   On the somewhat puzzling allusion to the judgement of Paris in *Iliad* 24, see M. Davies, 'The Judgment of Paris and *Iliad* Book XXIV', *Journal of Hellenic Studies* ci (1981), pp. 56–62. K. Reinhardt, 'The judgement of Paris', in G.M. Wright and P.V. Jones (eds), *Homer: German Scholarship in Translation* (Oxford, 1997), pp. 170–91, persuasively demonstrated that the story is implicitly present throughout the Homeric epic.

7   The prophecy is told in Pindar, *Isthmian* 8. On its significance for the *Iliad*, see L. Slatkin, *The Power of Thetis* (Berkeley, 1991). The gods' attendance of the wedding is referenced at *Iliad* 24.59 ff.

8   J. Burgess's *The Death and Afterlife of Achilles* (Baltimore, 2009) explores this and other stories about Achilles.

9   On the Epic Cycle, see: M. Davies, *The Greek Epic Cycle* (Bristol, 1989); J. Burgess, *The Tradition of the Trojan War in Homer and the Epic Cycle* (Baltimore, 2001); A. Debiasi, *L'epica perduta. Eumelo, il Ciclo, l'occidente* (Rome, 2005); M.L. West, *The Epic Cycle: A Commentary on the Lost Troy Epics* (Oxford, 2013). The surviving fragments and testimony are provided in Greek with facing translation by M.L. West, in *Greek Epic Fragments: From the Seventh to the Fifth Centuries BC* (Cambridge, MA, 2003). The summary is attributed to Proclus, perhaps the Neoplatonist of the fifth century CE (although this is disputed). It is preserved in the oldest completely surviving manuscript of the *Iliad*, the tenth-century 'Venetus A' (summaries of the *Cypria* are found in some other manuscripts).

10   Henceforth when uncapitalized, 'cyclic' shall refer to the general content of the Epic Cycle.

11   J. Griffin, 'The Epic Cycle and the uniqueness of Homer', *Journal of Hellenic Studies* xcvii (1977), pp. 39–53, points out (with some exaggeration) that Homeric poetry is relatively less fantastic and more humane.

II. PLOTS

1   See N. Lowe, *The Classical Plot and the Invention of Western Narrative* (Cambridge, 2000), Chapters 2 and 6 (for the *Odyssey* and the *Iliad* respectively).

2   The translations of Homer used here and throughout this book (unless otherwise stated) are those by A.T. Murray in the Loeb Classical Library. For the *Iliad* we use the 1999 edition, revised by W.F. Wyatt, and for the *Odyssey* we use the 1995 edition, revised by G.E. Dimock.

3   For an analysis of how the epic's opening introduces the plot, see M. Clark, 'The concept of plot and the plot of the *Iliad*', *Phoenix* lv/1–2 (2001), pp. 1–8.

4   Although full of insights, the concise remarks of the *Poetics* can be difficult to unpack, and Aristotle's view need not always be followed. See S. Halliwell, *Aristotle's Poetics* (London, 1986), especially Chapter 9 on Aristotle's remarks about epic and other genres.

5   For the *Cypria*'s 'plan of Zeus', see M. Christopoulos, '*Casus belli*: Causes of the Trojan War in the Epic Cycle', *Classics@* vi (2010), The Center for Hellenic Studies of Harvard University, <http://chs.harvard.edu/wa/pageR?tn=ArticleWrapper&bdc=12&mn=3367> (accessed 4 April 2014). For an insightful discussion of the Iliadic 'plan of Zeus', see also: S. Murnaghan, 'Equal honor and future glory: The plan of Zeus in the *Iliad*', in D. Roberts, F. Dunn and D. Fowler (eds), *Classical Closure: Reading the End in Greek and Latin Literature* (Princeton, 1997), pp. 23–42; J.S. Clay, 'The whip and will of Zeus', *Literary Imagination* i/1 (1999), pp. 40–60; W. Allan, 'Performing the will of Zeus: The Διὸς Βουλή and the scope of early Greek epic', in M. Revermann and P. Wilson (eds), *Performance, Iconography, Reception* (Oxford, 2008).

6   On Achilles' modelling his actions on other characters like Chryses and Heracles, see R.J. Rabel, *Plot and Point of View in the* Iliad (Ann Arbor, 1997).

7   Besides the Afterword and Appendix of C. Dué's *Homeric Variations on a Lament by Briseis* (Lanham, MD, 2002), see now Chapter 3 of M. Fantuzzi's *Achilles in Love* (Oxford, 2012) for ancient reception of the relationship between Achilles and Briseis.

8   See J. Burgess, *The Death and Afterlife of Achilles* (Baltimore, 2009), Chapter 2.

9   Cf. the subtitle of J.M. Redfield, *Nature and Culture in the* Iliad*: The Tragedy of Hector* (Chicago, 1975).

10 On the topic of the wooden or Trojan horse, see C.A. Faraone, *Talismans and Trojan Horses* (Oxford, 1992), and look for forthcoming publications by Robin Mitchell-Boyask on the topic. G.F. Franko, 'The Trojan horse at the close of the "Iliad"', *The Classical Journal* ci/2 (2005–6), pp. 121–3, makes the case that the end of the *Iliad* repeatedly alludes to the wooden horse.

11 See: A.M. Snodgrass, *Homer and the Artists* (Cambridge, 1998); J. Burgess, *The Tradition of the Trojan War in Homer and the Epic Cycle* (Baltimore, 2001).

12 See Burgess, *Death and Afterlife of Achilles*, Chapter 3.

13 W. Kullmann's *Die Quellen der* Ilias (Wiesbaden, 1960) is a magisterial and classic study of the *Iliad*'s explicit and implicit employment of the larger tradition of the Trojan War. See also Burgess, *Tradition of the Trojan War*.

14 C.H. Whitman's *Homer and the Heroic Tradition* (Cambridge, MA, 1958) outlines (and graphs) such correspondences throughout the poem. Cf. K. Stanley, *The Shield of Homer: Narrative Structure in the* Iliad (Princeton, 1993); B. Heiden, *Homer's Cosmic Fabrication: Choice and Design in the* Iliad (Oxford, 2008); B. Louden, *The* Iliad*: Structure, Myth, and Meaning* (Baltimore, 2006). One should be cautious about overdevelopment of this line of argument, however.

15 On the *Odyssey*'s plot, see: S.V. Tracy, 'The structures of the *Odyssey*', in I. Morris and B. Powell (eds), *A New Companion to Homer* (Leiden, 1997), pp. 360–79; B. Louden, *The* Odyssey*: Structure, Narration, and Meaning* (Baltimore, 1999).

16 On the divine manipulation of the plot in the *Odyssey*, see especially J. Marks, *Zeus in the* Odyssey (Washington, DC, 2008).

17 See J. Burgess, 'Framing Odysseus: The death of the suitors', in M. Christopoulos (ed.), *Crime and Punishment in Homeric and Archaic Epic* (in press), with reference to non-Homeric versions of Odysseus' post-return adventures.

18 On the tale type 'the returning husband', see: J. Foley, *Traditional Oral Epic: The* Odyssey*, Beowulf, and the Serbo-Croatian* Return Song (Berkeley, 1990); and, more generally, W. Hansen, *Ariadne's Thread: A Guide to International Tales Found in Classical Literature* (Ithaca, NY, 2002), pp. 201–11.

19 On the role of Athena in the *Odyssey*, see J.S. Clay, *The Wrath of Athena* (Princeton, 1983).

20 'The Odysseys within the *Odyssey*' in I. Calvino, *Why Read the Classics?*, trans. M. McLaughlin (New York, 1987) interestingly portrays Telemachus as searching for a non-existing story that becomes the *Odyssey*.

21 A.M. Snodgrass, 'An historical Homeric society?', *Journal of Hellenic Studies* xciv (1974), pp. 114–25, influentially argued that the question of Penelope's re-marriage reflects a mixture of historical practices; as a consequence, the Homeric world cannot be thought to reflect a single time period.

22 T. Zielinski, 'Die Behandlung gleichzeitiger Ereignisse im antiken Epos', *Philologus Supplementband* viii (1899–1901), pp. 405–49. For revisionist discussion, see R. Scodel, 'Zielinski's Law reconsidered', *Transactions of the American Philological Association* cxxxviii (2008), pp. 107–25.

23 See: M.L. West, *The Epic Cycle: A Commentary on the Lost Troy Epics* (Oxford, 2013), pp. 307–15; Burgess, *Tradition of the Trojan War*, pp. 153–4.

24 See J. Peradotto, *Man in the Middle Voice* (Princeton, 1990), pp. 59–93; here is a discussion of the 'inland journey' as an example of a centrifugal voice in the Homeric epic that

counters its centripetal, controlling vision. The centripetal–centrifugal dichotomy for Odysseus' wanderings is employed in W. Stanford's *The Ulysses Theme* (Oxford, 1954), but goes back to Joyce's *Ulysses*.

25   See S. Saïd, *Homer & the Odyssey*, trans. R. Webb (Oxford, 2011), pp. 249–57.

III. POETICS

1   For the paradoxical role of Athena in the *Odyssey*, see J.S. Clay, *The Wrath of Athena* (Princeton, 1983).

2   For the actions of divinities in the *Odyssey*, see: ibid.; E.F. Cook, *The* Odyssey *in Athens* (Ithaca, NY, 1995); J. Marks, *Zeus in the* Odyssey (Washington, DC, 2008).

3   On the 'Aegisthus' tale in the *Odyssey*, see S.D. Olson, *Blood and Iron: Stories and Storytelling in Homer's* Odyssey (Leiden, 1995), pp. 24–8. On ad hoc employment of paradigmatic myth, see: M. Willcock, 'Ad hoc invention in the *Iliad*', *Harvard Studies in Classical Philology* lxxxi (1977), pp. 41–53; J. Burgess, *The Death and Afterlife of Achilles* (Baltimore, 2009), pp. 56–71. W. Allan, 'Divine justice and cosmic order in early Greek epic', *Journal of Hellenic Studies* cxxvi (2006), pp. 1–35, convincingly demonstrates that both Homeric epics, and indeed all early Greek epics, share the same basic theological concepts.

4   See P. Pucci, 'Theology and poetics in the *Iliad*', *Arethusa* xxxv (2002), pp. 17–34. For the profundity that many perceive in Homeric theology, see J. Griffin, *Homer on Life and Death* (Oxford, 1980), pp. 144–204. W. Burkert, *Greek Religion: Archaic and Classical*, trans. J. Raffan (Cambridge, MA, 1985), provides a dependable survey of Greek religion in all its aspects.

5   On the system of reciprocal relations between Homeric heroes, see D. Wilson, *Ransom, Revenge and Heroic Identity in the* Iliad (Cambridge, 2002). For recent engaging discussions of competition and cooperation in Homeric society, see: E.T.E. Barker, *Entering the Agon: Dissent and Authority in Homer, Historiography, and Tragedy* (Oxford, 2009); D.F. Elmer, *The Poetics of Consent: Collective Decision Making and the* Iliad (Baltimore, 2013).

6   On Homeric *kleos*, cf. G. Nagy, *The Best of the Achaeans* (Baltimore, 1979); C. Segal, *Singers, Heroes, and Gods in the* Odyssey (Ithaca, NY, 1994), pp. 85–109; E.J. Bakker, *Pointing at the Past: From Formula to Performance in Homeric Poetics* (Washington, DC, 2005), pp. 92–113; J.C.B. Petropoulos, *Kleos in a Minor Key* (Washington, DC, 2011).

7   On Homeric characterization and character speech, see Griffin, *Homer on Life and Death*, pp. 50–80, and 'The speeches', in R.L. Fowler (ed.), *The Cambridge Companion to Homer* (Cambridge, 2004), pp. 156–70.

8   A. Parry, 'The language of Achilles', *Transactions of the American Philological Association* lxxxvii (1956), influentially argued that Achilles stretches the language of traditional epic speech in his scrutiny of the heroic code. R. Martin, *The Language of Heroes* (Ithaca, NY, 1989), employing speech-act theory, focuses particularly on how Achilles performs speech.

9   L.C. Muellner, *The Anger of Achilles: Menis in Greek Epic* (Ithaca, NY, 1996), is the essential study of *menis* in the *Iliad* and beyond.

10   See P. Gainsford, 'Achilles' views on death: succession and the Odyssey', *Classical Bulletin* lxxxiv (2009), pp. 7–26, for a summary of different scholarly opinions, with bibliography.

11 For an excellent study of the lament of Briseis and all its implications, see C. Dué, *Homeric Variations on a Lament by Briseis* (Lanham, MD, 2002).

12 On these qualities of Odysseus, see: D. Beck, *Speech Presentation in Homeric Epic* (Austin, TX, 2012), pp. 30–8; J. Ready, *Character, Narrator, and Simile in the* Iliad (Cambridge, 2011), pp. 9–10, 264–5.

13 Athena disguised as the visiting Mentes reports that the return of Odysseus is imminent (1.195 ff.), as does an anonymous visitor recalled by Eumaeus (14.372 ff.). Eumaeus does not trust such claims, but reports Penelope can't resist them, although she excuses her delayed acceptance of Odysseus by saying she mistrusts strangers (23.215–17).

14 On the rhetorical import of hospitality in the hero's account, see G. Most, 'The structure and function of Odysseus' *apologoi*', *Transactions of the American Philological Association* cxxix (1989), pp. 15–30.

15 On the *Odyssey*'s incorporation of anti-Odyssean perspectives, see J. Burgess, 'Framing Odysseus: The death of the suitors', in M. Christopoulos (ed.), *Crime and Punishment in Homeric and Archaic Epic* (forthcoming).

16 For example, see W.J. Woodhouse, *The Composition of Homer's Odyssey* (Oxford, 1930), pp. 200–3 ('without any gift of intellect or strength of character').

17 On the Homeric simile, H. Fränkel's 'Essence and nature of the Homeric similes', in G.M. Wright and P.V. Jones (eds), *Homer: German Scholarship in Translation* (Oxford, 1997), pp. 103–23 (originally 1920), is seminal. For analysis, cf. W.C. Scott, *The Oral Nature of the Homeric Simile* (Leiden, 1974) (an Oralist approach); C. Moulton, *Similes in the Homeric Poems* (Göttingen, 1977) (on patterning and larger poetic function); E. Minchin, *Homer and the Resources of Memory: Some Applications of Cognitive Theory to the* Iliad *and the* Odyssey (Oxford, 2001), pp. 132–69 (a cognitive analysis); Ready, *Character, Narrator, and Simile* (a well-theorized study). M.W. Edwards, *Homer: Poet of the* Iliad (Baltimore, 1987), masterfully surveys the simile and all other aspects of Homeric poetic technique with a generous number of examples.

18 On the reverse similes of the *Odyssey*, see H. Foley, '"Reverse similes" and sex roles in the *Odyssey*', *Arethusa* xi (1978), p. 7–26.

19 See Burgess, *Tradition of the Trojan War*, pp. 117–26.

20 W. Burkert, *Structure and History in Greek Mythology and Ritual* (Berkeley, 1979), pp. 30–4, describes the stake as a Palaeolithic weapon.

21 A clear exposition of Homeric metre, as well as other aspects of oral poetics discussed further in the next chapter, is provided by M. Clark, 'Formulas, metre, and type-scenes', in R. Fowler (ed.), *The Cambridge Companion to Homer* (Cambridge, 2004), pp. 117–38.

22 On dialect in Homer, see G.C. Horrocks, 'Homer's dialect', in I. Morris and B. Powell (eds), *A New Companion to Homer* (Leiden, 1997).

23 For this theory, see now A. Debiasi, 'Homer αγωνιστής in Chalcis', in F. Montanari, A. Rengakos and C. Tsagalis (eds), *Homeric Contexts: Neoanalysis and the Interpretation of Oral Poetry* (Berlin, 2012), pp. 471–500.

24 The issue of metre will return in the discussion of translations of Homer in Chapter 7. For use of the limerick form to discuss Homeric metrics, see M.S. Silk, *Homer: The* Iliad (Cambridge, 1987), pp. 22–4. My own compositions 'There once was a Trojan named Hector' and 'There once was a clever non-slacker' did not survive revision of this book.

25 See Clark, 'Formulas, metre, and type-scenes'.

IV. TEXTS AND PRE-TEXTS

1   On this so-called 'Venetus A' manuscript, see C. Dué, *Recapturing a Homeric Legacy: Images and Insights from the Venetus: A Manuscript of the* Iliad (Washington, DC, 2009).

2   For overviews of Homeric *scholia*, see: G. Nagy, 'Homeric *scholia*', in I. Morris and B. Powell (eds), *A New Companion to Homer* (Leiden, 1997), pp. 101–22; M. Schmidt, 'The Homer of the *scholia*: What is explained to the reader?', in F. Montanari (ed.), *Omero tremila anni dopo* (Rome, 2002), pp. 159–83. More generally on *scholia* and ancient scholarship, see E. Dickey, *Ancient Greek Scholarship* (Oxford, 2007).

3   Grafton, Most, and Zetzel (1985) provide an English translation of Wolf's *Prolegomena to Homer*, originally composed in Latin.

4   See A. Parry (ed.), *The Making of Homeric Verse* (Oxford, 1971), a collection of the Oralist scholarship of Milman Parry by his son.

5   J.A. Davison, 'The transmission of the text', in A.J.B. Wace and F.H. Stubbings (eds), *A Companion to Homer* (London, 1962), pp. 215–33, is a classic study of the transmission of Homeric texts, although it should be supplemented with reference to other works cited in this chapter.

6   The licensed *Thesaurus Linguae Graecae* (<http://www.tlg.uci.edu/>) is an almost comprehensive online compilation of ancient Greek literary texts. The *Chicago Homer* (<http://digital.library.northwestern.edu/homer/>) contains the Homeric poems in Greek and in translation. The exciting new project *The Homer Multitext* (<http://www.homermultitext.org/>) will enable exploration of the multiformity of Homeric texts.

7   For a catalogue of Homeric texts and translations in the Gutenberg era, see P.H. Young, *The Printed Homer* (Jefferson, NC, 2003).

8   For the medieval and ancient forms of recording the Homeric epics, see: M. Haslam, 'Homeric papyri and transmission of the text', in I. Morris and B. Powell (eds), *A New Companion to Homer* (Leiden, 1997), pp. 55–100; 'The physical media: Tablet, scroll, codex', in J. Foley (ed.), *A Companion to Ancient Epic* (Oxford, 2005), pp. 142–63.

9   General information on Alexandrian scholarship can be found in R. Pfeiffer, *History of Classical Scholarship from the Beginnings to the End of the Hellenistic Age* (Oxford, 1968). For more specific information on ancient Homeric philology in the Alexandrian period, see: F. Montanari, 'Zenodotus, Aristarchus, and the *Ekdosis* of Homer', in G.W. Most (ed.), *Editing Texts – Texte Edieren* (Göttingen, 1998), pp. 1–21; 'Alexandrian Homeric philology: The form of the *Ekdosis* and the *Variae Lectiones*', in M. Reichel and A. Rengakos (eds), *Epea Pteroenta* (Stuttgart, 2002), pp. 119–40.

10   G.D. Bird, *Multitextuality in the Homeric* Iliad: *The Witness of Ptolemaic Papyri* (Cambridge, MA, 2010), argues for the multiformity of ancient transmission of Homeric poetry on the evidence of the papyri.

11   For ancient readers of Homer, such as Aristotle, see R. Lamberton and J. Keaney (eds), *Homer's Ancient Readers* (Princeton, 1992).

12   T.W. Allen's *Homer: The Origins and Transmission* (Oxford, 1924) is still a useful compilation of ancient quotations and other evidence for knowledge of Homer. Through the close study of a Homeric quotation by Aeschines, an orator of the fourth century BCE, C. Dué, 'Achilles' golden amphora in Aeschines' *Against Timarchus* and the afterlife of oral tradition', *Classical Philology* xcvi (2001), pp. 33–47, illuminates the possibility

of continuing variability in Homeric poetic traditions. Nagy has extensively argued for an evolving multiformity of the Homeric epics in antiquity; see in particular G. Nagy, *Poetry as Performance* (Cambridge, 1996).

13   J. Burgess, *The Tradition of the Trojan War in Homer and the Epic Cycle* (Baltimore, 2001), pp. 122–3.

14   On the significance of biographies of Homer for the ancient reception of Homer, see B. Graziosi, *Inventing Homer: The Early Reception of Epic* (Cambridge, 2002). Translations of them can be found in M.L. West, *Greek Epic Fragments: From the Seventh to the Fifth Centuries BC* (Cambridge, MA, 2003).

15   For a discussion of this simile in early Greek literature and beyond, see Burgess, *Tradition of the Trojan War*, pp. 122–6.

16   Our fetishization of Shakespeare is explored in M. Garber, 'Shakespeare as fetish', *Shakespeare Quarterly* xli (1990), pp. 242–50, reprinted in M. Garber, *Profiling Shakespeare* (New York, 2008).

17   Greek culture would remain predominantly oral; see R. Thomas, *Literacy and Orality in Ancient Greece* (Cambridge, 1992).

18   For different perspectives on rhapsodes, cf. R. Sealey, 'From Phemios to Ion', *Revue des études grecques* lxx (1957), pp. 312–55; G. Nagy, *Plato's Rhapsody and Homer's Music* (Washington, DC, 2002); H. Pellicia, 'Two points about Rhapsodes', in M. Finkelberg and G.G. Stroumsa (eds), *Homer, the Bible, and Beyond* (Leiden, 2003), pp. 98–116.

19   For the Panathenaea and epic performance there, see: J.A. Davison, 'Pisistratus and Homer', *Transactions of the American Philological Association* lxxxvi (1955), pp. 1–21; M.S. Jensen, *The Homeric Question and the Oral-Formulaic Theory* (Copenhagen, 1980); J. Neils (ed.), *Goddess and Polis: The Panathenaic Festival in Ancient Athens* (Princeton, 1992); Nagy, *Poetry as Performance*, pp. 69–113; J. Burgess, 'Performance and the Epic Cycle', *The Classical Journal* c/1 (2004), pp. 1–23.

20   J. Gleick, *The Information: A History, a Theory, a Flood* (New York, 2012), offers a fascinating discussion on the variety of information exchange in human history.

21   On the pan-Ionian festival in Asia Minor and its potential relation to performance or even composition of the Homeric epics, see D.F. Frame, *Hippota Nestor* (Washington, DC, 2009), Part 4. In the second half of the *Homeric Hymn to Apollo*, the bard speaks as if he is performing at the Delian festival, as well as being the 'man from Chios'. Some speculate this half of the hymn was composed for a festival at Delos organized in late sixth century BCE by Polycrates, tyrant of Samos; see W. Burkert, 'Kynaithos, Polycrates and the Homeric hymn to Apollo', in G.W. Bowersock, W. Burkert and M.C.J. Putnam (eds), *Arktouros* (Berlin, 1979), pp. 53–62. For an exploration of how the *Iliad* might be performed orally, see O. Taplin, *Homeric Soundings: The Shaping of the* Iliad (Oxford, 1992).

22   The performance of long works of world oral literature is surveyed in J.M. Foley, *How to Read an Oral Poem* (Urbana-Champaign, 2002), and M.S. Jensen, *Writing Homer* (Copenhagen, 2011).

23   For good general studies of the historical periods of the Archaic Age, Dark Age and Bronze Age, see: A.M. Snodgrass, *The Dark Age of Greece*, 2nd ed. (Edinburgh, 2000) and *Archaic Age: An Age of Experiment* (Berkeley, 1980); O. Dickinson, *The Aegean Bronze Age* (Cambridge, 1994). For the transition through the Dark Age to the Archaic Age, see R. Osborne, *Greece in the Making, 1200–479 BC* (New York, 1996).

24   General overviews of the contents of the Linear B documents and their evidence for the Mycenaean world are given in J. Chadwick, *The Decipherment of Linear B*

(Cambridge, 1958) and *The Mycenaean World* (Cambridge, 1976). The texts themselves are gathered at M. Ventris and J. Chadwick, *Documents in Mycenaean Greek*, 2nd ed. (Cambridge, 1973).

25 A concise overview of potential connections between Homer and the Mycenaean world is provided at J. Bennet, 'Homer and the Bronze Age', in I. Morris and B. Powell (eds), *A New Companion to Homer* (Leiden, 1997), pp. 513–36.

26 On Schliemann's initial excavations at Troy, see D.F. Easton, *Schliemann's Excavations at Troia, 1870–1873* (Mainz, 2002). For a biography of Schliemann that reflects modern scepticism about his motivation, method, and honesty, see D.A. Traill, *Schliemann of Troy: Treasure and Deceit* (New York, 1995). On the essential role of Frank Calvert in the discovery of Troy, see S.H. Allen, *Finding the Walls of Troy: Frank Calvert and Heinrich Schliemann at Hisarlık* (Berkeley, 1999). For a fictional portrayal of a Schliemannesque character, bombastic and disturbingly duplicitous, see Peter Ackroyd's *The Fall of Troy* (London, 2006). See R. Stoneman, 'Die Idee Trojas: Resonanzen in England und Deutschland im zwanzigsten Jahrhundert', in E. Koczisky (ed.), *Ruinen in der Moderne: Archäologie und die Kunste* (Berlin, 2010), pp. 337–58, for the twentieth-century reception of 'the idea of Troy' in England and Germany, including not just literary responses such as Ackroyd's but also the symbolic resonance of Troy's excavation for such figures as Wagner, Freud and Joyce.

27 1183 BCE is given by the prominent names of Eratosthenes and Apollodorus, but there was a scattershot of other guesses; see W. Burkert, 'Lydia between East and West, or How to date the Trojan War: A study in Herodotus', in J.B. Carter and S.P. Morris (eds), *The Ages of Homer* (Austin, 1995), pp. 139–48.

28 Arguing for the historicity of the Trojan War, J. Latacz's *Troy and Homer: Towards a Solution of an Old Mystery* (Oxford, 2004) employs the Hittite evidence extensively. In a penetrating and decisive discussion, J. Grethlein in 'From imperishable glory to history: The *Iliad* and the Trojan War', in D. Konstan and K. A. Raaflaub (eds), *Epic and History* (Malden, MA, and Oxford, 2010), pp. 122–44, counters this type of historicist argument.

29 For the results of the Korfmann expedition, see the online site for Project Troia (< http://www.uni-tuebingen.de/troia/eng/index.html>), as well as the German-language *Troia: Traum und Wirklichkeit* (Stuttgart, 2001), which has excellent illustrations. J. Haubold, 'Wars of *Wissenschaft*: The new quest for Troy', *International Journal of the Classical Tradition* viii/4 (2002), pp. 564–79, contextualizes the often bitter and sometimes bizarre controversies over the expedition by reference to the modern reunification of Germany.

30 See: W. Burkert, *The Orientalizing Revolution: Near Eastern Influence on Greek Culture in the Early Archaic Age*, trans. M. Pinder (Cambridge, MA, 1992) and *Babylon, Memphis, Persepolis: Eastern Contexts of Greek Culture* (Cambridge, MA, 2004); M.L. West, *The East Face of Helicon: West Asiatic Elements in Greek Poetry and Myth* (Oxford, 1997). J. Haubold's *Greece and Mesopotamia: Dialogues in Literature* (Cambridge, 2013) is an advance on this line of research.

31 The most trustworthy translation of the *Gilgamesh Epic* is A.R. George, *The Epic of Gilgamesh: The Babylonian Epic Poem and Other Texts in Akkadian and Sumerian* (London, 2000); S. Mitchell's *Gilgamesh: A New English Version* (New York, 2006) is agreeably readable. The best critical edition is A.R. George, *The Babylonian Gilgamesh Epic: Introduction, Critical Edition and Cuneiform Texts*, 2 vols (Oxford, 2003).

32　On the personal relationship between Achilles and Patroclus in the *Iliad* and beyond, see M. Fantuzzi, *Achilles in Love* (Oxford, 2012), Chapter 4.

33　For comparisons of Homeric epic to the Gilgamesh story, see: J. Burgess, 'Gilgamesh and Odysseus in the Otherworld', *Echos du Monde Classique/Classical Views* xviii (1999), pp. 171–210; E.J. Bakker, 'The Greek Gilgamesh, or the immortality of return', in M. Païsi-Apostolopoulou (ed.), *Eranos* (Ithaca, 2001), pp. 331–53; B. Currie, 'The *Iliad*, *Gilgamesh*, and neoanalysis', in F. Montanari, A. Rengakos and C. Tsagalis (eds), *Homeric Contexts* (Berlin, 2012), pp. 543–80.

34　M.L. West's *Indo-European Poetry and Myth* (Oxford, 2007) comprehensively catalogues potential Indo-European motifs in Greek literature; see also C. Watkins, *How to Kill a Dragon: Aspects of Indo-Europen Poetics* (New York, 1995).

35　For the heel motif and Achilles, see: J. Burgess, 'Achilles' heel: The death of Achilles in ancient myth', *Classical Antiquity* xiv/2 (1995), pp. 217–44; *The Death and Afterlife of Achilles* (Baltimore, 2009), pp. 9–15.

36　On the Dumézilian analysis of the judgement of Paris, see C. Littleton, *The New Comparative Mythology: An Anthropological Assessment of the Theories of Georges Dumézil*, 3rd ed. (Berkeley, 1982), pp. 14–15.

37　On the seemingly Indo-European nature of 'undying glory', see G. Nagy, *The Best of the Achaeans* (Baltimore, 1979), pp. 244–55.

38　On the possibility of an Indo-European motif of a bow contest, see S.W. Jamison, 'Penelope and the pigs: Indic perspectives on the *Odyssey*', *Classical Antiquity* xviii/2 (1999), pp. 227–72.

39　As noted above, translations of the ancient biographies of Homer can be found in West, *Greek Epic Fragments*; Graziosi, *Inventing Homer*, explores how legends about Homer might reflect ancient conceptions of Homer. M.R. Lefkowitz's *The Lives of the Greek Poets* (London, 1981) demonstrates that ancient biographies of Greek poets typically mined the poetry itself in order to construct a portrayal of the authors.

40　E.S. Sherratt, 'Reading the texts: Archaeology and the Homeric Question', *Antiquity* lxiv (1990), pp. 807–24, applies the archaeological concept of 'layers' to the content of Homeric epic; cf. the title of J.B. Carter and S.P. Morris's *The Ages of Homer* (Austin, TX, 1995). For a general discussion on the 'world of Homer' see Osborne, *Greece in the Making*, pp. 137–60 (where one can find a bibliography on topics below). For an analysis of the latest datable elements in Homer, see particularly: J.P. Crielaard, 'Homer, history and archaeology: Some remarks on the date of the Homeric world', in J.P. Crielaard (ed.), *Homeric Questions* (Amsterdam, 1995), pp. 201–88; H. van Wees, 'Homer and early Greece', *Colby Quarterly* xxxviii (2002), p. 94–117.

41　The classic study employing this methodology is R. Janko, *Homer, Hesiod and the Hymn* (Cambridge, 1982); this is revisited by Janko and others in Ø. Andersen and D.T.T. Haug (eds), *Relative Chronology in Early Greek Epic Poetry* (Cambridge, 2012). See also B. Jones, 'Relative chronology within (an) oral tradition', *Classical Journal* cv/4 (2010), pp. 289–318.

42　In my remarks on the complication of performance traditions for the dating of Homer, I am thinking of Nagy's evolutionary approach (e.g. in Nagy, *Poetry as Performance*).

43　Cf. *Iliad* 9.404–5 (Delphi), 11.699–702 (Olympia?), *Odyssey* 6.162 (Delos), 8.80 (Delphi) and, for possible reflections of colonization, Odysseus' colonial gaze over 'Goat Island' at *Odyssey* 9.116–51, as well as the Phaeacian settlement at Scheria at 6.2–10. See further in Chapter 6.

44 The text is fragmented, so translation can vary; at least one of the three lines scans as a hexameter. Schliemann called a golden cup excavated from the sixteenth century BCE shaft graves at Mycenae the 'Cup of Nestor', but it does not exactly match Nestor's cup in Homer. The Ischian wine cup's playful remarks on the goddess of love and a heroic hero seem sympotic, or perhaps proto-sympotic, since the symposium in its developed form is dated to the later Archaic Age; see O. Murray, 'Nestor's cup and the origins of the Greek *symposion*', in B. D'Agostino and D. Ridgway (eds), *Apoikia* (Naples, 1994), pp. 47–54. Some Homeric passages have been described as sympotic in nature; cf. A. Ford, 'Odysseus after dinner: *Od.* 9.2–11, and the traditions of sympotic song', in A. Rengakos and J. Kazazis (eds), *Euphrosyne* (Leipzig, 1999), pp. 109–23; M. Węcowski, 'Homer and the origins of the *symposion*', in F. Montanari and P. Ascheri (eds), *Omero tremila anni dopo* (Rome, 2002), pp. 625–37; L. Mawhinney, 'Sympotic and rhapsodic discourse in the Homeric epics', Ph.D. dissertation (University of Toronto, 2012).

45 For different perspectives on Homeric influence on early lyric poetry, cf. W. Burkert, 'The making of Homer in the sixth century B.C.: Rhapsodes versus Stesichorus', in D. von Bothmer (ed.), *Papers on the Amasis Painter and His World* (Malibu, 1987), pp. 43–62; A. Ford, 'The inland ship: Problems in the performance and reception of Homeric epic', in E. Bakker and A. Kahane (eds), *Written Voices, Spoken Signs* (Cambridge, MA, 1997), pp. 83–109; Burgess, *Tradition of the Trojan War*, pp. 115–27.

46 See: A.M. Snodgrass, *Homer and the Artists* (Cambridge, 1998), pp. 67–100; Burgess, *Tradition of the Trojan War*, pp. 94–112. See also the analysis of L. Giuliani, *Image and Myth*, trans. J. O'Donnell (Chicago, 2013), pp. 70–88, which ultimately desires to ascribe the early Polyphemus images to the influence of Homer. M. Squire, *Image and Text in Graeco-Roman Antiquity* (Cambridge, 2009), pp. 300–56, provides an interesting discussion of Polyphemus imagery in Hellenistic and Roman art.

47 On the question of what time period Homeric epic on the whole reflects, see Chapter 6.

V. THE HOMERIC QUESTION

1 J.A. Davison, 'The Homeric Question', in A.J.B. Wace and F.H. Stubbings (eds), *A Companion to Homer* (London, 1962), pp. 234–65, is still an informative overview of the 'Homeric Question'. For a recent, thoughtful essay on the subject, see R.L. Fowler, 'The Homeric Question', in R.L. Fowler (ed.), *The Cambridge Companion to Homer* (Cambridge, 2004), pp. 220–34.

2 *Chorizontes* ('separators') is the term for Alexandrian scholars who itemized differences between the two epics, countering the single-author position of such prominent figures as Aristotle and Aristarchus.

3 On *Iliad* 10, see C. Dué and M. Ebbott, Iliad *10 and the Poetics of Ambush* (Washington, DC, 2010). Already on an early-sixth-century cup Dolon, a key character in Book 10, is shown with other Trojan War characters, if distinctly separated.

4 A survey of such depictions of Homer as illiterate is provided at A. Parry (ed.), *The Making of Homeric Verse* (Oxford, 1971), pp. ix–lxii. Celebration of Hebrew culture in contrast to Greek culture is the context of the polemic by Josephus.

5 J. DeJean, *Ancients against Moderns: Culture Wars and the Making of a Fin de Siècle* (Chicago, 1997), engagingly compares the *querelle des Anciens et des Modernes* to

modern American culture wars. Controversy over Homer preceded the *querelle*; R. Sowerby, 'Early humanist failure with Homer (I)', *International Journal of the Classical Tradition* iv/1 (1997–8), pp. 37–63, thoroughly demonstrates how ignorance of Homer in the Middle Ages was followed by widespread ambivalence towards Homer by early humanists.

6   On the Ossian controversy and its relevance to Homeric studies, see C. Dué, 'The invention of Ossian', *Classics@* iii (2006), The Center for Hellenic Studies of Harvard University, <http://chs.harvard.edu/wa/pageR?tn=ArticleWrapper&bdc=12&mn=1334> (accessed 4 April 2014).

7   For a defence of the *Odyssey*'s ending, employing a close lexical analysis, see H. Erbse, 'The ending of the *Odyssey*: Linguistic problems', in G.M. Wright and P.V. Jones (eds), *Homer: German Scholarship in Translation* (Oxford, 1997), pp. 263–320. It can also be pointed out that possible retribution for the slaughter of the suitors, an issue that emerges in *Odyssey* 24, is referenced early and often in the poem (see 1.376–80, 2.141–5; 20.40–2, 23.117–40). *Iliad* 10 is portrayed by Dué and Ebbott, Iliad *10*, as integral to the *Iliad* as well as generally harmonious with early epic and myth.

8   A. Parry (ed.), *The Making of Homeric Verse* (Oxford, 1971) is a collection of the works of Milman Parry by his son.

9   For Milman Parry on Ruskin, see ibid., p. 125.

10   A seminal revisionist study of the formula is J.B. Hainsworth, *The Flexibility of the Homeric Formula* (Oxford, 1968); for an overview, see M.W. Edwards, 'Homer and oral tradition: The formula, Part I', *Oral Tradition* i/2 (1986), pp. 171–230; 'Homer and oral tradition: The formula, Part II', *Oral Tradition* iii/1–2 (1988), pp. 11–60. E.J. Bakker, *Poetry in Speech: Orality and Homeric Discourse* (Ithaca, NY, 1997), innovatively discusses the formula and orality by recourse to linguistic-discourse theory. Others polemically challenge the Parryist conception of the formula; see: D. Shive, *Naming Achilles* (Oxford, 1987); R. Friedrich, *Formular Economy in Homer: The Poetics of the Breaches* (Stuttgart, 2007).

11   The seminal study of type scenes in Homer is W. Arend, *Die typischen Scenen bei Homer* (Berlin, 1933). See also B. Fenik, *Typical Battle Scenes in the* Iliad (Wiesbaden, 1968) and S. Reece, *The Stranger's Welcome: Oral Theory and the Aesthetics of the Homeric Hospitality Scene* (Ann Arbor, 1993), with M.W. Edwards, 'Homer and oral tradition: The type-scene', *Oral Tradition* vii/2 (1992), pp. 284–330.

12   The most prominent modern argument for faithful transmission of the Homeric epics by memory is G.S. Kirk, *The Songs of Homer* (Cambridge, 1962). Cf. the views of Robert Wood, discussed above.

13   A.B. Lord, *The Singer of Tales* (Cambridge, MA, 1960); this view is advocated, for example, at R. Janko, 'The Homeric poems as oral dictated texts', *Classical Quarterly* xlviii/1 (1998), pp. 135–67. See S. Reece, 'Homer's *Iliad* and *Odyssey*: From oral performance to written text', in M.C. Amodio (ed.), *New Directions in Oral Theory* (Tempe, AZ, 2005), pp. 43–89; after a thoughtful survey of theories of Homeric transmission, Reece ultimately supports the dictation theory on the basis of linguistic and manuscript evidence. An unlikely variation on this hypothesis is the notion that the invention of the Greek alphabet was motivated by a need to record the Homeric epics; see: H.T. Wade-Gery, *The Poet of the* Iliad (Cambridge, 1952); revisited by B.B. Powell, *Homer and the Origin of the Greek Alphabet* (Cambridge, 1991).

14   G. Nagy's *Poetry as Performance* (Cambridge, 1996) is a convenient statement of

the evolutionary theory, argued extensively in many other publications. More recent argumentation of Nagy is discussed below.

15 For Neoanalyst method, see: J.T. Kakridis, *Homeric Researches* (Lund, 1949); W. Schadewaldt, *Von Homers Welt und Werk* (Stuttgart, 1959); W. Kullmann, *Die Quellen der* Ilias (Wiesbaden, 1960) (the last one of the greatest works of Homeric scholarship).

16 Kakridis, *Homeric Researches*, pp. 65–75; see further J. Burgess, *The Death and Afterlife of Achilles* (Baltimore, 2009), pp. 83–5; 'Intertextuality without text in early Greek epic', in Ø. Andersen and D.T.T. Haug (eds), *Relative Chronology in Early Greek Epic Poetry* (Cambridge, 2012), pp. 171–6. Apparent irregularities in the scene are rejected as interpolations, in an Analyst manner, by M.L. West, *Studies in the Text and Transmission of the* Iliad (Munich–Leipzig, 2000), pp. 243–4. The Oralist argument of A. Kelly, 'The mourning of Thetis: "Allusion" and the future in the *Iliad*', in F. Montanari, A. Rengakos, and C. Tsagalis (eds), *Homeric Contexts: Neoanalysis and the Interpretation of Oral Poetry* (Berlin, 2012), pp. 221–68, makes the case, at length, that the scene is typological.

17 W. Kullmann, 'Oral poetry theory and neoanalysis in Homeric research', *GRBS* xxv (1984), pp. 307–23, attempts to reconcile Neoanalysis with Oralist theory, to a point. For Oralist employment of Neoanalyst method, see Burgess, *Death and Afterlife of Achilles*, with further bibliography.

18 The allusion is to an epigram on the Homeric Question by J.V. Cunningham: 'Homer was poor. His scholars live at ease, / Making as many Homers as you please, / And every Homer furnishes a book. / Though guests be parasitic on the cook / The moral is: It is the guest who dines. / I'll write a book to prove I wrote these lines.' Cf. Goethe's epigram on the Homeric Question: 'Seven cities quarrelled over which had given birth to him; now, since the "wolf" has torn him up, each can have a piece' (my translation).

19 Whatever its origin, Mark Twain records the story in his essay 'English as she is taught'.

VI. THEORY

1 For a survey of theoretical approaches to Homer, see J. Peradotto, 'Contemporary theory', in M. Finkelberg (ed.), *The Homer Encyclopedia* (Malden, MA, 2011). An introductory survey of literary theory for classicists is provided by T.A. Schmitz, *Modern Literary Theory and Ancient Texts: An Introduction* (Malden, MA, 2007).

2 For ancient allegorical and philosophical employment of Homeric poetry, see: R. Lamberton, *Homer the Theologian* (Berkeley, 1989); R. Lamberton and J. Keaney (eds), *Homer's Ancient Readers* (Princeton, 1992). For Odysseus, see S. Montiglio, *From Villain to Hero: Odysseus in Ancient Thought* (Ann Arbor, 2011). See also B. Sammons, 'History and *hyponoia*: Herodotus and early literary criticism', *Histos* vi (2012), pp. 52–66, for the Classical Age conception of *hyponoia*, 'hidden meaning', in reference to Herodotus' interpretation of Homer.

3 N. Frye, *Anatomy of Criticism* (Princeton, 1957), p. 89: 'It is not often realized that all commentary is allegorical interpretation, an attaching of ideas to the structure of poetic imagery [...] A writer is being allegorical whenever it is clear that he is saying "by this I also (*allos*) mean that".'

4   See, for example, E. Minchin, *Homer and the Resources of Memory: Some Applications of Cognitive Theory to the* Iliad *and the* Odyssey (Oxford, 2001).

5   See, for example, A. Purves, 'Falling into time in Homer's *Iliad*', *Classical Antiquity* xxv (2006), pp. 179–209; 'Homer and the art of overtaking', *American Journal of Philology* cxxxii (2011), pp. 523–51.

6   The primitivist approach of B. Snell, *The Discovery of the Mind*, trans. T.G. Rosenmeyer (Cambridge, MA, 1953), which doubted there was psychological unity in Homeric characters, has also been abandoned (though exploration of Homeric conceptions of mind, body and soul continue; see, for example: J. Bremer, *The Early Greek Concept of the Soul* [Princeton, 1987]; H. Pellicia, *Mind, Body, and Speech in Homer and Pindar* [Göttingen, 1995]). Note that the Greek word for 'soul' (or just 'breath') is *psyche*, the key root for our word 'psychology'.

7   J. Shay, *Achilles in Vietnam: Combat Trauma and the Undoing of Character* (New York, 1994) and *Odysseus in America: Combat Trauma and the Trials of Homecoming* (New York, 2002). Shay employs the *Iliad* and *Odyssey* respectively during discussions of post-traumatic stress disorder.

8   G. Devereux, 'Penelope's character', *Psychoanalytic Quarterly* xxvi (1957), pp. 378–86, is a seminal publication on the subconscious of Penelope.

9   For Polydamas and Hector, see M. Clark, 'Poulydamas and Hektor', *College Literature* xxxiv/2 (2007), pp. 84–106.

10 On the psychology of Achilles, see: W.T. MacCary, *Childlike Achilles* (New York, 1982); R.K. Holway, *Becoming Achilles* (Lanham, MD, 2012).

11 The structuralist analysis of Theban myth can be found in C. Lévi-Strauss, *Structural Anthropology*, trans. Claire Jacobson and Brooke Grundfest Schoepf (New York, 1963), pp. 206–31.

12 See P. Vidal-Naquet, 'Land and sacrifice in the *Odyssey*: A study of religious and mythical meaning', in S. Schein (ed.), *Reading the Odyssey* (Princeton, 1995), pp. 33–54.

13 For Wood, Ossian and Parry, see Chapter 5; for the Cambridge school of ritual theory, see R. Ackerman, *The Myth and Ritual School: J.G. Frazer and the Cambridge Ritualists* (New York, 1991).

14 Cf. the arguments of E.F. Cook's *The* Odyssey *in Athens* (Ithaca, NY, 2005) for a sixth-century Athenian context for the ultimate form of the *Odyssey*, and D.F. Elmer's *The Poetics of Consent: Collective Decision Making and the* Iliad (Baltimore, 2013), which links resolution of Iliadic conflict not to historical context but to the pan-Hellenic reception of its long-term performance.

15 For the socio-economic aspects of Homeric epic, see: S. von Reden, *Exchange in Ancient Greece* (London, 1995); D.W. Tandy, *Warriors into Traders* (Berkeley, 1997).

16 On late-eighth-century aristocratic identification with Homeric heroes, see: I. Morris, 'The use and abuse of Homer', *Classical Antiquity* v (1986), pp. 81–138; J.P. Crielaard, 'Past or present? Epic poetry, aristocratic self-representation and the concept of time in the eighth and seventh centuries BC', in F. Montari and P. Ascheri (eds), *Omero tremila anni dopo* (Rome, 2002), 239–95.

17 See also R. Rosen, *Making Mockery* (Oxford, 2007), which in chapters on Thersites and the Polyphemus episode suggests there is an ambiguous iambic strain within Homeric epic.

18 J. Marks, 'The ongoing *neikos*: Thersites, Odysseus and Achilleus', *American Journal of Philology* cxxvi/1 (2005), pp. 1–31, explores the class and mythological contexts of Thersites.

19 A.M. Bowie, *Homer:* Odyssey *Books XIII–XIV* (Cambridge, 2014), pp. 16–32, argues that the Homeric poem's interest in lower-class characters is innovative.

20 See P. Rose, *Sons of the Gods, Children of Earth: Ideology and Literary Form in Ancient Greece*, (Ithaca, NY, 1992). P. Rose's *Class in Archaic Greece* (Cambridge, 2012) is a more recent discussion of social class in the Archaic Age, including in Homer.

21 See W.G. Thalmann, *The Swineherd and the Bow: Representations of Class in the* Odyssey (Ithaca, NY, 1998).

22 Although ecocriticism has made some inroads into classical studies, it is rare in Homeric studies. My comments are indebted to E. Schultz, 'Odysseus comes to know his place: Reading the *Odyssey* ecocritically', *Neohelicon* xxxvi (2009), pp. 299–310. A convincing case for the cultural symbolism of freshwater and saltwater in the *Iliad* is J. Fenno, '"A great wave against the stream": Water imagery in Iliadic battle scenes', *American Journal of Philology* cxxvi (2005), pp. 475–504. M.G. Hopman, *Scylla: Myth, Metaphor, Paradox* (Cambridge, 2013), discusses Scylla and Charybdis as personifications of natural phenomena. For the environment and antiquity, see: R. Sallares, *The Ecology of the Ancient Greek World* (Cornell, NY, 1991); D. Hughes, *Pan's Travail: Environmental Problems of the Ancient Greeks and Romans* (Baltimore, 1994); P. Horden and N. Purcell, *The Corrupting Sea* (Oxford, 2000).

23 For Homeric geography, see: F.H. Stubbings and H. Thomas, 'Lands and peoples in Homer', in A.J.B. Wace and F.H. Stubbings (eds), *A Companion to Homer* (London, 1962), pp. 283–310; M.W. Dickie, 'The geography of Homer's world', in O. Anderson and M. Dickie (eds), *Homer's World: Fiction, Tradition, Reality* (Bergen, 1995), pp. 29–56. For a wide-ranging survey of geographical and spatial aspects of Homer, see C. Bocchetti, 'Cultural geography in Homer', *Eras* v (2003), <http://www.arts.monash.edu.au/publications/eras/edition-5/bocchettiarticle.php> (accessed 4 April 2014).

24 For the spatiality of the *Iliad*, see E. Minchin, 'Spatial memory and the composition of the *Iliad*', in E.A. Mackay (ed.), *Orality, Literacy, Memory in the Ancient Greek and Roman World* (Leiden, 2008), pp. 9–34; J.S. Clay, *Homer's Trojan Theater: Space, Vision, and Memory in the* Iliad (Cambridge, 2011); C. Tsagalis, *From Listeners to Viewers: Space in the* Iliad (Washington, DC, 2012); A. Purves, *Space and Time in Ancient Greek Narrative* (Cambridge, 2010), Chapter 1.

25 See A. Edwards, 'Homer's ethical geography: Country and city in the *Odyssey*', *Transactions of the American Philological Association* cxxiii (1993), pp. 27–78.

26 For spatial patterning of the wanderings, see: A. Ballabriga, *Les Fictions d'Homère. L'Invention mythologique et cosmographique dans l'Odyssée* (Paris, 1998); J. Burgess, 'Gilgamesh and Odysseus in the Otherworld', *Echos du Monde Classique/Classical Views* xviii (1999), pp. 171–210; G. Cursaro, 'Entre l'est et l'ouest, à midi: Structures spatio-temporelles de l'île de Circé', *Les Études classiques* lxxvi/1 (2008), pp. 39–64; D. Nakassis, 'Gemination at the horizons: East and West in the mythical geography of archaic Greek epic', *Transactions of the American Philological Association* cxxxiv (2004), pp. 215–33. For the structure of the wanderings, see E.F. Cook, *The* Odyssey *in Athens* (Ithaca, NY, 1995).

27 Aimé Césaire's 1969 version of *The Tempest*, a key target of post-colonial theory, evokes the *Odyssey* (see J. McConnell, *Black Odysseys* [Oxford, 2013], pp. 11, 29). On post-colonial creative and critical takes on *The Tempest*, see P. Hulme and W.H. Sherman (eds), *The Tempest and Its Travels* (London, 2000). See T.W. Adorno and M. Horkheimer, *Dialectic of Enlightenment*, trans. E. Jephcott (Redwood City, CA, 2002 [orig. 1947]), p. 39, for an early identification of Odysseus' colonialist attitude. More

recently, M. Torgovnick's *Gone Primitive* (Chicago, 1991) compares Odysseus to Stanley in Africa. In classical studies C. Dougherty's *The Raft of Odysseus: The Ethnographic Imagination of Homer's* Odyssey (Oxford, 2001) and now McConnell's *Black Odysseys* are post-colonial examinations of the *Odyssey* and its reception, respectively.

28 See also J. Burgess, '"If peopled and cultured": Bartram's travels and the *Odyssey*', in G.R. Ricci, *Travel, Discovery, Transformation* (New Brunswick, NJ, 2014), pp. 19–44, with a focus on Odysseus' description of 'Goat Island', and further post-colonial bibliography.

29 For a well-theorized survey of Homeric portrayal of women, see especially C. Franco, 'Women in Homer', in S.L. James and S. Dillon (eds), *A Companion to Women in the Ancient World* (Malden, MA, 2012), pp. 54–65.

30 On Penelope's *agnoia* ('ignorance'), see S. Murnaghan, 'Penelope's *agnoia*: Knowledge, power, and gender in the *Odyssey*', in L.E. Doherty (ed.), *Homer's* Odyssey (Oxford, 2009), pp. 231–46.

31 On Penelope's potential 'recognition' of Odysseus, see N. Yamagata, 'Penelope and early recognition: Vlahos, Harsh, and Eustathius', *College Literature* xxxviii/2 (2011), pp. 122–30, with the bibliography cited there.

32 For further examples of post-structuralist Homeric interpretation, see: M. Lynn-George, *Epos: Word, Narrative and the* Iliad (Atlantic Highlands, NJ, 1988); S. Goldhill, *The Poet's Voice* (Cambridge, 1990), Chapter 1; M. Buchan, *The Limits of Heroism: Homer and the Ethics of Reading* (Ann Arbor, 2004); J. Burgess, 'Framing Odysseus: The death of the suitors', in M. Christopoulos (ed.), *Crime and Punishment in Homeric and Archaic Epic* (forthcoming).

33 T. Eagleton's *After Theory* (London, 2003) is nuanced (and unrelentingly aphoristic); in general, see: R. Selden, P. Widdowson and P. Brooker, *A Reader's Guide to Contemporary Literary Theory*, 5th ed. (Harlow, 2005), Conclusion; P. Barry, *Beginning Theory* (Manchester, 2009), Chapter 15.

34 To paraphrase the well-known aphorism at T. Eagleton, *Literary Theory: An Introduction* (Oxford, 1983), p. xiv.

35 Readers of *Iliad* 6 in Greek will benefit from the recent and excellent commentary provided by B. Graziosi and J. Haubold, *Homer:* Iliad *Book VI* (Cambridge, 2010); its introductory essays will interest all readers of Book 6. A classic Unitarian analysis can be found at W. Schadewaldt, 'Hector and Andromache', in G.M. Wright and P.V. Jones (eds), *Homer: German Scholarship in Translation* (Oxford, 1997), pp. 124–42.

36 For the erosion of humanity by war in the *Iliad*, cf. J.M. Redfield, *Nature and Culture in the* Iliad: *The Tragedy of Hector* (Chicago, 1975); C. Segal, *The Theme of Mutilation of the Corpse in the* Iliad (Leiden, 1971); J.P. Holoka, *Simone Weil's the* Iliad *or the Poem of Force: A Critical Edition* (New York, 2003).

37 On the role of gender in *Iliad* 6, see M.A. Katz, 'The divided world of *Iliad* VI', *Women's Studies* viii/1–2 (1981), pp. 21–46.

38 On the 'Nobody/Myself' ruse, cf. J. Glenn, 'The Polyphemus folktale and Homer's *Kyklôpeia*', *Transactions of the American Philological Association* cii (1971), pp. 133–81; W. Hansen, *Ariadne's Thread: A Guide to International Tales Found in Classical Literature* (Ithaca, NY, 2002), pp. 289–301. The 'magic ring' motif found in the ogre-blinding tale type does not appear in the Homeric episode.

39 For comparison of the Homeric Cyclopes to traditional portrayals, see R. Mondi, 'The Homeric Cyclopes: Folktale, tradition, and theme', *Transactions of the American Philological Association* cxiii (1983), pp. 17–38.

40   The *pithos* depicting Medusa is located in the Louvre (CA 795).
41   Porphyry, *On the Cave of the Nymphs* 79. For a discussion, see Lamberton, *Homer the Theologian*, pp. 130–1.
42   On an infantile Odysseus in the womb of the Cyclops cave, see N. Austin, 'Odysseus and the Cyclops: Who is who?', in C.A. Rubino and C.W. Shelmerdine (eds), *Approaches to Homer* (Austin, TX, 1983), pp. 3–37.
43   For employment of the post-structuralist psychoanalyst theory of Jacques Lacan on the Polyphemus episode, see Buchan, *Limits of Heroism*, pp. 18–35; further Lacanian explication of the *Odyssey* occurs elsewhere in this book.
44   For a structuralist interpretation of the episode, see: G.S. Kirk, *Myth: Its Meaning and Function* (Berkeley, 1970), pp. 162 ff.; Vidal-Naquet, 'Land and sacrifice'.
45   On the essential differences between the land of the Cyclopes and 'Goat Island', see C.S. Byre, 'The rhetoric of description in *Odyssey* 9.116–41: Odysseus and Goat Island', *The Classical Journal* lxxxix/4 (1994), pp. 357–67.
46   For the wanderings functioning as a survey of non-Greek 'otherness', see F. Hartog, *Memories of Odysseus*, trans. J. Lloyd (Chicago, 2001), Chapter 1.
47   On the guest-gift theme in the Polyphemus episode, see A. Podlecki, 'Guest-gifts and nobodies in *Odyssey* 9', *Phoenix* xv (1961), pp. 125–33.
48   See K.S. Calhoon, 'Charming the carnivore: Bruce Chatwin's Australian odyssey', in J. Zilcosky (ed.), *Writing Travel* (Toronto, 2008), pp. 179, 185–6; the author discusses the 'sacrifice' of companions by Odysseus.
49   For ancient and modern localization of wanderings of Odysseus, see *In the Wake of Odysseus*, <http://homes.chass.utoronto.ca/~jburgess/rop/od.voyage.html> (accessed 4 April 2014).
50   On the post-colonial treatment of Greek colonization, see: I. Malkin, 'Postcolonial concepts and ancient Greek colonization', *Modern Language Quarterly* lxv/3 (2004), pp. 341–64; F. de Angelis, 'Colonies and colonization', in G. Boys-Stones, B. Graziosi and P. Vasunia (eds), *The Oxford Handbook of Hellenic Studies* (Oxford, 2009), pp. 48–64. It would, of course, be anachronistic to equate Greek colonization (the term preferred by classicists) with the colonialism and imperialism of the modern period.

VII. RECEPTION

1   Entries in M. Finkelberg (ed.), *The Homer Encyclopedia*, 3 vols (Malden, MA, 2011) comprehensively survey reception in all time periods. R.L. Fowler (ed.), *The Cambridge Companion to Homer* (Cambridge, 2004) is the Homeric 'companion' most dedicated to reception. Particularly informative on the reception of Trojan War myth, including the *Iliad*, is J. Solomon,'The vacillations of the Trojan myth: Popularization & classicization, variation & codification', *International Journal of the Classical Tradition* xiv/3–4 (2007), pp. 482–534. For a classic study of Odysseus, see W. Stanford, *The Ulysses Theme* (Oxford, 1954). For a more modern approach to *Odyssey* reception, see: E. Hall, *The Return of Ulysses: A Cultural History of Homer's* Odyssey (Baltimore, 2008); P. Boitani, *The Shadow of Ulysses*, trans. A. Weston (Oxford, 1994).
2   For a translation of essays on audience-reception theory, including the 'horizon of expectations', see H.R. Jauss, *The Shadow of Ulysses*, trans. A. Weston (Oxford, 1994).

3   See T. Morgan, *Literate Education in the Hellenistic and Roman Worlds* (Cambridge, 1998), pp. 105–6, 111–12. On the nature of Homeric papyri, see also R. Cribiore, *Gymnastics of the Mind: Greek Education in Hellenistic and Roman Egypt* (Princeton, 2001), pp. 193–6. Although Homeric papyri are quantitatively the greatest, the *Odyssey* is much less popular than its sister epic, and in both educational and literary papyri the later books of both epics are notably neglected.

4   Though many places claimed Homer, Chios was often associated with the poet in legend. On the variety of the fluid ancient biographical tradition, see B. Graziosi, *Inventing Homer: The Early Reception of Epic* (Cambridge, 2002).

5   Athenaeus *The Sophists at Dinner*, 8.347e; 'crumbs' is often given in translation. Athenaeus also claims that Sophocles composed his dramas from the material of the Epic Cycle (277c). Karakantza references these remarks in sensibly arguing that Sophocles is both Cyclic and Homeric in nature; see E. Karakantza, 'Eating from the tables of others: Sophocles' *Ajax* and the Greek Epic Cycle', *Classics@* vi (2010), The Center for Hellenic Studies of Harvard University, <http://chs.harvard.edu/wa/pageR?tn=ArticleWrapper&bdc=12 &mn=3228> (accessed 4 April 2014).

6   Below, the correspondence between a scene in the *Ajax* by Sophocles and the encounter between Hector and Andromache is noted. For the potential Homeric aspects of the *Philoctetes* by Sophocles, see S.L. Schein, *Sophocles: Philoctetes* (Cambridge, 2013), pp. 15–18. The intertextuality is complex, depending heavily on subjective analysis. Philoctetes at once can seem like Achilles in his independence, like Odysseus in his lonely exile on an island, and like Polyphemus in his habitation amid nature in a cave. See M. Robinson, 'Ways of hearing in Sophokles: Auditory spaces and social dynamics in the *Elektra*, *Philoktetes*, *Trachiniai*, and *Oidipous Tyrannos*', Ph.D. dissertation (University of Toronto, 2013), p. 67, n. 63; Robinson notes that both Philoctetes and Polyphemus think of animals as constituting their social community.

7   For Homer envisioned as a flowing source (ocean, mother's milk, vomit, etc.), see, for example, Longinus *On the Sublime*, 9.13; Heraclitus *Homeric Problems*, 76; Aelian *Various Histories*, 13.22.

8   M. Squire's *The Iliad in a Nutshell: Visualizing Epic on the* Tabulae Iliacae (Oxford, 2011) explores Hellenistic and Roman material culture as a context for the Iliac Tables, albeit with little interest in their primary motivation, the Epic Cycle.

9   On 'anti-Homeric' trends in literature of the Roman Empire, with comparison to earlier treatment of Homer in early Greek history, see L. Kim, *Homer between History and Fiction in Imperial Greek Literature* (Cambridge, 2010).

10 For translation, see R.M. Frazer, *The Trojan War: The Chronicles of Dictys of Crete and Dares the Phrygian* (Bloomington, IN, 1966). For discussion, see: S. Merkle, 'The truth and nothing but the truth', in G.L. Schmeling (ed.), *The Novel in the Ancient World* (Leiden, 1996), pp. 563–80; P. Gainsford, 'Diktys of Crete', *Classical Journal* lviii (2012), pp. 58–87.

11 For a well-theorized exploration of the Epic Cycle poems as Homeric sequels, see: I. Holmberg, 'The creation of the ancient Epic Cycle', *Oral Tradition* xiii/2 (1998), pp. 456–78; 'Homer and the beginning of the sequel', in P. Budra and B. Schellenberg (eds), *Part Two: Reflections on the Sequel* (Toronto, 1998), pp. 19–33. On the nature of traditional cycles, see J.M. Foley, 'Epic cycles and epic traditions', in J.N. Kazazis and A. Rengakos (eds), *Euphrosyne* (Stuttgart, 1999), pp. 99–108.

12 'Homer now seems so obviously essential to whatever we mean by the classical tradition

that it is difficult to grasp that in Western Europe for almost a thousand years the great epic poems that bear his name were not part of anyone's account of the most significant relics of antiquity.' S. Greenblatt and J.L. Koerner, 'Glories of classicism', *New York Review of Books* lx/3 (2013).

13 On the imperial subtext of Tennyson's poem, see M. McKinsey, *Hellenism and the Postcolonial Imagination: Yeats, Cavafy, Walcott* (Cranbury, NJ, 2010).

14 The translation employed is from E. Keeley and P. Sherrard (trans.), *C.P. Cavafy: Collected Poems*, ed. G. Savidis (Princeton, 1992).

15 On the cycles of Pastan and Glück, see S. Murnaghan and D.H. Roberts, 'Penelope's song: The lyric odysseys of Linda Pastan and Louise Glück', *Classical and Modern Literature* xxii (2002), pp. 1–33.

16 On the Homeric nature of *Ulysses*, see: Boitani, *Shadow of Ulysses*, pp. 144–8; L. Culligan-Flack, '1922's "UnUlyssean" Ulysses: Modernist visions and revisions of the Homeric *nostos*', in H. Gardner and S. Murnaghan (eds), *Odyssean Identities in Modern Cultures: The Journey Home* (Athens, OH, 2014), pp. 133–52, with bibliography. For the Nausicaa scene in *Ulysses*, see S. Minta, 'Homer and Joyce: The case of Nausicaa', in B. Graziosi and E. Greenwood (eds), *Homer in the Twentieth Century* (Oxford, 2007), pp. 92–119.

17 On the Odyssean nature of Hugh MacLennan's oeuvre, see G. Woodcock, *Odysseus Ever Returning* (Toronto, 1970), pp. 12–23. Transformative reception of the *Odyssey* in Canadian novels continues: Theresa Kishkan's *A Man in a Distant Field* (2004) features a grieving Irishman who moves to the coast of British Columbia, and then eventually back home, while obsessed with translating the *Odyssey*; in Wayne Johnston's *The Son of a Certain Woman* (2013), set in St John's, Newfoundland, the protagonist is the son of a missing father named Jim Joyce and a mother named Penelope, whose voluptuousness attracts all, including her son.

18 For *Cold Mountain* and the *Odyssey*, see 'Ambiguous homecomings: *Cold Mountain* and the *Odyssey*', in H. Gardner and S. Murnaghan (eds), *Odyssean Identities in Modern Cultures: The Journey Home* (Athens, OH, 2014), pp. 173–91.

19 For Odyssean elements in Sebald's *The Emigrants*, see A. Purves, 'Sleeping outside in Homer's *Odyssey* and W. G. Sebald's *The Emigrants*', in H. Gardner and S. Murnaghan (eds), *Odyssean Identities in Modern Cultures: The Journey Home* (Athens, OH, 2014), pp. 213–39.

20 For the relationship between Achilles and Patroclus in antiquity, see M. Fantuzzi, *Achilles in Love* (Oxford, 2012), Chapter 4.

21 For Homer in cinema, see J. Paul, *Film and the Classical Epic Tradition* (Oxford, 2013), Chapter 2.

22 M.M. Winkler's *Troy: From Homer's* Iliad *to Hollywood Epic* (Malden, MA, 2007) contains chapters on various aspects of the film, but see also J. Burgess, 'Achilles' heel: The historicism of *Troy* the movie', in K. Myrsiades (ed.), *Reading Homer: Film and Text* (Madison, NJ, 2009), pp. 163–85.

23 On the Coen brothers' Odyssean film, cf. J. Siegel, 'The Coens' O Brother, Where Art Thou? and Homer's *Odyssey*', *Mouseion* vii (2007), pp. 213–45; S. Goldhill, '*Naked* and *O Brother, Where Art Thou*? The politics and poetics of epic cinema', in B. Graziosi and E. Greenwood (eds), *Homer in the Twentieth Century* (Oxford, 2007), pp. 245–67.

24 For a concise survey of Homeric reception in modern art, see C. Dué, 'Homer's post-classical legacy', in J.M. Foley (ed.), *A Companion to Ancient Epic* (Oxford, 2005), pp. 397–414.

25 Goldhill's 'Naked and O Brother, Where Art Thou?' engagingly explores Naked's potential correspondences to the Odyssey; the discussion of reception is all the more informative because it includes the very different case of O Brother, Where Art Thou?

26 An equally profound film by the same Inuit studio, Before Tomorrow (2008), also encompasses Odyssean motifs: in the nineteenth century an old Inuit woman and her son wait out a long winter alone on an island, only to find their home village completely wiped out by European disease upon return.

27 The remark is attributed by Margaret Atwood to an unnamed BBC reviewer in 'Atanarjuat: The Fast Runner, a film by Zacharias Kunuk', a review reprinted at M. Atwood, Writing with Intent: Essays, Reviews, Personal Prose, 1983–2005 (New York, 2005), pp. 220–3. Atwood allows that the story's background in oral tradition evokes Homer, but suggests the content is more reminiscent of the saga of the House of Atreus.

28 For the historical sources and context of the Martin Guerre story, see N.Z. Davis, The Return of Martin Guerre (Cambridge, 1983). Davis was a consultant for the French film of the same name (1982) starring Gérard Depardieu.

29 On the Odyssean nature of Sommersby's fictional transformation of the Martin Guerre story, see: R.J. Rabel, 'Impersonation and identity: Sommersby, The Return of Martin Guerre, and the Odyssey', International Journal of the Classical Tradition ix/3 (2003), pp. 391–406; J. McConnell, Black Odysseys (Oxford, 2013), pp. 155–80.

30 See B. Graziosi and J. Haubold, Homer: Iliad Book VI (Cambridge, 2010), pp. 47–56.

31 On the 'anti-colonialist' nature of Lucian's dialogue, see McConnell, Black Odysseys, p. 8.

32 For a discussion of 'Al-Sindibad' and Polyphemus, which concludes it is probably independent of Homer, see J.E. Montgomery, 'Al-Sindibad and Polyphemus', in A. Neuwirth et al. (eds), Myths, Historical Archetypes and Symbolic Figures in Arabic Literature (Stuttgart, 1999), pp. 437–66.

33 On the reception of the Odyssey by The Tempest and The Adventures of Huckleberry Finn, look for the future appearance of publications by the author.

34 On the significance of the Kubrick movie, cf. (with caution): L.F. Wheat, Kubrick's 2001: A Triple Allegory (Lanham, MD, 2000); P. Kuberski, 'Kubrick's Odyssey: Myth, technology, gnosis', Arizona Quarterly lxiv/3 (2008), pp. 51–73. Clarke's 1948 short story 'The Sentinel' is the germ of the screenplay co-written with Kubrick.

35 See: P.D. Rankine, Ulysses in Black: Ralph Ellison, Classicism, and African American Literature (Madison, WI, 2006); McConnell, Black Odysseys, pp. 71–105, with further bibliography cited there. As an African-American, Ellison received criticism for portraying Polyphemus negatively, despite post-colonial interest in Polyphemus as a victim (see Chapter 6 and below).

36 For an illuminating survey of the varying portrayals of Polyphemus as a tyrant and victim, see Hall, Return of Ulysses, pp. 89–100.

37 P.H. Young, The Printed Homer (Jefferson, NC, 2003) comprehensively reports on translations as well as critical editions of the Homeric epics. A concise online listing of translators can be found at <https://records.viu.ca/~johnstoi/homer/homertranslations. htm> (accessed 4 April 2014). The compiler is a Homeric translator himself; his and several other translations are now readily available on the internet for free. G. Steiner (ed.), Homer in English (London, 1996) provides selections from a wide range of translations with concise introductions.

38 The essay on Odyssey translations can be found in J.L. Borges, Selected Non-Fictions, ed. E. Weinberger, trans. E. Allen, S.J. Levine and E. Weinberger (New York, 1999).

Borges made use of Homer in his fiction as well: for example, 'The Immortal' from *The Aleph* (1949; printed in J.L. Borges, *Selected Fictions*, trans. A. Hurley [New York, 1999]) subtly interweaves Homeric poetry, the Homeric Question and the persona of 'Homer'.

39   To be fair to the metre, R. Merrill has produced skilled translations of the *Iliad* (2007) and *Odyssey* (2002).

40   From A. Nicoll (ed.), *Chapman's Homer. The Iliad* (Princeton, 1956).

41   Recent hexameter-like translators of Homer include Edward McCrorie (*Odyssey*, 2004; *Iliad*, 2012). S. Lombardo (*Iliad*, 1997; *Odyssey*, 2000) employs metreless verse that is notably plain and vernacular. The prolific translator of world literature Stephen Mitchell (*Iliad*, 2011; *Odyssey*, 2013) employs a pentameter that avoids iambs. A curiosity of his translation of the *Iliad* is that it omits lines that M.L. West deems suspicious (but does not necessarily omit); so Book 10 is absent! A similarly Analyst approach is taken with the *Odyssey*, although long-deleted passages from the two underworld scenes (Books 11 and 24) reappear in appendices.

42   *Odyssey*: 1946, revised by his son D.C.H. Rieu in 1991; *Iliad*: 1950; revised by his son and P. Jones in 2003.

43   See E. Greenwood, 'Logue's tele-vision: Reading Homer from a distance', in B. Graziosi and E. Greenwood (eds), *Homer in the Twentieth Century* (Oxford, 2007), pp. 145–76. Notably Logue creates his versions without knowledge of Greek.

44   See Graziosi, *Inventing Homer*, for the role of the biographies in ancient reception of Homer. In M.L. West's *The Making of the* Iliad (Oxford, 2011), the poet's experiential travel in Asia Minor informs his composition. In G. Nagy, *Homer the Preclassic* (Berkeley, 2010) and M.S. Jensen, *Writing Homer* (Copenhagen, 2011), the wanderings of Homer in the ancient biographical traditions are seen as symbolic of historical reception and rhapsodic practice respectively. Cf. Keats on reading Chapman's Homer: the poet notionally aligns his cultural experience with Odysseus' travels (the opening lines allude to the *Odyssey*'s opening) and Homer's world with the Pacific gazed at by an explorer of the New World.

45   R. Bittlestone, J. Diggle and J. Underhill, *Odysseus Unbound: The Search for Homer's Ithaca* (Cambridge, 2005), revisit, with much geological data, an old theory that Cephalonia, not modern Thiaki, was the Ithaca of historical antiquity. Karl Dörpfeld, the German archaeologist who assisted Schliemann at Troy, insisted that Leukas was Homeric Ithaca, a theory that died with him. We know that the Thiaki of historical antiquity was considered the island of Odysseus.

46   For ancient and modern localization of the wanderings of Odysseus, see the website 'In the Wake of Odysseus': <http://homes.chass.utoronto.ca/~jburgess/rop/od.voyage.html> (accessed 4 April 2014).

47   For the geographical reality of the ancient Troad, see J.M. Cook, *The Troad: An Archaeological and Topographical Study* (Oxford, 1973); on the location of heroic tumuli in the area, see J. Burgess, *The Death and Afterlife of Achilles* (Baltimore, 2009), pp. 111–31; Nagy, *Homer the Preclassic*, pp. 147–70.

48   J.V. Luce, *Celebrating Homer's Landscapes: Troy and Ithaca Revisited* (New Haven, CT, 1998) is a recent attempt to verify Homeric topography at Troy and Ithaca.

49   On the proto-ethnographic nature of Robert Woods's travels, see J. Sachs, 'On the road: Travel, antiquarianism, philology', in S. Gurd (ed.), *Philology and Its Histories* (Athens, OH, 2010), pp. 127–47.

50 For reactions to Butler by classicists, see M. Beard, 'Why Homer was (not) a woman: The reception of the authoress of the *Odyssey*', in J.D. Paradis (ed.), *Samuel Butler: Victorian against the Grain* (Toronto, 2007), pp. 317–42.

51 On Butler and modern feminism, see: B. Clayton, *A Penelopean Poetics* (Lanham, MD, 2004), Chapter 1; M. Ebbott, 'Butler's authoress of the *Odyssey*: Gendered readings of Homer, then and now', *Classics@* iii (2006), The Center for Hellenic Studies of Harvard University, <http://chs.harvard.edu/wa/pageR?tn=ArticleWrapper&bdc=1 2&mn=1313> (accessed 4 April 2014).

52 See: V. Bérard, *Les Phéniciens et l'Odyssée*, 2 vols (Paris, 1902–3); *Les navigations d'Ulysse*, 4 vols (Paris, 1927–9). For a publication of photographs of Bérard's localizations and a convenient summary of his views, see F. Boissonnas, *Dans le sillage d'Ulysse* (Paris, 1933).

53 See: H. Kenner, *The Pound Era* (Berkeley, 1971), pp. 41–53; (and cautiously) M. Seidel, *Epic Geography: James Joyce's* Ulysses (Princeton, 1976).

Bibliography

Ackerman, R., *The Myth and Ritual School: J.G. Frazer and the Cambridge Ritualists* (New York, 1991).

Adorno, T.W., and M. Horkheimer, *Dialectic of Enlightenment*, trans. E. Jephcott (Redwood City, CA, 2002).

Allan, W., 'Divine justice and cosmic order in early Greek epic', *Journal of Hellenic Studies* cxxvi (2006), pp. 1–35.

—— 'Performing the will of Zeus: The Διὸς Βουλή and the scope of early Greek epic', in M. Revermann and P. Wilson (eds), *Performance, Iconography, Reception* (Oxford, 2008), pp. 204–18.

Allen, S.H., *Finding the Walls of Troy: Frank Calvert and Heinrich Schliemann at Hisarlık* (Berkeley, 1999).

Allen, T.W., *Homer: The Origins and Transmission* (Oxford, 1924).

Angelis, F. de, 'Colonies and colonization', in G. Boys-Stones, B. Graziosi and P. Vasunia (eds), *The Oxford Handbook of Hellenic Studies* (Oxford, 2009), pp. 48–64.

Arend, W., *Die typischen Scenen bei Homer* (Berlin, 1933).

Atwood, M., *Writing with Intent: Essays, Reviews, Personal Prose, 1983–2005* (New York, 2005).

Austin, N., 'Odysseus and the Cyclops: Who is who?', in C.A. Rubino and C.W. Shelmerdine (eds), *Approaches to Homer* (Austin, TX, 1983), pp. 3–37.

Bakker, E.J., *Poetry in Speech: Orality and Homeric Discourse* (Ithaca, NY, 1997).

—— 'The Greek Gilgamesh, or the immortality of return', in M. Païsi-Apostolopoulou (ed.), *Eranos* (Ithaca, 2001), pp. 331–53.

—— *Pointing at the Past: From Formula to Performance in Homeric Poetics* (Washington, DC, 2005).

Ballabriga, A., *Les Fictions d'Homère. L'Invention mythologique et cosmographique dans l'Odyssée* (Paris, 1998).

Barker, E.T.E., *Entering the Agon: Dissent and Authority in Homer, Historiography, and Tragedy* (Oxford, 2009).

Barry, P., *Beginning Theory* (Manchester, 2009).

Beard, M., 'Why Homer was (not) a woman: The reception of the authoress of the *Odyssey*', in J.D. Paradis (ed.), *Samuel Butler: Victorian against the Grain* (Toronto, 2007), pp. 317–42.

Beck, D., *Speech Presentation in Homeric Epic* (Austin, TX, 2012).

Bennet, J., 'Homer and the Bronze Age', in I. Morris and B. Powell (eds), *A New Companion to Homer* (Leiden, 1997), pp. 513–36.

Bérard, V., *Les Phéniciens et l'Odyssée*, 2 vols (Paris, 1902–3).

—— *Les navigations d'Ulysse*, 4 vols (Paris, 1927–9).

Bing, P., *The Well-Read Muse* (Göttingen, 1988).

Bird, G.D., *Multitextuality in the Homeric* Iliad*: The Witness of Ptolemaic Papyri* (Cambridge, MA, 2010).

Bittlestone, R., J. Diggle and J. Underhill, *Odysseus Unbound: The Search for Homer's Ithaca* (Cambridge, 2005).

Bocchetti, C., 'Cultural geography in Homer', *Eras* v (2003), <http://www.arts.monash.edu.au/publications/eras/edition-5/bocchettiarticle.php> (accessed 4 April 2014).

Boissonnas, F., *Dans le sillage d'Ulysse* (Paris, 1933).

Boitani, P., *The Shadow of Ulysses*, trans. A. Weston (Oxford, 1994).

Borges, J.L.; *Selected Non-Fictions*, ed. E. Weinberger, trans. E. Allen, S.J. Levine and E. Weinberger (New York, 1999).

—— *Selected Fictions*, trans. A. Hurley (New York, 1999).

Bowie, A.M., *Homer:* Odyssey *Books XIII–XIV* (Cambridge, 2014).

Bremer, J., *The Early Greek Concept of the Soul* (Princeton, 1987).

Buchan, M., *The Limits of Heroism: Homer and the Ethics of Reading* (Ann Arbor, 2004).

Burgess, J., 'Achilles' heel: The death of Achilles in ancient myth', *Classical Antiquity* xiv/2 (1995), pp. 217–44.

—— 'Gilgamesh and Odysseus in the Otherworld', *Echos du Monde Classique/Classical Views* xviii (1999), pp. 171–210.

—— *The Tradition of the Trojan War in Homer and the Epic Cycle* (Baltimore, 2001).

—— 'Performance and the Epic Cycle', *The Classical Journal* c/1 (2004), pp. 1–23.

—— *The Death and Afterlife of Achilles* (Baltimore, 2009).

—— 'Achilles' heel: The historicism of *Troy* the movie', in K. Myrsiades (ed.), *Reading Homer: Film and Text* (Madison, NJ, 2009), pp. 163–85.

—— 'Intertextuality without text in early Greek epic', in Ø. Andersen and D.T.T. Haug (eds), *Relative Chronology in Early Greek Epic Poetry* (Cambridge, 2012), pp. 168–83.

—— '"If peopled and cultured": Bartram's travels and the *Odyssey*', in G.R. Ricci, *Travel, Discovery, Transformation* (New Brunswick, NJ, 2014), pp. 19–44.

—— 'Ambiguous homecomings: *Cold Mountain* and the *Odyssey*', in H. Gardner and S. Murnaghan (eds), *Odyssean Identities in Modern Cultures: The Journey Home* (Athens, OH, 2014), pp. 173–91.

—— 'Framing Odysseus: The death of the suitors', in M. Christopoulos (ed.), *Crime and Punishment in Homeric and Archaic Epic* (in press).

Burkert, W., *Structure and History in Greek Mythology and Ritual* (Berkeley, 1979).

—— 'Kynaithos, Polycrates and the Homeric hymn to Apollo', in G.W. Bowersock, W. Burkert and M.C.J. Putnam (eds), *Arktouros* (Berlin, 1979), pp. 53–62.

—— *Greek Religion: Archaic and Classical*, trans. J. Raffan (Cambridge, MA, 1985).

—— 'The making of Homer in the sixth century B.C.: Rhapsodes versus Stesichorus', in D. von Bothmer (ed.), *Papers on the Amasis Painter and His World* (Malibu, 1987), pp. 43–62.

—— *The Orientalizing Revolution: Near Eastern Influence on Greek Culture in the Early Archaic Age*, trans. M. Pinder (Cambridge, MA, 1992).

—— 'Lydia between East and West, or How to date the Trojan War: A study in Herodotus', in J.B. Carter and S.P. Morris (eds), *The Ages of Homer* (Austin, 1995), pp. 139–48.

——*Babylon, Memphis, Persepolis: Eastern Contexts of Greek Culture* (Cambridge, MA, 2004).

Butler, S. *The Authoress of the Odyssey* (London, 1987).

Byre, C.S., 'The rhetoric of description in *Odyssey* 9.116–41: Odysseus and Goat Island', *The Classical Journal* lxxxix/4 (1994), pp. 357–67.

Calhoon, K.S., 'Charming the carnivore: Bruce Chatwin's Australian odyssey', in J. Zilcosky (ed.), *Writing Travel* (Toronto, 2008), pp. 173–94.

Calvino, I., *Why Read the Classics?*, trans. M. McLaughlin (New York, 1987).

Chadwick, J., *The Decipherment of Linear B* (Cambridge, 1958).

——*The Mycenaean World* (Cambridge, 1976).

Christopoulos, M., '*Casus belli*: Causes of the Trojan War in the Epic Cycle', *Classics@* vi (2010), The Center for Hellenic Studies of Harvard University, <http://chs.harvard.edu/wa/pageR?tn=ArticleWrapper&bdc=12&mn=3367> (accessed 4 April 2014).

Clark, M., 'The concept of plot and the plot of the *Iliad*', *Phoenix* lv/1–2 (2001), pp. 1–8.

——'Formulas, metre, and type-scenes', in R. Fowler (ed.), *The Cambridge Companion to Homer* (Cambridge, 2004), pp. 117–38.

——'Poulydamas and Hektor', *College Literature* xxxiv/2 (2007), pp. 84–106.

Clay, J.S., *The Wrath of Athena* (Princeton, 1983).

——'The whip and will of Zeus', *Literary Imagination* i/1 (1999), pp. 40–60.

——*Homer's Trojan Theater: Space, Vision, and Memory in the* Iliad (Cambridge, 2011).

Clayton, B., *A Penelopean Poetics* (Lanham, MD, 2004).

Cook, E.F., *The Odyssey in Athens* (Ithaca, NY, 1995).

Cook, J.M., *The Troad: An Archaeological and Topographical Study* (Oxford, 1973).

Cribiore, R., *Gymnastics of the Mind: Greek Education in Hellenistic and Roman Egypt* (Princeton, 2001).

Crielaard, J.P., 'Homer, history and archaeology: Some remarks on the date of the Homeric world', in J.P. Crielaard (ed.), *Homeric Questions* (Amsterdam, 1995), pp. 201–88.

——'Past or present? Epic poetry, aristocratic self-representation and the concept of time in the eighth and seventh centuries BC', in F. Montari and P. Ascheri (eds), *Omero tremila anni dopo* (Rome, 2002), 239–95.

Culligan-Flack, L., '1922's "UnUlyssean" Ulysses: Modernist visions and revisions of the Homeric *nostos*', in H. Gardner and S. Murnaghan (eds), *Odyssean Identities in Modern Cultures: The Journey Home* (Athens, OH, 2014), pp. 133–52.

Currie, B., 'The *Iliad, Gilgamesh*, and neoanalysis', in F. Montanari, A. Rengakos and C. Tsagalis (eds), *Homeric Contexts* (Berlin, 2012), pp. 543–80.

Cursaru, G., 'Entre l'est et l'ouest, à midi: Structures spatio-temporelles de l'île de Circé', *Les Etudes classiques* lxxvi/1 (2008), pp. 39–64.

Davies, M., 'The Judgment of Paris and *Iliad* Book XXIV', *Journal of Hellenic Studies* ci (1981), pp. 56–62.

——*The Greek Epic Cycle* (Bristol, 1989).

Davis, N.Z., *The Return of Martin Guerre* (Cambridge, 1983).

Davison, J.A., 'Pisistratus and Homer', *Transactions of the American Philological Association* lxxxvi (1955), pp. 1–21.

——'The transmission of the text', in A.J.B. Wace and F.H. Stubbings (eds), *A Companion to Homer* (London, 1962), pp. 215–33.

——'The Homeric Question', in A.J.B. Wace and F.H. Stubbings (eds), *A Companion to Homer* (London, 1962), pp. 234–65.

Debiasi, A., *L'epica perduta. Eumelo, il Ciclo, l'occidente* (Rome, 2005).

—— 'Homer αγωνιστής in Chalcis', in F. Montanari, A. Rengakos and C. Tsagalis (eds), *Homeric Contexts: Neoanalysis and the Interpretation of Oral Poetry* (Berlin, 2012), pp. 471–500.

DeJean, J., *Ancients against Moderns: Culture Wars and the Making of a Fin de Siècle* (Chicago, 1997).

Devereux, G., 'Penelope's character', *Psychoanalytic Quarterly* xxvi (1957), pp. 378–86.

Dickey, E., *Ancient Greek Scholarship* (Oxford, 2007).

Dickie, M.W., 'The geography of Homer's world', in O. Anderson and M. Dickie (eds), *Homer's World: Fiction, Tradition, Reality* (Bergen, 1995), pp. 29–56.

Dickinson, O., *The Aegean Bronze Age* (Cambridge, 1994).

Dodds, E., *The Greeks and the Irrational* (Berkeley, 1951).

Doherty, L., *Siren Songs: Gender, Audiences, and Narrators in the* Odyssey (Ann Arbor, 1995).

Dougherty, C., *The Raft of Odysseus: The Ethnographic Imagination of Homer's* Odyssey (Oxford, 2001).

Dué, C., 'Achilles' golden amphora in Aeschines' *Against Timarchus* and the afterlife of oral tradition', *Classical Philology* xcvi (2001), pp. 33–47.

—— *Homeric Variations on a Lament by Briseis* (Lanham, MD, 2002).

—— 'Homer's post-classical legacy', in J.M. Foley (ed.), *A Companion to Ancient Epic* (Oxford, 2005), pp. 397–414.

—— 'The invention of Ossian', *Classics@* iii (2006), The Center for Hellenic Studies of Harvard University, <http://chs.harvard.edu/wa/pageR?tn=ArticleWrapper&bdc=12&mn=1334> (accessed 4 April 2014).

—— *Recapturing a Homeric Legacy: Images and Insights from the Venetus: A Manuscript of the* Iliad (Washington, DC, 2009).

Dué, C., and M. Ebbott, Iliad *10 and the Poetics of Ambush* (Washington, DC, 2010).

Eagleton, T., *Literary Theory: An Introduction* (Oxford, 1983).

—— *After Theory* (London, 2003).

Easton, D.F., *Schliemann's Excavations at Troia, 1870–1873* (Mainz, 2002).

Ebbott, M., 'Butler's authoress of the *Odyssey*: Gendered readings of Homer, then and now', *Classics@* iii (2006), The Center for Hellenic Studies of Harvard University, <http://chs.harvard.edu/wa/pageR?tn=ArticleWrapper&bdc=12&mn=1313> (accessed 4 April 2014).

Edwards, A.T., *Achilles in the* Odyssey (Königstein, 1985).

—— 'Homer's ethical geography: Country and city in the *Odyssey*', *Transactions of the American Philological Association* cxxiii (1993), pp. 27–78.

Edwards, M.W., 'Homer and oral tradition: The formula, Part I', *Oral Tradition* i/2 (1986), pp. 171–230.

—— *Homer: Poet of the* Iliad (Baltimore, 1987).

—— 'Homer and oral tradition: The formula, Part II', *Oral Tradition* iii/1–2 (1988), pp. 11–60.

—— 'Homer and oral tradition: The type-scene', *Oral Tradition* vii/2 (1992), pp. 284–330.

Elmer, D.F., *The Poetics of Consent: Collective Decision Making and the* Iliad (Baltimore, 2013).

Erbse, H., 'The ending of the *Odyssey*: Linguistic problems', in G.M. Wright and P.V. Jones (eds), *Homer: German Scholarship in Translation* (Oxford, 1997), pp. 263–320.

Fantuzzi, M., *Achilles in Love* (Oxford, 2012).

Faraone, C.A., *Talismans and Trojan Horses* (Oxford, 1992).

Felson-Rubin, N., *Regarding Penelope: From Character to Poetics* (Princeton, 1997).

Fenik, B., *Typical Battle Scenes in the* Iliad (Wiesbaden, 1968).

Fenno, J., '"A great wave against the stream": Water imagery in Iliadic battle scenes', *American Journal of Philology* cxxvi (2005), pp. 475–504.

Finkelberg, M. (ed.), *The Homer Encyclopedia*, 3 vols (Malden, MA, 2011).

Finley, M.I., *The World of Odysseus* (Cambridge, 1954).

Foley, H., '"Reverse similes" and sex roles in the *Odyssey*', *Arethusa* xi (1978), p. 7–26.

Foley, J.M., *Traditional Oral Epic: The* Odyssey, Beowulf, *and the Serbo-Croation* Return Song (Berkeley, 1990).

—— 'Epic cycles and epic traditions', in J.N. Kazazis and A. Rengakos (eds), *Euphrosyne* (Stuttgart, 1999), pp. 99–108.

—— *How to Read an Oral Poem* (Urbana-Champaign, 2002).

Ford, A., 'The classical definition of PAΨΩIΔIΑ', *Classical Philology* lxxxiii (1988), pp. 300–7.

- —— 'The inland ship: Problems in the performance and reception of Homeric epic', in E. Bakker and A. Kahane (eds), *Written Voices, Spoken Signs* (Cambridge, MA, 1997), pp. 83–109.

—— 'Odysseus after dinner: *Od.* 9.2–11 and the traditions of sympotic song', in A. Rengakos and J. Kazazis (eds), *Euphrosyne* (Leipzig, 1999), pp. 109–23.

Fowler, R.L., 'The Homeric Question', in R.L. Fowler (ed.), *The Cambridge Companion to Homer* (Cambridge, 2004), pp. 220–34.

Fowler, R.L. (ed.), *The Cambridge Companion to Homer* (Cambridge, 2004).

Frame, D.F., *Hippota Nestor* (Washington, DC, 2009).

Franco, C., 'Women in Homer', in S.L. James and S. Dillon (eds), *A Companion to Women in the Ancient World* (Malden, MA, 2012), pp. 54–65.

Fränkel, H., 'Essence and nature of the Homeric similes', in G.M. Wright and P.V. Jones (eds), *Homer: German Scholarship in Translation* (Oxford, 1997), pp. 103–23.

Franko, G.F., 'The Trojan horse at the close of the "Iliad"', *The Classical Journal* ci/2 (2005–6), pp. 121–3.

Frazer, J.G. (ed.), *Apollodorus: The Library*, vols 1–2 (Cambridge, MA, 1921).

Frazer, R.M., *The Trojan War: The Chronicles of Dictys of Crete and Dares the Phrygian* (Bloomington, IN, 1966).

Friedrich, R., *Formular Economy in Homer: The Poetics of the Breaches* (Stuttgart, 2007).

Frye, N., *Anatomy of Criticism* (Princeton, 1957).

Gainsford, P., 'Diktys of Crete', *Classical Journal* lviii (2012), pp. 58–87.

Gantz, T., *Early Greek Myth: A Guide to Literary and Artistic Sources* (Baltimore, 1993).

Garber, M., 'Shakespeare as fetish', *Shakespeare Quarterly* xli (1990), pp. 242–50.

—— *Profiling Shakespeare* (New York, 2008).

Gainsford, P., 'Achilles' views on death: succession and the *Odyssey*', *Classical Bulletin* lxxxiv (2009), pp. 7–26.

George, A.R., *The Epic of Gilgamesh: The Babylonian Epic Poem and Other Texts in Akkadian and Sumerian* (London, 2000).

—— *The Babylonian Gilgamesh Epic: Introduction, Critical Edition and Cuneiform Texts*, 2 vols (Oxford, 2003).

Giuliani, L., *Image and Myth*, trans. J. O'Donnell (Chicago, 2013).

Gleick, J., *The Information: A History, a Theory, a Flood* (New York, 2012).

Glenn, J., 'The Polyphemus folktale and Homer's *Kyklôpeia*', *Transactions of the American Philological Association* cii (1971), pp. 133–81.

Goldhill, S., *The Poet's Voice* (Cambridge, 1990).

—— 'Naked and O Brother, Where Art Thou? The politics and poetics of epic cinema', in B. Graziosi and E. Greenwood (eds), Homer in the Twentieth Century (Oxford, 2007), pp. 245–67.

Graziosi, B., Inventing Homer: The Early Reception of Epic (Cambridge, 2002).

Graziosi, B. and J. Haubold, Homer: Iliad Book VI (Cambridge, 2010).

Greenblatt, S., and J.L. Koerner, 'Glories of classicism', New York Review of Books lx/3 (2013).

Greenwood, E., 'Logue's tele-vision: Reading Homer from a distance', in B. Graziosi and E. Greenwood (eds), Homer in the Twentieth Century (Oxford, 2007), pp. 145–76.

Grethlein, J., 'From imperishable glory to history: The Iliad and the Trojan War', in D. Konstan and K.A. Raaflaub (eds), Epic and History (Malden, MA, and Oxford, 2010), pp. 122–44.

Griffin, J., 'The Epic Cycle and the uniqueness of Homer', Journal of Hellenic Studies xcvii (1977), pp. 39–53.

—— Homer on Life and Death (Oxford, 1980).

—— 'The speeches', in R.L. Fowler (ed.), The Cambridge Companion to Homer (Cambridge, 2004), pp. 156–70.

Hainsworth, J.B., The Flexibility of the Homeric Formula (Oxford, 1968).

Hall, E., The Return of Ulysses: A Cultural History of Homer's Odyssey (Baltimore, 2008).

Halliwell, S., Aristotle's Poetics (London, 1986).

Hansen, W., Ariadne's Thread: A Guide to International Tales Found in Classical Literature (Ithaca, NY, 2002).

Hartog, F., Memories of Odysseus, trans. J. Lloyd (Chicago, 2001).

Haslam, M., 'Homeric papyri and transmission of the text', in I. Morris and B. Powell (eds), A New Companion to Homer (Leiden, 1997), pp. 55–100.

—— 'The physical media: Tablet, scroll, codex', in J. Foley (ed.), A Companion to Ancient Epic (Oxford, 2005), pp. 142–63.

Haubold, J., Homer's People (Cambridge, 2000).

—— 'Wars of Wissenschaft: The new quest for Troy', International Journal of the Classical Tradition viii/4 (2002), pp. 564–79.

—— Greece and Mesopotamia: Dialogues in Literature (Cambridge, 2013).

Heiden, B., Homer's Cosmic Fabrication: Choice and Design in the Iliad (Oxford, 2008).

Holmberg, I., 'The creation of the ancient Epic Cycle', Oral Tradition xiii/2 (1998), pp. 456–78.

—— 'Homer and the beginning of the sequel', in P. Budra and B. Schellenberg (eds), Part Two: Reflections on the Sequel (Toronto, 1998), pp. 19–33.

Holoka, J.P., Simone Weil's the Iliad or the Poem of Force: A Critical Edition (New York, 2003).

Holway, R.K., Becoming Achilles (Lanham, MD, 2012).

Hopman, M.G., Scylla: Myth, Metaphor, Paradox (Cambridge, 2013).

Horden, P., and N. Purcell, The Corrupting Sea (Oxford, 2000).

Horrocks, G.C., 'Homer's dialect', in I. Morris and B. Powell (eds), A New Companion to Homer (Leiden, 1997), pp. 193–217.

Hughes, D., Pan's Travail: Environmental Problems of the Ancient Greeks and Romans (Baltimore, 1994).

Hulme, P., and W.H. Sherman (eds), The Tempest and Its Travels (London, 2000).

Jamison, S.W., 'Penelope and the pigs: Indic perspectives on the Odyssey', Classical Antiquity xviii/2 (1999), pp. 227–72.

Janko, R., Homer, Hesiod and the Hymn (Cambridge, 1982).

——— 'The Homeric poems as oral dictated texts', *Classical Quarterly* xlviii/1 (1998), pp. 135–67.

Jauss, H.R., *Towards an Aesthetic of Reception*, trans. T. Bahti (Minneapolis, 1982).

Jensen, M.S., *The Homeric Question and the Oral-Formulaic Theory* (Copenhagen, 1980).

——— *Writing Homer* (Copenhagen, 2011).

Jones, B., 'Relative chronology within (an) oral tradition', *Classical Journal* cv/4 (2010), pp. 289–318.

Jong, I.J.F. de, *Narrators and Focalizers: The Presentation of the Story in the* Iliad (Amsterdam, 1987).

——— *A Narratological Commentary on the* Odyssey (Cambridge, 2001).

——— 'The Helen *logos* and Herodotus' fingerprint', in E. Baragwanath and M. de Bakker (eds), *Myth, Truth, and Narrative in Herodotus* (Oxford, 2012), pp. 127–42.

Kakridis, J.T., *Homeric Researches* (Lund, 1949).

Karakantza, E., 'Eating from the tables of others: Sophocles' Ajax and the Greek Epic Cycle', *Classics@* vi (2010), The Center for Hellenic Studies of Harvard University, <http://chs.harvard.edu/wa/pageR?tn=ArticleWrapper&bdc=12&mn=3228> (accessed 4 April 2014).

Katz, M.A. [=Arthur, M.], 'The divided world of *Iliad* VI', *Women's Studies* viii/1–2 (1981), pp. 21–46.

——— *Penelope's Renown* (Princeton, 1991).

Kelly, A., 'The mourning of Thetis: "Allusion" and the future in the *Iliad*', in F. Montanari, A. Rengakos, and C. Tsagalis (eds), *Homeric Contexts: Neoanalysis and the Interpretation of Oral Poetry* (Berlin, 2012), pp. 221–68.

Kenner, H., *The Pound Era* (Berkeley, 1971).

Kim, L., *Homer between History and Fiction in Imperial Greek Literature* (Cambridge, 2010).

Kirk, G.S., *The Songs of Homer* (Cambridge, 1962).

——— *Myth: Its Meaning and Function* (Berkeley, 1970).

Kuberski, P., 'Kubrick's *Odyssey*: Myth, technology, gnosis', *Arizona Quarterly* lxiv/3 (2008), pp. 51–73.

Kullmann, W., *Die Quellen der* Ilias (Wiesbaden, 1960).

——— 'Oral poetry theory and neoanalysis in Homeric research', *GRBS* xxv (1984), pp. 307–23.

Lamberton, R., *Homer the Theologian* (Berkeley, 1989).

Lamberton, R., and J. Keaney (eds), *Homer's Ancient Readers* (Princeton, 1992).

Latacz, J., *Troy and Homer: Towards a Solution of an Old Mystery*, trans. K. Windle and R. Ireland (Oxford, 2004).

Lateiner, D., *Sardonic Smile: Nonverbal Behavior in Homeric Epic* (Ann Arbor, 1995).

Lefkowitz, M.R., *The Lives of the Greek Poets* (London, 1981).

Leopold, A., *A Sand County Almanac* (New York, 1949).

Lévi-Strauss, C., *Structural Anthropology*, trans. Claire Jacobson and Brooke Grundfest Schoepf (New York, 1963).

Littleton, C., *The New Comparative Mythology: An Anthropological Assessment of the Theories of Georges Dumézil*, 3rd ed. (Berkeley, 1982).

Lord, A.B., *The Singer of Tales* (Cambridge, MA, 1960).

Louden, B., *The* Odyssey: *Structure, Narration, and Meaning* (Baltimore, 1999).

——— *The* Iliad: *Structure, Myth, and Meaning* (Baltimore, 2006).

Lowe, N., *The Classical Plot and the Invention of Western Narrative* (Cambridge, 2000).

Luce, J.V., *Celebrating Homer's Landscapes: Troy and Ithaca Revisited* (New Haven, CT, 1998).

Lynn-George, M., *Epos: Word, Narrative and the* Iliad (Atlantic Highlands, NJ, 1988).

MacCary, W.T., *Childlike Achilles* (New York, 1982).

McConnell, J., *Black Odysseys* (Oxford, 2013).

McKinsey, M., *Hellenism and the Postcolonial Imagination: Yeats, Cavafy, Walcott* (Cranbury, NJ, 2010).

Malkin, I., 'Postcolonial concepts and ancient Greek colonization', *Modern Language Quarterly* lxv/3 (2004), pp. 341–64.

Marks, J., 'The ongoing *neikos*: Thersites, Odysseus and Achilleus', *American Journal of Philology* cxxvi/1 (2005), pp. 1–31.

—— *Zeus in the* Odyssey (Washington, DC, 2008).

Martin, R., *The Language of Heroes* (Ithaca, NY, 1989).

Mawhinney, L., 'Sympotic and rhapsodic discourse in the Homeric epics', Ph.D. dissertation (University of Toronto, 2012).

Merkle, S., 'The truth and nothing but the truth', in G.L. Schmeling (ed.), *The Novel in the Ancient World* (Leiden, 1996), pp. 563–80.

Minchin, E., *Homer and the Resources of Memory: Some Applications of Cognitive Theory to the* Iliad *and the* Odyssey (Oxford, 2001).

—— 'Spatial memory and the composition of the *Iliad*', in E.A. Mackay (ed.), *Orality, Literacy, Memory in the Ancient Greek and Roman World* (Leiden, 2008), pp. 9–34.

Minta, S., 'Homer and Joyce: The case of Nausicaa', in B. Graziosi and E. Greenwood (eds), *Homer in the Twentieth Century* (Oxford, 2007), pp. 92–119.

Mitchell, S., *Gilgamesh: A New English Version* (New York, 2006).

Mondi, R., 'The Homeric Cyclopes: Folktale, tradition, and theme', *Transactions of the American Philological Association* cxiii (1983), pp. 17–38.

Montanari, F., 'Zenodotus, Aristarchus, and the *Ekdosis* of Homer', in G.W. Most (ed.), *Editing Texts – Texte Edieren* (Göttingen, 1998), pp. 1–21.

—— 'Alexandrian Homeric philology: The form of the *Ekdosis* and the *Variae Lectiones*', in M. Reichel and A. Rengakos (eds), *Epea Pteroenta* (Stuttgart, 2002), pp. 119–40.

Montgomery, J.E., 'Al-Sindibad and Polyphemus', in A. Neuwirth et al. (eds), *Myths, Historical Archetypes and Symbolic Figures in Arabic Literature* (Stuttgart, 1999), pp. 437–66.

Montiglio, S., *From Villain to Hero: Odysseus in Ancient Thought* (Ann Arbor, 2011).

Morgan, T., *Literate Education in the Hellenistic and Roman Worlds* (Cambridge, 1998).

Morris, I., 'The use and abuse of Homer', *Classical Antiquity* v (1986), pp. 81–138.

Most, G., 'The structure and function of Odysseus' *apologoi*', *Transactions of the American Philological Association* cxxix (1989), pp. 15–30.

Moulton, C., *Similes in the Homeric Poems* (Göttingen, 1977).

Muellner, L.C., *The Anger of Achilles: Menis in Greek Epic* (Ithaca, NY, 1996).

Murnaghan, S., 'Equal honor and future glory: The plan of Zeus in the *Iliad*', in D. Roberts, F. Dunn and D. Fowler (eds), *Classical Closure: Reading the End in Greek and Latin Literature* (Princeton, 1997), pp. 23–42.

—— 'Penelope's *agnoia*: Knowledge, power, and gender in the *Odyssey*', in L.E. Doherty (ed.), *Homer's* Odyssey (Oxford, 2009), pp. 231–46.

Murnaghan, S. and D.H. Roberts, 'Penelope's song: The lyric odysseys of Linda Pastan and Louise Glück', *Classical and Modern Literature* xxii (2002), pp. 1–33.

Murray, O., 'Nestor's cup and the origins of the Greek *symposion*', in B. D'Agostino and D. Ridgway (eds), *Apoikia* (Naples, 1994), pp. 47–54.

Murray, P., 'The Muses and their arts', in P. Murray and P. Wilson (eds), *Music and the Muses* (Oxford, 2004), pp. 365–89.

Nagy, G., *The Best of the Achaeans* (Baltimore, 1979).

—— *Poetry as Performance* (Cambridge, 1996).

—— 'Homeric *scholia*', in I. Morris and B. Powell (eds), *A New Companion to Homer* (Leiden, 1997), pp. 101–22.

—— *Plato's Rhapsody and Homer's Music* (Washington, DC, 2002).

—— *Homer the Classic* (Washington, DC, 2009).

—— *Homer the Preclassic* (Berkeley, 2010).

Nakassis, D., 'Gemination at the horizons: East and West in the mythical geography of archaic Greek epic', *Transactions of the American Philological Association* cxxxiv (2004), pp. 215–233.

Neils, J. (ed.), *Goddess and Polis: The Panathenaic Festival in Ancient Athens* (Princeton, 1992).

Olson, S.D., *Blood and Iron: Stories and Storytelling in Homer's* Odyssey (Leiden, 1995).

Osborne, R., *Greece in the Making, 1200–479 BC* (New York, 1996).

Parry, A., 'The language of Achilles', *Transactions of the American Philological Association* lxxxvii (1956), pp. 1–7.

Parry, A. (ed.), *The Making of Homeric Verse* (Oxford, 1971).

Paul, J., *Film and the Classical Epic Tradition* (Oxford, 2013).

Pellicia, H., *Mind, Body, and Speech in Homer and Pindar* (Göttingen, 1995).

—— 'Two points about Rhapsodes', in M. Finkelberg and G.G. Stroumsa (eds), *Homer, the Bible, and Beyond* (Leiden, 2003), pp. 98–116.

Peradotto, J., *Man in the Middle Voice* (Princeton, 1990).

—— 'Contemporary theory', in M. Finkelberg (ed.), *The Homer Encyclopedia* (Malden, MA, 2011).

Petropoulos, J.C.B., *Kleos in a Minor Key* (Washington, DC, 2011).

Pfeiffer, R., *History of Classical Scholarship from the Beginnings to the End of the Hellenistic Age* (Oxford, 1968).

Podlecki, A., 'Guest-gifts and nobodies in *Odyssey* 9', *Phoenix* xv (1961), pp. 125–33.

Powell, B.B., *Homer and the Origin of the Greek Alphabet* (Cambridge, 1991).

Pucci, P., *Odysseus Polutropos* (Ithaca, NY, 1987).

—— 'Theology and poetics in the *Iliad*', *Arethusa* xxxv (2002), pp. 17–34.

Purves, A., 'Falling into time in Homer's *Iliad*', *Classical Antiquity* xxv (2006), pp. 179–209.

—— *Space and Time in Ancient Greek Narrative* (Cambridge, 2010).

—— 'Homer and the art of overtaking', *American Journal of Philology* cxxxii (2011), pp. 523–51.

—— 'Sleeping outside in Homer's *Odyssey* and W. G. Sebald's *The Emigrants*', in H. Gardner and S. Murnaghan (eds), *Odyssean Identities in Modern Cultures: The Journey Home* (Athens, OH, 2014), pp. 213–39.

Rabel, R.J., *Plot and Point of View in the* Iliad (Ann Arbor, 1997).

—— 'Impersonation and identity: *Sommersby*, *The Return of Martin Guerre*, and the *Odyssey*', *International Journal of the Classical Tradition* ix/3 (2003), pp. 391–406.

Rankine, P.D., *Ulysses in Black: Ralph Ellison, Classicism, and African American Literature* (Madison, WI, 2006).

Ready, J., *Character, Narrator, and Simile in the* Iliad (Cambridge, 2011).

Reden, S. von, *Exchange in Ancient Greece* (London, 1995).

Redfield, J.M., *Nature and Culture in the* Iliad: *The Tragedy of Hector* (Chicago, 1975).

Reece, S., *The Stranger's Welcome: Oral Theory and the Aesthetics of the Homeric Hospitality Scene* (Ann Arbor, 1993).

—— 'Homer's *Iliad* and *Odyssey*: From oral performance to written text', in M.C. Amodio (ed.), *New Directions in Oral Theory* (Tempe, AZ, 2005), pp. 43–89.

Reinhardt, K., 'The judgement of Paris', in G.M. Wright and P.V. Jones (eds), *Homer: German Scholarship in Translation* (Oxford, 1997), pp. 170–91.

Robinson, M., 'Ways of hearing in Sophokles: Auditory spaces and social dynamics in the *Elektra*, *Philoktetes*, *Trachiniai*, and *Oidipous Tyrannos*', Ph.D. dissertation (University of Toronto, 2013).

Rose, P., *Sons of the Gods, Children of Earth: Ideology and Literary Form in Ancient Greece* (Ithaca, NY, 1992).

—— *Class in Archaic Greece* (Cambridge, 2012).

Rosen, R., *Making Mockery* (Oxford, 2007).

Sachs, J., 'On the road: Travel, antiquarianism, philology', in S. Gurd (ed.), *Philology and Its Histories* (Athens, OH, 2010), pp. 127–47.

Saïd, S., *Homer & the Odyssey*, trans. R. Webb (Oxford, 2011).

Sallares, R., *The Ecology of the Ancient Greek World* (Cornell, NY, 1991).

Sammons, B., 'History and *hyponoia*: Herodotus and early literary criticism', *Histos* vi (2012), pp. 52–66.

Schadewaldt, W., *Von Homers Welt und Werk* (Stuttgart, 1959).

—— *Iliasstudien*, 3rd ed. (Darmstadt, 1966 [orig. 1938]).

—— 'Hector and Andromache', in G.M. Wright and P.V. Jones (eds), *Homer: German Scholarship in Translation* (Oxford, 1997), pp. 124–42.

Schein, S.L., *Sophocles: Philoctetes* (Cambridge, 2013).

Schmidt, M., 'The Homer of the *scholia*: What is explained to the reader?', in F. Montanari (ed.), *Omero tremila anni dopo* (Rome, 2002), pp. 159–83.

Schmitz, T.A., *Modern Literary Theory and Ancient Texts: An Introduction* (Malden, MA, 2007).

Schultz, E., 'Odysseus comes to know his place: Reading the *Odyssey* ecocritically', *Neohelicon* xxxvi (2009), pp. 299–310.

Scodel, R., 'Zielinski's Law reconsidered', *Transactions of the American Philological Association* cxxxviii (2008), pp. 107–25.

Scott, W.C., *The Oral Nature of the Homeric Simile* (Leiden, 1974).

Sealey, R., 'From Phemios to Ion', *Revue des études grecques* lxx (1957), pp. 312–55.

Segal, C., *The Theme of Mutilation of the Corpse in the* Iliad (Leiden, 1971).

—— *Singers, Heroes, and Gods in the* Odyssey (Ithaca, NY, 1994).

Seidel, M., *Epic Geography: James Joyce's* Ulysses (Princeton, 1976).

Selden, R., P. Widdowson and P. Brooker, *A Reader's Guide to Contemporary Literary Theory*, 5th ed. (Harlow, 2005).

Shay, J., *Achilles in Vietnam: Combat Trauma and the Undoing of Character* (New York, 1994).

—— *Odysseus in America: Combat Trauma and the Trials of Homecoming* (New York, 2002).

Sherratt, E.S., 'Reading the texts: Archaeology and the Homeric Question', *Antiquity* lxiv (1990), pp. 807–24.

Shive, D., *Naming Achilles* (Oxford, 1987).

Siegel, J., 'The Coens' *O Brother, Where Art Thou?* and Homer's *Odyssey*', *Mouseion* vii (2007), pp. 213–45.

Silk, M.S., *Homer: The* Iliad (Cambridge, 1987).

Slatkin, L., *The Power of Thetis* (Berkeley, 1991).

Snell, B., *The Discovery of the Mind*, trans. T.G. Rosenmeyer (Cambridge, MA, 1953).

Snodgrass, A.M., 'An historical Homeric society?', *Journal of Hellenic Studies* xciv (1974), pp. 114–25.

——*Archaic Age: An Age of Experiment* (Berkeley, 1980).

——*Homer and the Artists* (Cambridge, 1998).

——*The Dark Age of Greece*, 2nd ed. (Edinburgh, 2000).

Solomon, J., 'The vacillations of the Trojan myth: Popularization & classicization, variation & codification', *International Journal of the Classical Tradition* xiv/3–4 (2007), pp. 482–534.

Sowerby, R., 'Early humanist failure with Homer (I)', *International Journal of the Classical Tradition* iv/1 (1997–8), pp. 37–63.

Squire, M., *Image and Text in Graeco-Roman Antiquity* (Cambridge, 2009).

——*The* Iliad *in a Nutshell: Visualizing Epic on the* Tabulae Iliacae (Oxford, 2011).

Stanford, W., *The Ulysses Theme* (Oxford, 1954).

Stanley, K., *The Shield of Homer: Narrative Structure in the* Iliad (Princeton, 1993).

Steiner, G. (ed.), *Homer in English* (London, 1996).

Steinrück, M., *The Suitors in the* Odyssey (New York, 2008).

Stoneman, R., 'Die Idee Trojas: Resonanzen in England und Deutschland im zwanzigsten Jahrhundert', in E. Koczisky (ed.), *Ruinen in der Moderne: Archäologie und die Kunste* (Berlin, 2010), pp. 337–58.

Stubbings, F.H., and H. Thomas, 'Lands and peoples in Homer', in A.J.B. Wace and F.H. Stubbings (eds), *A Companion to Homer* (London, 1962), pp. 283–310.

Tandy, D.W., *Warriors into Traders* (Berkeley, 1997).

Taplin, O., *Homeric Soundings: The Shaping of the* Iliad (Oxford, 1992).

Thalmann, W.G., *The Swineherd and the Bow: Representations of Class in the* Odyssey (Ithaca, NY, 1998).

Thomas, R., *Literacy and Orality in Ancient Greece* (Cambridge, 1992).

Torgovnick, M., *Gone Primitive* (Chicago, 1991).

Tracy, S.V., 'The structures of the *Odyssey*', in I. Morris and B. Powell (eds), *A New Companion to Homer* (Leiden, 1997), pp. 360–79.

Traill, D.A., *Schliemann of Troy: Treasure and Deceit* (New York, 1995).

Tsagalis, C., *From Listeners to Viewers: Space in the* Iliad (Washington, DC, 2012).

Ventris, M., and J. Chadwick, *Documents in Mycenaean Greek*, 2nd ed. (Cambridge, 1973).

Vidal-Naquet, P., 'Land and sacrifice in the *Odyssey*: A study of religious and mythical meaning', in S. Schein (ed.), *Reading the Odyssey* (Princeton, 1995), pp. 33–54.

Wade-Gery, H.T., *The Poet of the* Iliad (Cambridge, 1952).

Watkins, C., *How to Kill a Dragon: Aspects of Indo-European Poetics* (New York, 1995).

Weçowski, M., 'Homer and the origins of the *symposion*', in F. Montanari and P. Ascheri (eds), *Omero tremila anni dopo* (Rome, 2002), pp. 625–37.

Wees, H. van, 'Homer and early Greece', *Colby Quarterly* xxxviii (2002), p. 94–117.

West, M.L., *The East Face of Helicon: West Asiatic Elements in Greek Poetry and Myth* (Oxford, 1997).

——*Studies in the Text and Transmission of the* Iliad (Munich-Leipzig, 2000).

——*Greek Epic Fragments: From the Seventh to the Fifth Centuries BC* (Cambridge, MA, 2003).

——*Indo-European Poetry and Myth* (Oxford, 2007).

——*The Making of the* Iliad (Oxford, 2011).

—— *The Epic Cycle: A Commentary on the Lost Troy Epics* (Oxford, 2013).

Wheat, L.F., *Kubrick's* 2001: *A Triple Allegory* (Lanham, MD, 2000).

Whitman, C.H., *Homer and the Heroic Tradition* (Cambridge, MA, 1958).

Wilamowitz-Moellendorff, U. von, *Die* Ilias *und Homer* (Berlin, 1916).

Willcock, M., 'Ad hoc invention in the *Iliad*', *Harvard Studies in Classical Philology* lxxxi (1977), pp. 41–53.

Wilson, D., *Ransom, Revenge and Heroic Identity in the* Iliad (Cambridge, 2002).

Winkler, M.M., *Troy: From Homer's* Iliad *to Hollywood Epic* (Malden, MA, 2007).

Wolf, F., *Prolegomena ad Homerum*, trans. A. Grafton, G. Most and J. Zetzel (Princeton, 1985 [1795]).

Woodcock, G., *Odysseus Ever Returning* (Toronto, 1970).

Woodhouse, W.J., *The Composition of Homer's* Odyssey (Oxford, 1930).

Yamagata, N., 'Penelope and early recognition: Vlahos, Harsh, and Eustathius', *College Literature* xxxviii/2 (2011), pp. 122–30.

Young, P.H., *The Printed Homer* (Jefferson, NC, 2003).

Zeitlin, F.I., 'Visions and revisions of Homer in the Second Sophistic', in S. Goldhill (ed.), *Greek Identity in the Second Sophistic* (Cambridge, 2001), pp. 195–266.

Zielinski, T., 'Die Behandlung gleichzeitiger Ereignisse im antiken Epos', *Philologus Supplementband* viii (1899–1901), pp. 405–49.

INDEX